WHY THEATRE MATTERS

Urban Youth, Engagement, and a Pedagogy of the Real

What makes young people value and care about themselves, others, their communities, and their futures? In this book, Kathleen Gallagher uses the drama classroom as a window into student engagement and the daily challenges of marginalized youth in Toronto, Boston, Taipei, and Lucknow. An ethnographic study that combines quantitative and qualitative methodologies, *Why Theatre Matters* presents a framework for understanding student involvement in the context of school, family, and community, as well as changing social, political, and economic realities around the world.

Focusing on the voices of the students themselves, Gallagher illustrates how creative expression through theatre can act as a rehearsal space for real-life struggles and for democratic participation. An invigorating challenge to the myths that surround urban youth, *Why Theatre Matters* is a testament to theatre's transformative potential.

KATHLEEN GALLAGHER is Canada Research Chair in Theatre, Youth, and Research in Urban Schools and a professor in the Department of Curriculum, Teaching and Learning at the Ontario Institute for Studies in Education, University of Toronto.

KATHLEEN GALLAGHER

Why Theatre Matters

Urban Youth, Engagement, and a Pedagogy of the Real

UNIVERSITY OF TORONTO PRESS
Toronto Buffalo London

© University of Toronto Press 2014
Toronto Buffalo London
www.utppublishing.com
Printed in the U.S.A.

ISBN 978-1-4426-4957-6 (cloth)
ISBN 978-1-4426-2694-2 (paper)

Printed on acid-free, 100% post-consumer recycled paper with vegetable-based inks.

Library and Archives Canada Cataloguing in Publication

Gallagher, Kathleen, 1965–, author
Why theatre matters : urban youth, engagement, and a pedagogy of the real / Kathleen Gallagher.

Includes bibliographical references and index.
ISBN 978-1-4426-4957-6 (bound). – ISBN 978-1-4426-2694-2 (pbk.)

1. Drama in education – Case studies.   2. Theater and society –
Case studies.   3. Arts in education – Case studies.   4. Urban
youth–Education–Case studies.   5. Urban youth–Social Conditions–
Case studies.   I. Title.

PN3171.G34 2014   371.39′9   C2014-904127-6

This book has been published with the help of a grant from the Canadian Federation for the Humanities and Social Sciences, through the Awards to Scholarly Publications Program, using funds provided by the Social Sciences and Humanities Research Council of Canada.

University of Toronto Press acknowledges the financial assistance of the Canada Council for the Arts and the Ontario Arts Council, an agency of the Government of Ontario.

Canada Council   Conseil des Arts
for the Arts   du Canada

ONTARIO ARTS COUNCIL
CONSEIL DES ARTS DE L'ONTARIO
an Ontario government agency
un organisme du gouvernement de l'Ontario

University of Toronto Press acknowledges the financial support of the Government of Canada through the Canada Book Fund for its publishing activities.

For Caroline, whose virtues as a parent and partner are resplendent.

For Liam, whose future has stirred my every research instinct and desire to communicate.

How can we both preserve and develop our freedom as humans? It is precisely by cultivating the between-us, but not only as individuals who simply belong to a same people … Rather it is at every moment, in the relation with the one whom we are meeting, that we must cultivate the energy born thanks to this encounter … Starting from desire we can do so many things, and first of all become humans, alone and together, always safeguarding the relationship between two different beings … Transforming our needs into desire requires the mediation of art, in our gestures, in our words, in all our ways of relating to ourselves, to the other(s), to the world … Art does not amount to a kind of unnecessary work that is suitable only for some artists. Art ought to be a basic daily undertaking carried out by everyone for passing from nature to culture, from the satisfaction of instincts to a sharing of desire, that is, for preserving and cultivating the between-us. Art is more critical than morality if we are to enter a culture of humanity formed by beings-in-relation …

Luce Irigaray, *In the Beginning, She Was* (pp. 21–2)

Contents

Figures and Tables

Figures

Tables

Foreword

"It's us rather than me ..."

These are a few of the words spoken by Chrysanthemum, one of the student voices in this book (p. 171). She is talking about the pressures of performing on a stage and says, "And we were all back there jumping around like, it was kind of like trying to ramp each other up, and I think that one of the most important things that we were saying to each other was like 'you know what, we're on there. If you make a mistake, you know, we got you.'" When I first read that I heard it as a threat – make a mistake, let us down and we'll get you. I was confronted with my own ease in assuming that urban youth were prone to aggression and coercion. Only on a second read did I get it: *And it was kind of like, you have to be able to tell that person that you're not going up there alone, you're going up there with those people behind you and those people beside you to like catch you when you make a mistake.* It was in fact a statement of solidarity, of community, of the power of communal action. That is what this book does – it takes our prejudgments, popular folk devil myths, and our "othering" of urban youth and painstakingly seeks to test, fragment, and disturb outsider perceptions of what it is to be young and urban.

Writing a foreword for a book, which is as elegantly written and crafted as this one, is a daunting task. Kathleen Gallagher has produced a groundbreaking work that carefully unravels some of the dominant perceptions of "urban youth," and of the various theoretical and methodological claims that have attempted to capture the living experience and "troubles" of these young people – particularly those who often find themselves forgotten or underserved by institutions, policymakers,

and the media. Kathleen's work with young people in a diversity of settings has no simple solutions but painstakingly outlines the need for
a complex and comprehensive set of heuristics to be applied to questions around "disengagement" from school. It should be said from the
start that the diversity of research settings and sampling does not lead
to a heterogeneous global claim about the young. Rather the diversity
within these pages powerfully reinforces the particularities and differences among young people within their sites of inquiry and broader
communities. Bakhtin's idea of the "mutuality of difference" permeates
the text.

School, of course, should provide all children with the means of
acquiring the necessary armour to succeed in an increasingly unfair
world. "Disengagement" from this opportunity is a concern for us all.
But why are some young people in our urban schools struggling to
attend and gain from education? Are they "feckless" and "hopeless"?
Kathleen's exquisitely woven tapestry of responses to these questions
emerges from case studies in the urban cores of Toronto, Boston, Lucknow,
and Taipei. The commentary and findings of these cases are interpolated
with the findings from a significant survey of attitudes and phenomena
in young people's lives that show the particularity and heterogeneity
of "youth." Importantly, there is a highly sophisticated discussion of
the interdependence of quantitative and qualitative methodologies
and purposes. In the context of this book, quantitative data is vital in
both disturbing received "truths" about the causes of "disengagement"
and in describing the scale of social injustice that tips the qualitative
findings. Recently, for instance, Oxfam in the United Kingdom has produced a meta-analysis of detailed socio-economic surveys, which in a
popular form at least demonstrates that 85 people in the world own
more wealth than the bottom 3.5 billion people who share the world
with them.[1] Kathleen's book speaks for the many, not the few.

To this crucible of research data she adds a lucid and accessible inquiry
into a diversity of theoretical fields in order to confuse and deepen any
outsider understanding of what it is like to be young and urban in the
twenty-first century. The contribution that this book makes to this body
of transdisciplinary thought is immense. This is a scholarly and mas-
terful book in which the author feels confident enough with complex
theory to explicate it in an accessible and compelling way.

Underpinning the work are the voices of young people themselves,
often heard through extensive transcripts that allow the reader to capture some of the processes of delicate negotiations between students,

their teachers, and the researcher. The "voices" are carefully worked with; a safe and transparent research environment allows for the lowering of the barricades of resistance, where they exist, and the possibility of hearing "a truth" from the subjects of the study. We are led through the complexity of the work by Kathleen's own voice as a committed researcher – reflexive and urgent, and committed to producing a necessarily complex understanding of the implications of the chorus of "voices" in the text. The mixture is both polyphonic and heteroglossic. The vernacular is carefully positioned and valued within the more academic discourses of critical theory and ethnographic research.

This is a rigorous and impressively well-researched and well-informed study. And it's full of heart – of pathos and ethos; a restless heart seeking out ways to better understand those who bear, what Bourdieu called, the "weight of the world." It is a mindful work that combines the codes of the academy with the means of artistry in its questing. It's a disciplined academic mind and voice at work, but it seeks the possibility and hope of transformative action. This marks Kathleen out in terms of her own position. The book successfully interpolates activism, social science, artistic practice, and critical pedagogy to produce a complex and nuanced "take" on urban youth. Interestingly, for me, at the core of the study are the analogies between drama and critical ethnographic practices. Theatre was the first invention of democracy – it offered a necessary socio-aesthetic mirror to the Athenian polis so that they could see themselves sharing socially in the questioning of who they were and who they were becoming. In its comic/satiric guise it punctured in public the hubris of the rich, the overbearing, and the corrupt. Drama in society, and particularly in schools, offers students the vernacular and aesthetic opportunity to examine and understand who they are and what their bonds are with others. This attempt to understand one's own understandings and get inside the understandings of others is also the work of a more formal ethnographic method. Whilst the book is a substantive work of social science it does not offer scientific certainties in its findings and discussions. Like drama, it seeks moments of "phronein" – wisdom based on experience, argument, and understanding forged through social interactions and negotiations.

In its discussion of findings, the book points towards a heterotopian possibility for urban youth that eschews the often dystopian cultural misrecognitions that are imposed on them. There is hope, but it is a complex hope partly supported by the dignity, pride, and caring among urban youth and partly by our need to fully understand as many of the layers of skin that make up their beings as they are prepared to reveal. Or at least to discover and understand the many variables that shape their lives in and beyond school.

We are reminded that young people feel most engaged when there is at least the possibility of community in their lives, the opportunity for dialogue, and the chance that participation may lead to transformations in their immediate worlds. This sense of community, family, and social interaction in the wider world is experienced most forcibly, by some young people, outside in the playground rather than within classrooms. Kathleen shows that youth who enjoy and are cared for in this way are more likely to be "engaged" in a school's normative academic and social trajectories. Those who are less fortunate may slip away both from their own worlds and from education.

The sites of school-based inquiry in this book are often drama classrooms and other theatre spaces. Kathleen's experiences as drama practitioner and theatre activist give her expert insights into the ways in which many drama teachers seek to create a temporary world, at least in their learning spaces. The Scottish director Michael Boyd asked whether the ensemble – which characterizes the best work in theatre and drama classrooms – can serve as a model for a better world. This is the ambition of the drama practices in this book – to create a temporary culture that fosters and even demands participation, dialogue, and interaction in both the social and aesthetic planes of the teaching and learning experience. In this sense, drama work is political. It allows young people to negotiate rules that are freely accepted rather than fearfully followed, to practise freedom and restraint of speech and action, and to act in significant ways in both social and aesthetic spheres. Drama is by choice. It cannot be imposed or taught without student engagement. Drama teachers in every class work as if the students have the choice to be there. This is a significant and often exhausting challenge in schools with high levels of often misunderstood "disengagement." The transcripts reveal the delicate negotiations between students and teachers who "uncrown" their power and seek to leverage the "illusion of equality," which Richard Sennett associates with all forms of social play. Can these teachers, students, spaces, and socio-artistic politics model a better world? For urban youth? For the world?

But Kathleen reminds us that even these often institutionally marginalized episodes of political and artistic engagement in drama classrooms are supported, or not, by the deeper and wider contextual experiences and realities that young people bring to school. Issues of "disengagement" in drama and schooling are contingent on the actual and perceived rights and wrongs and material advantages and disadvantages that constitute students' wider worlds and life experiences. From an activist perspective, participation and engagement in schools and drama classrooms is most likely when students feel that they are participating and engaging with the social in their own lives – be this in the family, among carers, or community. We can't fix the classroom without fixing the wider world that houses it.

And therein lies the problem. What promise can we make to the young that through their "engagement" in authentic forms of democracy they can combat the owned and self-interested politics determined by the already powerful, über-rich fractions of society? Inequality, disengagement, and self-interest are the antitheses of both drama and democracy. Yet they are mirrored to urban youth in the wider world and replicated in their classrooms. In his state-of-the-nation speech delivered in January 2014, Barack Obama promised to "create" *ladders of opportunity* for the disadvantaged majority. After reading this book I am caused to ask, alongside the subjects of this book: How high will these ladders take me? Where will these ladders be placed – ground zero or just out of reach? Who will be first in the queue? What happens if you fall off the third rung? What happens if I'm scared of heights? In this game of ladders will there still be snakes for me that slide me right back to where I began?

In closing, Michelle Obama, as chair of the President's Committee on the Arts and the Humanities, reminds us both of the importance of rich arts experiences to the life chances of the poor and also to the inequity of the distribution of cultural resources.[2]

> At this moment in our nation's history, there is great urgency around major transformation in America's schools. Persistently high dropout rates (reaching 50% or more in some areas) are evidence that many schools are no longer able to engage and motivate their students … In such a climate, the outcomes associated with arts education – which include increased academic achievement, school engagement, and creative thinking – have become increasingly important…
>
> Just when they need it most, the classroom tasks and tools that could best reach and inspire these students – art, music, movement and performing – are less available to them.

Sadly, this is especially true for students in urban schools such as those featured in this book. Analyses of similar schools in the United

Kingdom and the United States show that access to the arts is disproportionately absent in comparison to suburban and middle-class schools. Just when they need it most many young urban students are denied, both in schools and increasingly in their communities, access to the tools and platforms that are necessary to Kathleen's sense of a socially vital "socio-artistic voice."

This book emerges from a period of profound changes in both the urban schooling system and the wider government support for communities and individuals. In the United Kingdom these are historical changes on an unprecedented scale. This book captures this moment of "disengagement" of urban youth from these changes, and documents the complexity and struggles of their everyday existence now. The book is unfinished, of course; it's the kind of book that doesn't rest still with its conclusions. But it does contain portents for the future, which are going to be challenging for us all.

> And I think that if you're able to convince and like make the actors, or like us the students feel that we're not alone up there when you go up. Because when you go up, you're not thinking like, "OK, well it's us together." You're thinking, "oh my god, all those people are looking at me." And I think the idea of getting people to think, "it's us rather than me." I think that would help it if we were all talking about it. Help each other and know that we're not alone when we're going up there.
>
> (Individual Interview, Chrysanthemum, Middleview, June 2, 2009, p. 171)

Thank you Chrysanthemum, whoever you are, wherever you are.

Jonothan Neelands
University of Warwick, 2014

NOTES

1 Oxfam. (2014). Working for the few: Political capture and economic inequality. Oxfam Briefing Paper 178. London: Oxfam.
2 President's Committee on the Arts and the Humanities. (2011). Reinvesting in arts education: Winning America's future through creative schools. http://www.pcah.gov

Acknowledgments

I begin this book with deep and abiding gratitude to my research team, my graduate student colleagues, who shaped my most important intellectual community over these last five years. When I discuss the observations "we" made or understandings "we" came to in this text, it is to this splendid team of scholars that I am referring. Of course, many academic writers owe their students a great debt for the skills and commitment they bring to the research. In addition to their enormous research talents and analytic minds, my students also brought a philosophical spirit and a humanity to the work that kept us on course when there were challenges. These challenges were sometimes technical or logistical, but also existential, as we together tried to reconcile ourselves to our own privilege in the face of untold trials for young people. They asked the hard questions of our research and negotiated the interpersonal and institutional challenges of work in struggling schools. And, they travelled the emotional terrain of the work with me at every turn. Many of our early post-field moments were spent in a deli on Bloor Street in Toronto while consuming matzo ball soup and pondering our emotional states; trying to understand the classroom events we'd witnessed or participated in. We collaborated on many publications throughout the project, and although I am writing this book on my own, it is without question the result of our work together. Anne Wessels has been with the project from its beginnings to the very end, followed by Burcu Yaman Ntelioglou and Ivan Service for over four years, Barry Freeman over three years, Heather Fitzsimmons-Frey, Rebecca Starkman, Heather Farragher, and Anne Rovers over two years, and Art Babayants, Chrissi Forte, Casey Scott Songin, Sarah Switzer, Alex Means, Ajit Yadav, Jingwei Zhang, Bodong Chen, and Chandi Desai for one year. To this tireless research team, working as researchers, translators, and technological support, I owe everything.

We also had important technical assistance over the last five years of the project as we pushed the boundaries of hypermedia ethnography and digital technology to new heights, using video, audio, and communications technology across our global sites in often very complex ways. Thanks especially to Neil Tinker, Joseph Caprara, Scott Hollows, Olesya Falenchuck, Seeta Nyari, and Dominic Goveas for their technology support, to Bessie Giannikos for her budgetary wisdom and Nina Lewis for her administrative support, and of course to the Social Sciences and Humanities Research Council of Canada for its generous support and the peer reviewers across the country for their validation of this research.

I would further like to acknowledge my international collaborators: artists, researchers, and teachers. They brought us into their worlds and provided important context to help us understand their cultures, aesthetics, and pedagogies. As well as in-person meetings, we kept lively project blogs and a wiki to keep one another informed about our sites and also to solicit responses from each other about empirical experiences we were having in our local sites. We did this mainly through posting video data from classroom or performance work. Thank you to Dr. Su Chien-ling of the General Education Centre, Ming Chuan University; Dr. Yu-hsuan Lin of the Department of Applied Sociology and Graduate Institute of Sociology of Education, Nanhua University; and independent artist Betsy Lan of Taiwan. To Dr. Christina Marin of Emerson College in Boston and to Dr. Urvashi Sahni and Anand Chitravanshi of Prerna Girls School in Lucknow, India.

For his unanticipated gift to this process, I would also like to thank playwright and actor Andrew Kushnir. Meeting Andrew and his colleagues at Project: Humanity through our shared interest in making theatre with young people, and seeing their breathtaking play *The Middle Place,* has been nothing short of inspirational. As I write, Andrew is also working with data from this research project to create a new Verbatim play.

It takes a village to make a book. To the schools, principals, teachers, and many students (appearing under pseudonyms in this book) who welcomed us into their busy, often tumultuous, lives, I am eternally grateful. I hope that what we have made, of what you so generously shared, is acceptable. A very special thank you to Ms. S, Ms. C, and Ms. K for their many insights, their boundless commitment to young people, and their significant contributions to this research. While our team did often and happily contribute to their classroom work, when I describe aspects of the drama curriculum and specific pedagogies in this book, I am speaking of the creative, striving, and generous work of these three teachers and their creative and curious students.

WHY THEATRE MATTERS

Urban Youth, Engagement, and a Pedagogy of the Real

Introduction

Being in the Real

> KATHLEEN: If I were writing something about my experience here, what do you think would be very important for me to communicate to the world about the perspective of young people in high schools, from your point of view?
>
> MARBLES: The truth?
>
> KATHLEEN: What's the truth?
>
> MARBLES: That we're not all wastrels that do drugs all the time. And we do learn ...
>
> (Focus Group Interview, Marbles, Twila, Joe,
Middleview, December 11, 2009)

As I begin the writing of this book after five years of ethnographic research in schools in Toronto, Canada; Boston, USA; Taipei, Taiwan; and Lucknow, India, I would like to suggest simply that in our times, and around the globe, young people have shouldered the weight of growing inequality in very real and tangible ways as their struggle for an education attests. But, they have struggled in ways beyond "the real" and the material; they have also withstood assaults on their imaginaries and their desires. And yet – and there is always a yet – I have had the privilege of spending time over the last five years with the most extraordinary young people in various parts of the world who are full of urgent searching, and who are indescribably creative, intelligent, and resilient in the face of so much adversity. Or, as one student in Toronto Asad put it to me: "We have one saying in our culture. We say that if you take one charcoal and you put it in a big sack of charcoal, it will light all of it. You get it?" This book is one small attempt to make some sense of these contradictions.

Two other "life events" have also significantly shaped my capacity to understand the worlds I've inhabited with young people. First, I became a mother and embarked on the most challenging and euphoric journey I've ever made. It has shaped me in unanticipated ways but it has also unsettled many assumptions I have had about my research and myself. Being a parent exposes one to oneself in ways that almost nothing else does. It also, for me, created an unexpected new understanding of others, which at turns made me both more patient and more enraged. Such subtle changes or bursts of consciousness have made their way into this ethnographic study, one that focuses on the basic human right of young people to learn, whether that learning is in a drafty downtown classroom in North America or a hot and dusty one in Asia.

The second unanticipated event was the death of my dear colleague Roger Simon. Roger was someone who informally "mentored" me in my early days as an academic at the University of Toronto. He was also a prolific writer, and while I had read many of his important works, I had by no means read them all because I had been spoiled by the "real" life conversations we would have informally over coffee, or institutionally through shared graduate student committee work or other sympathetic collaborations. Now we, so many of us who admired his great intelligence, are left with a silence and the desire to return to his writing, for there was never a gratuitous thought or word with Roger. They all mattered. Roger emphasized the important work of "remembrance-learning," where the task is to learn how to receive and translate the "terrible gift" of the past so that we can open the present to something new. These terrible gifts sometimes come in the form of historical events, but also, I have discovered, in the inheritance of inequalities and injustices played out on the bodies of young people in a hyper-globalized world. And in schools, where young people either have or lack a sense of belonging to a bounded sociality, what we make of these "terrible gifts" bears consideration. Roger's compassion and intelligence have had enormous effect on my sense of the vital place of social science and humanities research in the world.

I have included "a pedagogy of the real" in the subtitle of this book, because it has been a study of the so-called real lives of young people in urban schools, discovered ethnographically. Both the notion of ethnographic "discoveries" and "the real" in ethnography have been usefully challenged by critical, feminist, postcolonial, post-structural, and psychoanalytic theories to which I am very sympathetic. The historic abuses of ethnography have been well documented; I have previously written about ethnographic methods such as the use of cameras for documentation (Gallagher and Kim 2008). Some of these have not simply had the effect of exploring so-called distant cultures for mainstream consumption but have wreaked untold damage on marginalized communities while celebrating unethical practices oblivious to, or unconcerned with, issues of power and justice. In her analysis of colonizing knowledges, Tuhiwai Smith (1999) draws on Said's notion of "positional superiority" (p. 58) to explain how imperialism in the Enlightenment project not only has drawn everything into the centre but has also distributed ideas and materials outwards, illustrating "the ways in which knowledge and culture were as much a part of Imperialism as raw materials and military strength" (p. 58).

I have, moreover, been influenced by the Lacanian idea of "the real" in so far as he understood "the real" as something beyond the symbolic and even beyond language. There is a symbolic language used to represent youth, a language and discourse that is responsible for injecting particular images and ideas about young people, especially socio-economically marginalized and racialized young people, that has served them poorly both in the public record and in the vernacular. The "real" of the stories and life experiences that I share in this book interrupt some of those representations in important ways. These are stories of a "real" that disrupt and unsettle such sedimented and damaging representations.

But this book is not so much a representation of the lives of those who suffer marginalization because of poverty and discrimination as it is an attempt to document the difficulty and complexity of those who attempt to see it, study it, and make sense of it. I offer an important note at the outset about pseudonyms and social identity markers. I have taken the decision to include an appendix of all the youth and teachers cited in this book rather than to include their multiple identity markers within the text. The question of naming and fixing identities is always a difficult one. In this research, we invited students to invent their own pseudonyms and to include as many social identity categories as they wished to identify themselves to readers. I also invited the students to include any other thoughts or ideas about what they would wish readers to know about them should they be cited in a publication. This was a pragmatic way of trying to get at both what young people value about themselves, and also to assess how intersectionality – different aspects of their identity – work together or create contradictions. I trust the inconvenience of having to turn to the back of the book to look up specific students will not disrupt the flow of the book too much, and any awkwardness will be outweighed by the importance of finding a way to include all of the subject position choices made by them.

To make sense methodologically and analytically, I have drawn most often on sociological readings. Because the theatre/drama explored in this book is so deeply engaged with ideas of "community," "society," "youth," "empowerment," "subjectivity," and "social relations," the sociological lens has been central. But the art/theatre, too, demanded intellectual care; in this regard, I have found the disciplines and languages of philosophy and theatre/drama indispensable. Moving across disciplines and languages in this way had the effect, for me, of putting both art and the social into question. Thinking of the artistic and the social together created important tensions *and* continuities that I have found especially useful in understanding education in broader terms.

When I turn to the quantitative aspect of my study (in chapter 3), the reader will see a sharp turn towards educational research, and even positivist representations of research. It was important to understand this largely quantitative body of work in order to appreciate what our different approach and differently theoretically informed questions might be contributing to the literature on "engagement" in education. In education research, the idea of engagement has been studied and represented not only as a phenomenological or material experience but also as a psychological one, through conceptions of "motivation" and "behaviour." The post-structural, phenomenological, and art perspectives of my research needed then to be reconciled, to some extent, but also to be held in tension with this body of education research. And so, while necessarily turning to some of this more quantitative and psychological body of literature, I have attempted as well to bring a critical feminist perspective to my analysis of that work.

In my use of the term "the real," I am not simply pointing to "reality" – so it is important that I pin down further what I am meaning in this context of research. The real, material lives of youth often entered into the space with an unstoppable force in the classrooms where we worked. Some teachers, in the drama classrooms where our work was primarily situated, welcomed these intrusions, understanding that young people often choose to explore questions of relevance to them through the artifice of theatre in ways that are educationally powerful for individuals and communities. The pedagogies on offer in drama classrooms are often punctured by the "real," as it elbows its way into the curriculum or is invited to make a special appearance. The teachers of our study mainly understood this as responsive and responsible pedagogy, but I have also understood it as culturally sustainable pedagogy. Gone are the days, so it goes, of culturally irrelevant facts in learning. As we have discovered, the challenge for committed teachers is to make good and responsible use of cultural or personal student realities, and to simultaneously stretch the minds of young people beyond the scope of their current understandings, thus making their realities relevant to a broader social and political world.

The real is both a burden and a possibility. It is also relational. Owing to an age-old attraction to "the real," heightened by a steady contemporary popular culture diet of "reality shows," how the real makes its way into classrooms pedagogically and into research ethnographically was critical to this study. The instability of the real inside the fictionalizing frame of theatre, as well as the use of the real to effect political and social change for and with young people, is central to the interests of our research. This was confirmed by a serendipitous experience in the second year of the study with a professional Verbatim theatre production about homeless youth in Toronto, one that reverberated in form and content not only for students in Toronto schools but also for our research students in Lucknow. And so we began to understand how the interplay between real and fictional worlds came to matter so much to all of us.

Youth and Urban Education in Crisis

Back in 2007, when I proposed this research to the Social Sciences and Humanities Research Council of Canada, I gave it a suitably academic title – a mouthful – trying to somehow capture the multi-modality and multi-sitedness of the work I was proposing: *Urban School Performances: The interplay, through live and digital drama, of local-global knowledge about student engagement*. It was billed as an international research project that would examine how the relationships among culture, identity, multicultural and equity policies, and student engagement have an impact on the lives of youth in schools and communities traditionally labelled "disadvantaged" in the cities of Toronto (Canada), Taipei (Taiwan), Lucknow (India), and Boston (USA). As George Marcus (1995) outlined, such multi-sited imaginaries have catalysed a new way to think about ethnographic research, previously understood as local and deeply rooted in one place. He describes these new ethnographic research designs as moving "out from the single sites and local situations of conventional ethnographic research designs to examine the circulation of cultural meaning, objects, and identities in diffuse time-space" (p. 96).

Our project was proposing to bring together communities in these diverse cities to examine student engagement, pedagogical practices, and success at school from a local-global perspective and to illustrate how such a multi-sited ethnography is changed by arts-based, participatory, digital, and performative research methods. Going beyond comparative study, I wanted our multiple sites to help us understand self-other relations at this socio-historical moment; I learned early on that such an orientation would likely teach us about ourselves in unanticipated but important ways. What we would later learn is that our ethnography would need to also become multilingual as well as multi-sited. Shared digital video of theatre performances were translated from English to Hindi and Mandarin, and performances from India included English subtitles. Our quantitative survey was also developed in all three languages; our interviews in India involved translators. We also drew on digital tools and hypermedia contexts to enhance and give nuance to our understandings of student engagement and artistic practice while further challenging us to think in ever more sophisticated methodological ways and to take into consideration the politics of knowledge production across the global north and south. But, as I would learn over the course of our ethnography, engagement is not an easily observable event, but a complex interior experience.

At the time of developing the research proposal, there were three international studies that influenced how I was conceptualizing young people, schooling practices, and the notion of "engagement." The UNICEF Innocenti Research Centre *Report Card 7* (2007) on the well-being of children and young people in the world's advanced economies had Canada sitting at number 12 of 21 on the average ranking across six dimensions. The six dimensions taken to measure the well-being of children included material well-being, health and safety, education, peer and family relationships, behaviours and risks, and young people's own subjective sense of well-being. In the dimension of "education," however, Canada was sitting at number 2, just below Belgium in first place. Despite this impressive standing in the UNICEF study, the *Program for International Student Assessment (PISA* 2004) ranked Canada much lower in relation to its counterparts on the question of engagement in school. According to this study, the number of Canadian students with low levels of participation in school activities is considerably higher than the average number of low participation of students in all of the other OECD countries. While the average prevalence of poor school participation of students among OECD countries was 20 per cent, the prevalence for poor school participation of students in Canada was 26 per cent (Willms 2003, p. 21). Finally, I read the War Child Canada *Youth Opinion Poll: Canadian Youth Speak Out on Global Issues and Canada's Role in the World* (2006), whose goal it was to convince policymakers, community leaders, and the Canadian public of "the importance, relevance and value of youth participation – not simply because it is fundamental to the principle of inclusiveness within any democracy, but also because youth have a critical and important role to play in the articulation, development, and management of the current and future affairs of our country" (p. 6). Persuasive in its rhetoric, it also got me thinking about how I might want to pay particular attention to collaboration with young people in the study's design. My impetus then was to create a "youth knowledge base" on the subject of engagement; a subject I thought had been handled in the literature with relative disregard for young people's own perspectives. My sense was that many young people were participating in what Ross (2008) has called "spectator democracy," acceding to common understandings of democratic citizenship but not really engaging in the messy and active part of a thriving democracy, where different social realities, and political and cultural frameworks, come into contact with one another. What I realize now, however, is that a "youth knowledge base" is an unrealistic goal in the broad sense because youth experiences are so contextually situated, their "voice" so inadequately accessed. In effect, to "scale up" what we might learn from young people is a near impossible task.

Fast-forward six years to the latest UNICEF report (2013) on the well-being of children. Canada finds itself, or its children, in an undeniably worse position. Dropping to 17th position overall of 29 rich countries, Canada is 27th in the area of health and safety for children and has dropped to 14th in education. Two other measures also jumped off the page for me. Canada ranks 24th out of 29 countries when it comes to children's own views on their life satisfaction and 25th with respect to relationships with parents and peers. The rate of social mobility, an area where Canada had always excelled, is also weakened in this latest report. Young people seem to be getting trapped in poverty as income inequality grows, and Aboriginal children fare the very worst in this regard. Most analysts of the latest data suggest that Canada has not changed dramatically over the previous 10 years that UNICEF has been producing such a report card, but that this year (*Report Card 11*) signals many warning signs that Canada is losing its foothold and, many argue, its moral compass. The report card gives us a snapshot of how well children are doing today, according to specific measures, but it also presents a fairly comprehensive picture of life for children across the world's most affluent nations during the first decade of the new millennium. Especially relevant to this study, in the league tables presented, Canada falls into the lowest third of the pack on "participation in further education," considered by the report to be education between the ages 15 and 19. This indicator would be a marker of safe passage for young people in the final years of compulsory schooling, associated of course with a wider range of opportunities at the beginning of adult life. Poor standing here means that we have one of the highest percentages of young people not participating in education, employment, or training. Canadian youth seem to be doing quite well according to the latest PISA educational achievement charts by age 15, in second place just below Finland, signalling very good results for the "quality of education" as measured by students' abilities in the three basic competencies of reading, maths, and science. However, what happens after that in Canadian high schools – the numbers of young people not experiencing success after age 15 – paints a very different picture. As I pull together my five years of data and collect my ethnographically enriched thoughts on student engagement – so intricately related, as it is, to larger social, political, and cultural questions – the poignant summary on the UNICEF Canada website echoes in my ears:

> Failure to protect and promote the well being of children is associated with increased risk across a wide range of later-life outcomes. Children have the right to first call on their nations' resources and capacities, in good times and bad. There will always be some interest more immediate than protecting the well being of children. There will never be one more important. (http://www.UNICEF.ca/en/discover/article/child-well-being-in-rich-countries-a-comparative-overview)

In education scholarship, there continues to be much attention paid to the idea of student voice. However, where these ideas seem most fruitfully developed are in the particular projects imagined and conducted in spaces where youth and adults act in collaboration to re-imagine the conditions of their living and learning. Francine Joselowsky's (2007) study is a good example of project-based curriculum reform. Her project aimed to increase youth engagement by building partnerships between school districts and communities with various concrete activities in mind. In Boston and San Diego, for instance, students, schools, and communities conducted student surveys that became the foundation for new curriculum initiatives. In that work, young people were active participants and researchers. In our own ethnography, we too chose to engage with youth while operating under similar processes and values. John Smyth (2007) also asserts that student voice is a key component to identifying reasons for and reducing student dropout rates – inextricably tied to engagement in high school – and proposes an analytical framework he calls the "cultural geography of the school." Smyth presents the analysis of 209 student interviews in a cultural geography table, comparing hostile experiences and hospitable experiences in school, and how these affect a student's sense of belonging in the school. He then categorizes students' reasons for leaving into five themes (individual responsibility; opportunity to express views; care, respect, and consistency; quality of teaching; and maturity of treatment) that resonate strongly with my own analysis of students' reasons for, and experiences of, (dis)engagement with school. Smyth also discusses the all-important issue of trust and assent, drawing on Erickson's key point that "*not* learning can be seen as a form of political resistance" (p. 648, emphasis added).

Over the last two decades, the concept of engagement has certainly received much attention. This is the case, I believe, because engagement has been regarded as a way to explain low levels of academic achievement, as well as generalized boredom at school and high early-leaving rates, in urban areas. Also, because engagement is presumed to be a dynamic quality, it has been regarded as a field of potential for policy intervention aimed at increasing student success (Fredricks et al. 2004). And yet despite sensing the fervour with which scholars were pursuing studies of student engagement, I came away uncertain still about what engagement might look like and how we were managing, for all our research, to miss so patently young people's own perspectives on what engages and disengages them. Although aggregate rates of early-school leaving and academic achievement are well documented in Canada, both at the provincial and district board levels, less is known about the daily experiences, conditions, and interactions that shape long-term processes of students' engagement or disaffection with a school system.

In our study, we took a broad view of engagement and disengagement. We spent years of qualitative time in high school classrooms in our two local Toronto schools and creating two different cross-site surveys, while trying to capture a more expansive view of engagement across our very diverse local and global sites. We used two kinds of surveys in our study: an online survey completed by students across all sites and what we called a reflective survey completed in-person by students at the completion of classes judged by teachers to have been especially engaging.

The purpose of the online surveys was to quantitatively explore dynamics of student engagement that we were beginning to understand through our qualitative work. The reflective in-person survey provided specificity and helped us to tie student responses to particular pedagogies being used in the classrooms; these were not just generic survey questions. Teachers distributed these surveys to their students on a day that they, the teachers, considered to have been particularly engaging. On the heels of a successful class, we asked students to reflect on the particular pedagogies they experienced to see whether the teacher's idea of an engaging class was also shared by students. Ultimately, we could not easily validate these findings, so we took their responses more as indications of what aspects of the pedagogy we should pay particular attention to. Taken together, these two surveys represent our attempt, albeit through quantitative tools, to preserve some measure of the "liveness" of an engaging experience.

Nesting quantitative studies within a qualitative one also allowed us to ask broad questions about students' lives outside school that we wouldn't have come to understand ethnographically or through interviews. The process also allowed us to pursue questions of interest about student engagement, home-school relationships, and the drama space as a rehearsal site for broader civic engagement. In the associated literature, we found very little qualitative or quantitative research that signalled the relevance of life outside school to how young people choose to engage with, or disengage from, school. In our experience, it mattered hugely. There are studies that examine neighbourhood factors (see Daly et al. 2009, for instance) in determining in-school engagement, but these tend to disregard important in-school factors. In our research, we wanted to take a comprehensive look at environmental forces like neighbourhood, family, and peer and community supports, and how they are impacted by drama pedagogy and by responsive and relational teaching.

The study of student engagement also tells us about the degree to which young people perceive the value of their presence and participation in school. Our research made central the importance of student engagement in learning because the dramatic performances developed and then shared among the five research sites were imagined and created by the youth using, as sources, their experiences of the "hidden" or "corridor" curriculum of engagement. These performances were communicated to and discussed with researchers of other sites through the use of multilingual digital technology. Fredricks et al. (2004) suggest that, to date, research has not capitalized on the potential of engagement as a multidimensional construct that involves behaviour, emotion, and cognition. Our work, with its participatory arts-based design and affinity to the informal spaces of learning in schools, tapped into this multidimensionality.

Our three international and two local sites all embraced youth marked by socio-economic disadvantage. We knew that life both in and outside school, with its economic pressures, peer affiliations, stories of language and migration, and broader cultural politics, had tremendous influence on young people and how they could take up learning as the opportunity we mean it to be. In some ways, our study of engagement became a long rumination on how young people *come to care*, or in some cases, the ways in which social barriers and personal lives impede their commitment to an idea, a project, a community, an imaginary. Why do some young people care while others do not? Why do some young people have the luxury of caring while others do not? When is disengagement strategic, a survival instinct; when does it tell us educators, in no uncertain terms, that we have got it wrong? When is engagement a matter of choosing life over the grim alternatives? When is disengagement operating as social position or political resistance? And when and how does an artistic idea take hold?

In many countries, urban education is considered to be in "crisis" (see Gallagher and Fusco 2006; Anyon 2005; Fine and Weis 2003; Thomson 2002; Yon 2000) and the literature in urban schooling would suggest that this "crisis" has been in full throttle for at least 20 years. The "crisis" is characterized, in some studies, by (discursively) associating "urban" with "burden": that is, urban areas are drains on a city's and/or nation's financial and human resources (see Barber 1992 and Barber and Dann 1996 for a UK perspective; Cibulka and Boyd 2003 for a US perspective; Kalantzis 1995 for an Australian perspective; Kelly, Purvey, Jaipal, and Penberg 1995 for a Canadian perspective). Other studies tend to position "urban issues" as a set of opportunities to redress the inequality (economic and educational) that has prevailed in urban centres (see Dean 2001; Mirón 1996; Ziegler, Hardwick, and McCreath 1989).

Notions of urban and multicultural education continue to identify "diversity" and other "urban challenges" as the greatest obstructions to healthy, safe, and high-achieving classroom communities. The ideologies that help to constitute the phenomenon of "at risk," a pervasive term in the urban schooling literature, too often carelessly link failure with identity difference. As James's (2012) study of stereotyping and Black boys in Canada points out, the label of "at risk" often refers to student deficits rather than learning needs. Risk can denote class, neighbourhood, individual characteristics, parental behaviours, and teacher/administration expectations (p. 465). Fuelled by these misconceptions, our research attempted to address this familiar and problematic conflation by bringing youth together to take a local-global and virtual perspective in order to examine the crucial roles played by issues of diaspora and immigration, structures of racism, ideological constructions of home, fluid conceptions of culture, and malleable forms of identity in student engagement and school success.

Our project partners examined, in this context of "cities in crisis," the causes and consequences of changes brought about by globalization as they related especially to urban youth in local schools. Given, for instance, the over-representation of Chinese- and South Asian-born students in "disadvantaged" schools in Canada and their documented "under-performance" (see Reitz and Banerjee 2007) our relationship with youth in Taipei and Lucknow opened up particularly useful channels of communication about the "corridor" experiences lived by many of Canada's new immigrant students living in economically disadvantaged communities. The experience of seeing one another in the process of evaluating connectedness to "home" and "culture" contributed to local understanding for communities similarly searching for space and place within new multicultural realities. This is especially the case in cities like Toronto and Boston, but in Taipei, more recently, there has been growing interest in issues of multiculturalism, which are experienced there as an integration of Aboriginal Taiwanese students into mainstream schools.

In an early trip to Taiwan (December 2006), when I was conceptualizing this project, I was asked by those who invited me to identify aspects of multiculturalism in Canada that might offer particular insight for those attempting to manage this relatively new phenomenon in Taiwan. These ideas do not simply translate easily across geographic and cultural borders. I felt a longer and sustained relationship would offer so much more to all of us. In Lucknow, there are also many diverse groups living together – Muslims, Hindus, Christians, Buddhists, Sikhs, Jains, Parsis – and several linguistic groups from different states – Punjabis, Gujaratis, South Indians, Maharashtrians, Bengalis – working out a multi-cultural/lingual environment. And, of course, there are caste groups.

Such borders, though distinct, are sometimes more permeable in schools, which often prove to be especially productive laboratories. Canadian urban schools offer a particularly fertile context in which to ask such questions. As persuasively summarized in the War Child Canada report:

> Canadians live in an increasingly interconnected world. Technology, media, trade, disease, and the environment have no borders, drawing Canada – and all Canadians – into a complex reality where "local" and "global" can seem anachronistic; what happens *locally*, now matters *globally*, and what happens *globally*, now matters *locally*." (The War Child Canada Report 2006, p. 9).

Storytelling and Ethnography

Finally, a brief word about our experiments in collaborative ethnography and why and how we used theatre, methodologically, to make sense of the lives and stories we engaged with. I found the early thinking of Hannah Arendt to be particularly useful in our methodological experiments. It has been argued that storytelling is the term Arendt used to describe critical understanding that comes from experience. From much of her writing, it is clear that she understood that all abstract theories began as particular experiences. In her *Lectures on Kant's Political Philosophy*, Arendt describes storytelling as the way one trains the imagination to "go visiting," arguing that it is neither a vehicle for authentic critical voice, as some humanists might reason, nor a means by which one can postpone the authoritative moment necessary to criticism and action (1982, p. 43). For instance, in *Between Past and Future*, she writes:

> My assumption is that thought itself arises out of incidents of living experience and must remain bound to them as the only guideposts by which to take its bearings. (1977, p. 14)

Young-Bruehl (1977) described Arendt as having "an unfailing regard for the life of the story ... and a charming disregard for mere facts"

(p. 183). Storytelling, or as we often experienced storytelling through theatre that draws on symbol and metaphor, realism and abstraction, can act as a "methodological release point" to invite the unsaid, the masked, the contested, the contradictory. And here, I must thank Sara McLelland and Michelle Fine (2008) for their invention of this term to describe the sometimes halting or uneven bursts of understanding that can result from innovative qualitative methodologies.

Storytelling as a narrow, truth-telling method has had a strong foothold in education research. "Keeping it real" and telling "real stories," so much the expectation of traditional ethnography, often anchors researchers to only those things that can be or were spoken in the given context rather than using stories – methodologically – as spaces for exploration and rival musings. I desperately wanted to resist this reductive and appropriating form of reporting in my own work. There is a social science possible, I believe, that does not divest experience of its ambiguities and contradictions. Lyotard (1984) argues that it is their consensus-resisting capacities, their rejection of the linear, and their capacity to hold fragments together, that make stories a particularly powerful postmodern force. Stories, whether theatrical or narrative, demand interpretation; they cannot be taken literally. In my experience of using theatre with youth to tell and hear stories, I wanted to make the experiences we were having together theoretically and contextually rich, and to let their words not simply illustrate but also interact, critically, with the complexities of our research, the philosophical dimensions of our inquiry, and our own theoretical constructions as researchers.

As I have attempted to articulate at greater length elsewhere (Gallagher 2011), storytelling through theatre takes on a polyvocality, rather than a "telling it like it is." Storytelling also helps us see how it is that stories of cultures come to be taken as natural and unquestioned. Rather than taking experience and stories as the grounds for ethnographic authority, as more traditional forms of anthropological and educational ethnography have done, storytelling as method in "the field" with young people is often consensus-resisting and dialectical. Storytelling used in this way positions the story not as a place at which to arrive, but as a place from which to begin inquiry.

Storytelling is not a term Arendt defined precisely, but she does call on a most useful metaphor – "thinking without a banister" (*Hannah Arendt: The Recovery of the Public World*, 1979) in arguing how storytelling can invite critical thinking. Disch (1994) suitably describes the process of thinking without a banister as a call for a "way of proceeding in which critical categories are not imposed on but inspired by one's engagement with a phenomenon" (p. 144). This orientation positions storytelling, as I am suggesting, as a place to begin inquiry rather than as a place on which to fix pre-existing categories and meanings, resulting in what I have often thought of as a reality rut.

We worked in this way with the youth in our study. We used ideas and provocations raised in classroom discussion or in interviews as points of departure for further excavation. The interpretive work of understanding the embodied languages of theatre enlivens research for both researchers and research participants. It becomes a dialogue, a system of communication that is unlike any other form of research communication. It is about sharing a language to talk about, beside, and around shared concerns. It is, for researchers, about coming in through the back door, or the side door – not bursting in through the front door with contrived questions of rehearsed neutrality. This thinking-in-community approach exercised the imagination and stimulated a plurality of the mind that was important to us, as researchers, and to our research participants. In our work, we moved back and forth between the local and the global, between drama and education, between micro-pedagogies and broad social movements, between story and politics.

The book's structure comes from our five years of analysis and writing. We analysed both qualitative and quantitative data, using various software analysis programs like SPSS, Atlas ti, and Nvivo. We also used feminist sociologist Laurel Richardson's "writing as method" to help us make sense of the various pedagogies and the vastly different worlds of students we were encountering across sites. There were, of course, overarching contextual data that helped us understand the specificity of the sites we were encountering, such as understanding the persistent educational problems students encountered and the available educational supports in each site and in the larger social context. We took particular note of the empirical data associated with experiences and groupings of gender: our Toronto and Boston schools were co-educational; our Taiwanese school was vocational and predominantly male; our Indian school was exclusively for lowest caste girls. Paying attention to the social performances of young people, the teacher discourses, the various drama pedagogies and performances, and the unique forms of literacy became important points of cross-site comparison, as did our general reflection on how participating in such a research project affected different students in different sites.

In the second and third years of the study, when our Toronto sites experienced the Verbatim play *The Middle Place*, produced by Toronto theatre company Project: Humanity, and subsequently engaged in some of their own Verbatim storytelling, we were able to examine more closely the students' experiences of Verbatim theatre as a pedagogy and an artistic genre, the interesting relational engagements between artists and audiences provoked by such theatre, and also popular and media images of North American youth. Our research team conducted 75 post-show interviews with youth and adult audience members fresh from the experience of seeing the play. Through these interviews, we became particularly interested in a general audience's perceptions of youth and their reflections on theatre as a form and venue for social commentary.

This research was never intended to be a traditional comparative international study. Our ethnographic engagements with each site were different. There were some barriers to ethnographic work in Boston and Taipei. Consequently, the bulk of our phenomenological experiences and theatre activities occurred in our two Toronto sites and in our Indian site. We were not interested in how students in Lucknow compared to students in Toronto, but we were interested in how our understanding of young people and schools and teaching in North America was changed by our growing understandings of young people living and learning in vastly different environments. The multi-sitedness of the study has allowed us to think through the effects of what some have aptly called the "asymmetrical globalization" of youth culture (see Kennelly and Poyntz, forthcoming). What started as a hunch, that is, our attempt to take distance from something we thought we understood fairly well, usefully challenged our assumptions and generated new learning: new learning about ourselves, our cultural norms, our habits of thought. Seeing ourselves in relation to others was a conceptual and methodological focus throughout. To do this, we took a phenomenological stance, which involves suspending one's habitual acceptance of a shared world, the backdrop against which we typically interpret the experiences of others.

An experience of spectatorship, then, both in the theatres and in the classrooms where we researched, returned us to that beautiful paradox of the unique and individual experience, undertaken in the context of a pulsating sociality. Rancière (2011) captures it best:

> The collective power shared by spectators does not stem from the fact that they are members of a collective body or from some specific form of interactivity. It

is the power each of them has to translate what she perceives in her own way, to link it to the unique intellectual adventure that makes her similar to all the rest in as much as this adventure is not like any other. (pp. 16–17)

On the very first day of the study, when we arrived in one of our Toronto classroom sites, I was introduced to a Grade 11 class of students in our downtown school. I introduced myself, offering what I thought were my "street creds," explaining to the students that I'd been studying high school students for most of my academic career after having taught in a high school for 10 years. I shared with them some of my previous publications and proceeded "selling" myself as a capable researcher. At one point during my monologue, one young woman raised her hand: "How are you going to hear anything new? How are you going to hear *us* and not just all the other teenagers you've worked with in the past? How are you going to pay attention to what *we* have to say?" A very fair question. And one that I kept in the foreground of my mind for the next five years.

1 The Complexity of People, Conversation, and Space as Data

Middleview Technical School

Middleview has 1,797 students (62% male, 38% female, 56% of students with a primary language other than English) and is physically the largest technological school in the province of Ontario. It offers a comprehensive selection of academic and technological study programs. From their website, the school we're calling Middleview, located in downtown Toronto, describes itself as:

> a composite school offering a wide range of programs, including all core academic courses with modern computer technology integrated into all core subjects, as well as concentration and specialization in visual arts and technical studies. [Middleview] also offers enriched levels and special education, including resource room and monitoring for students who have been identified as having learning disabilities, and support for students in the transition from high school to university, college, or employment.
>
> We believe that each student's personal, intellectual, and social growth can be accomplished by a shared interaction with other students, staff, and the community. [Middleview] is committed to developing personal discipline, caring, and a respect for the rights of others. An active Students' Council adds to the excitement at [Middleview], supporting varied co-curricular programs in physical education, music, art, and student clubs.
>
> [Middleview] enjoys a fine reputation in the university, community college, and business communities for the calibre of its graduates.

Promotional in tone, as these things tend to be, the website paints a rather different picture from the one we came to understand from teachers and students, and from our own experiences there. I am not meaning to suggest that the website blurb is dishonest, or that what teachers and students and researchers say about a place is some kind of unadulterated truth. Instead, I am confirming that school spaces, and the social relations of schools, are complex and changeable. Cultural geographer Doreen Massey writes that while places may have boundaries, these borders are open and porous. Spaces inform, and are informed by, the outside. In this way, spaces should find definition not by exclusion, bordering, and ordering, but by the specific "constellation of social relations" (Massey 1994, p. 154) within and around them. Each person in the school experiences this constellation of social relations within and around the school differently; these sometimes contradictory accounts together constituted our sense of Middleview as a space for academic and social learning. Massey's notion of space and social relations in dynamic interplay best captures our sense, post-analysis, of how the physical spaces and diverse relationships came together in our understanding of the school.

The website continues:

> [Middleview] is a full service secondary school that provides programming at every level! Our motto: *"To strive, to seek, to find, and not to yield"* has inspired thousands of students to seek the best in themselves. Our school is a semestered school in the heart of downtown Toronto. We pride ourselves on serving a diverse student population of almost 2,000 students! *The world is welcome at [Middleview!]*. We boast outstanding technical programs and a visual arts centre second to none. [Middleview] staff, in partnership with families, employers, and community agencies is committed to the cultural and moral development of our students.

Despite the long description on the website about the importance of attendance and the rules governing absence, we found in both of our Toronto schools that absenteeism was in fact the greatest challenge for teachers and students.

Braeburn Secondary School

Our second Toronto site is really two schools housed in one building. We worked in the Ed-Vance program (students aged 18–20) rather than in the adult learning program (students 21 or older). From their website:

> [Braeburn] is a secondary school that offers an academic program for adult students who wish to earn the Ontario Secondary School Diploma

(OSSD). Under the same roof, [Braeburn] Secondary School offers the Ed-Vance Program, which provides an opportunity for adolescents aged 18–20 to re-enter the education system to earn credits quickly towards the completion of their diploma or post-secondary requirements.

[Braeburn] offers courses at the applied, academic, open, college, and university levels. All the usual academic courses are available, such as Mathematics, English, ESL, Science, Business, Computers, History and the Social Sciences. The school also offers a certificate program for Personal Support Workers and the first semester of the Practical Nursing and Police Foundations programs.

The school is located in downtown Toronto but draws students from the entire city. There are approximately 2,000 students in the Adult program at [Braeburn] and an additional 500 students in the Ed-Vance program.

In describing the Ed-Vance program, the mode of address shifts:

You've been out of school long enough to gain perspective, long enough to know that education is the answer to the career – and the life – you want. The trouble is: you need more credits. You need to brush up on reading, writing, and math skills. You need the right connections to universities, colleges, apprenticeships, and the workforce. But where do you turn?

Turn to Ed-Vance. And advance your talent, your skills, your creativity.

Many of the students we interviewed and worked with during our time at Braeburn had found out about the school through word of mouth, most considering that they had been lucky to have stumbled upon it. The school year at Braeburn Ed-Vance is divided into four quads (Quadmesters). A quad is like a semester in a regular high school, only it is approximately 10 weeks long. Students are required to take three courses each quad.

As part of their promotional and recruitment material, the website also explains:

Ed-Vance Demands Commitment
- Regular attendance
- Demonstrated dedication to learning and personal progress
- Transcript must be provided
- Mandatory interview

Ed-Vance Makes Learning Personal
- Enrolment is limited, class sizes are limited
- Specialized, pre-selected teachers commit to your success
- Strong co-op placements showcase your abilities

Ed-Vance Promotes New Ways to Learn
- Experiential learning is tied in with a variety of academic courses. Computer labs, software, digital cameras, a fully outfitted food and nutrition lab, science labs, and other technological devices are used for a variety of courses
- Mentoring is available for all students – whether it be individuals who have turned their lives around, teachers, teacher candidates, nurse candidates, community organization representatives, or community members

Are you an Ed-Vance Candidate?
- The Ed-Vance program is for students who have very clear educational and career goals and who are:
- 18–20 years old
- have earned at least 5 high school Applied or Academic credits to date

Gala Public School, Boston

We never worked inside our Boston site in person. Our knowledge of this school and its students came through our collaborator's qualitative work and our quantitative survey analysis. We would have preferred to spend time in this site as well, but our collaborator began in a New York school, and because she moved to Emerson College from New York University in the middle of the study, she had to find a new school, gain ethical clearance, and start the process again. Time was against us. It should also be noted that she never managed to get the New York City school board to agree to participate in our study, despite much effort. They were primarily concerned about the digital/video interests of the study and how sharing of data with other international collaborators might expose their schools in ways that were unacceptable to them. Once in Boston, Dr. Marin experienced some of the same issues with both university and school board ethics procedures but did finally, in the fourth year of the study, make her way into the school.

Consequently, this site offered contextual information but was mainly involved in the quantitative survey.

This urban Boston middle and high school is a pilot school but not a charter school and is part of the Boston Public Schools. The school has a student population of 490 students. Over half of the students are Asian, one quarter are African American/Black, one eighth of the students are Hispanic, and less than 10 per cent are White or Other. The 37 teachers in the school are Black (20.7%), Hispanic (6.9%), White (34.5%), and Asian (37.9%). There is a high attendance rate (93.9%) and a low drop-out rate (1.0%). Students are enrolled in one of two programs – Regular Education (78.9%) and Special Education (21.0%). International Baccalaureate and Advanced Placement courses are also offered.

On their website this is how they choose to feature the strengths of the school:

> A pilot school that builds on the [Gala] Elementary School program to create a rich, challenging, seamless K–12 educational program:
>
> - Four conceptual educational pavilions: *Information* for science, math, and technology; *Cultural* for developing historical and cultural sensitivities; *Pathfinding* for exploring 21st century issues and encouraging individual expression through art, music, and physical education; and *Renewal* for mental, physical, and emotional health
> - International Baccalaureate programs, an academically rigorous curriculum available in select schools around the world
> - Teacher involvement in decision-making
> - Teachers as instructional and operational leaders and peer mentors
> - Weekly professional development
> - Longer school day

We also learned that they offer an Advanced Placement English Course and that they help with the tests that lead to college admission and offer social work assistance to students. At Gala, a student would meet with a teacher-led advisory group daily to discuss concerns. From the school climate survey conducted by the Office of Research, Assessment, and Evaluation: Boston Public Schools, we also learned the following. Regarding "Standardized Climate Scores compared to the District," the school scored below the district mean on everything except "principal effectiveness." Here they scored right on the mean. The areas where they scored below the mean were "perceptions of the school," "student enthusiasm for learning," and "teacher effectiveness." On the question "My teacher expects me to make good grades," the percentage of student responses was above the district mean and evenly distributed across races. On the question "My teacher(s) provides daily opportunities for students to contribute in class," most racial groups were above the mean but African American/Blacks had the largest number who disagreed and the largest number who disagreed strongly. Also from the climate survey, we learned that the question asked of teachers: "What do you think is the most important factor influencing how much students learn in school?" produced the following:

- 28% of teachers selected family support as the most important factor.
- Approximately 16% of teachers selected intrinsic motivation of students as the most important factor.
- 38% of teachers selected one of four responses that are under the category "teachers" influence.

Si Fang High School of Commerce and Industry, Taipei

There are three types of senior high schools in Taiwan: Academic, Mixed, and Vocational. Our school, Si Fang High School of Commerce and Industry, was founded in 1917 and is located in the capital city of Taipei. It contains both mixed and vocational streams. There are 2,500 staff and students together and the male to female ratio is 4:1. The school is highly disciplined, has the reputation of low academic performance, and serves socio-economically disadvantaged families. Students attend eight classes a day between 8:10 a.m. and 4:50 p.m. Monday-Friday, and each class is 50 minutes long. The average commute to school for students is one hour. Educationally, the parents of students in the school had high school diplomas although some had college certificates. In the classes we worked with, most students were Taiwanese, although there was one Aboriginal and one Japanese student. The students identified their top three worries as academic performance, future career planning, and money.

Our collaborators in Taipei, Dr Yu-hsuan Lin, Dr Su Chien-ling, independent artist Betsy Lan, and research student Hui-wen Lo worked in two drama classrooms in the spring of 2009 and the fall of 2010. In the 2009 class there were 43 students (27 boys and 16 girls), and in the 2010 class there were 39 students (24 boys and 15 girls). The drama classes took place on Wednesday afternoons and were two hours long. The team spent 11 classes with the students, doing drama with them, and they also took a field trip together to see a play Betsy Lan was performing in, called in translation The One Who Boiled the Sea. The students engaged in a lot of physical theatre activities, games of concentration, and community building exercises. Near the end of the 11 weeks, the students watched a performance (*The Doors*) devised by the students at Middleview in Toronto, and engaged in visual art responses to the performance they watched on video. At the end of the workshops the students completed our online and reflective surveys.

At our first collaborator meeting in Toronto, our Taiwanese collaborators talked about how the students found "acting" intimidating. Doing drama was not a usual part of the curriculum; it was met with some scepticism by students and teachers. They were more accustomed to lecture-style teaching, and while some found the drama activities playful, they also found them "childish" and intimidating. The classroom teacher, who had no drama training, always kept a watchful eye and often seemed worried that important time for other, more academic, work would be lost. The researchers did manage to see how engagement in drama also provided some "escape" from the authoritarian structure of the school; the students seemed engaged even when they felt shy. The researchers completed 15 individual interviews with students in each of the two classes and an interview with the classroom teacher. But the classroom teacher insisted on being present at all student interviews, which considerably changed the dynamic, and the researchers found the conversations to be very limited as a result. The surveillance at the school was extraordinarily heavy.

Our Taiwanese collaborators spoke about the many challenges they faced, the unofficial status of drama in the Taiwanese curriculum, the cultural resistance to drama's pedagogies, the shame many students felt about not being viewed as "academically strong," but, most significantly, the highly authoritarian school system that privileged discipline and order over most everything else. After these two years of work, our Taiwanese collaborators found themselves without a site. The teacher, Miss Lee, had been unceremoniously fired from her position as public discipline for the poor test performance of her students. Consequently, we had the Taiwanese sites collaborate with us for only two of the five years of the ethnography. The first year gave us much of our contextual understanding and the second allowed students to participate in the quantitative survey.

Figure 1: Rehearsal of *The Doors* at Middleview

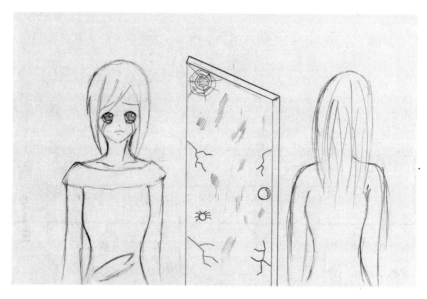

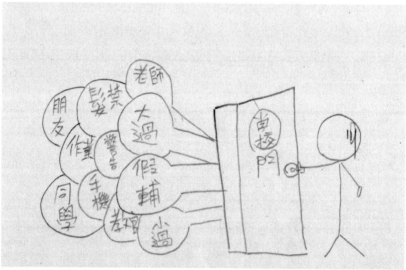

Figure 2a/2b: Artwork produced by students in Taipei from the metaphor of "doors" in their lives – inspired by their viewing of the Toronto students' performance of their play *The Doors*

George Marcus (1995) foresaw the challenge of multi-sitedness, warning that the quantity of fieldwork in each site will never be uniform. His description certainly reflects our experience of global, multi-sited ethnography. Though the Taiwanese and American students provided us with important quantitative data, and their school contexts created for us a broader backdrop against which to evaluate our own local experiences, it was the case that for both duration and quality our engagements with the two Toronto sites and the Indian site were strongest.

Prerna Girls School, Lucknow

Finally, we turn to Lucknow, the place where we spent time as ethnographers and the site with which we collaborated most profoundly over the course of five years. There were significant moments of sharing performance and pedagogical work between Middleview and Prerna. These moments of collaboration taught us a great deal about self-other relations not only in the context of our research collaboration but also with respect to how we came to understand artistic, academic, and social engagement for young people in an era of hyper-globalization. We learned the most from this site; it was free of the kinds of bureaucratic and institutional barriers in evidence in both the Boston and the Taipei sites. Prerna, founded in 2003, is an all-girl preschool to 12th grade formal school, run by a private foundation called Study Hall Educational Foundation (SHEF). SHEF's extensive website introduction bears consideration. Its tone and underlying philosophy stand in sharp contrast to those of the others:

> All testing and evaluation is done only with the motive of helping the children learn better and NOT with the idea of passing judgment on them. They are in school to learn and to be helped in learning, and NOT to perform and be judged. Learning is too complex a process to be gauged adequately by marks and grades. Moreover, these end up assuming a disproportionate importance in the minds of children, parents, and teachers, perverting the learning endeavour and becoming the end towards which learning is directed. As such we have abandoned the minimalistic and often humiliating practice of grading, ranking, or marking in our classrooms.
>
> We strive to create a friendly, collaborative learning environment in our classrooms, which enables our children to develop freely at their own pace, even as they move towards optimising their potential without the

fear and humiliation of unfair comparisons with their friends. We try to help our children and to ensure that they emerge not only with literacy and numerical skills, but more importantly, as secure individuals, sure of their special worth.

We believe that schools should be nurturing places where everyone – teachers, students and parents – should feel supported, cared for, and respected. We conceive of teaching as an extremely creative and complex process, one requiring much imagination, continuous thinking, caring, and commitment. Teachers are all very creative persons, needing the freedom and the opportunity to discover their own hidden depths, which flower and blossom, given a hospitable climate. We try to create an environment that nurtures the creativity and growth of our teachers too, because we believe that only those who are prepared to learn and grow all their lives can teach effectively. We work towards making our school a "community of learners," based upon a foundation of mutual support, caring and trust – one, in which we are constantly learning from each other.

The school was founded in January 1986 with the vision described above. Since then we have structured our school around the beliefs and values mentioned above. Our pedagogy, teaching methodology, our curriculum, organizational structure, teacher-student relationship, policies, and rules are all designed to actualize our vision of schooling and education. The happiness with which our children come to school, the joy with which they learn, the caring and imagination with which our teachers teach them, and the appreciative co-operation that we receive from our parent body, is sufficient validation of our efforts. This tells us that we are on the right path and encourages us to continue in this direction.

SHEF began its work in 1986, with the goal of providing quality education to all children in India. Its main area of work has been in Uttar Pradesh, which is one of the largest and most underdeveloped states in India. Currently SHEF is reaching out to over 300 teachers, 6,000 children, and 14,000 student teachers through its schools and other programs.

Prerna school is located in Lucknow, the capital city of Uttar Pradesh (UP). Uttar Pradesh is the most populous state of India, with a population of more than 199 million, and a sex ratio of 908 women to 1,000 men. Lucknow has a population of 2.81 million people. Prerna is located in the area of Gomti Nagar, which is a neighbourhood like many in Indian cities where affluent residential homes are situated alongside very poor slums. The majority of students come from the slums of Gomti Nagar, some travelling from other more distant slums. Prerna is housed in a fairly large, well-equipped, and well-furnished building of a private fee-paying school for middle-class children, called Study Hall, also established by SHEF. Prerna operates in a second shift in the afternoon, after the Study Hall day is over. Prerna is an all-girls' school and has a secure building with security guards. Its classes are held from 1:30 p.m. until 5:30 p.m. in the summer, and 2:00 p.m. until 6:00 p.m. in the winter.

Some further context setting about India is warranted. India's Parliament passed the Right to Education Act in 2009, but has struggled to fill the financing gap; consequently implementation has been thwarted. UNESCO estimates that there is an external financing gap of $16 billion a year to support basic education needs in low-income countries, over and above what developing country governments and donors currently resource (van der Gaag and Abetti 2011). This is why the Center for Universal Education says we are in a "global learning crisis." At the current pace, most countries, it has been argued, will fail to meet the "Education for All" and the Millennium Development Goals by 2015, by a wide margin.

Our collaborator, Dr. Urvashi Sahni, the founder of Prerna, runs the fee-paying school (Study Hall) in the day for middle-class students and uses their tuition to pay teachers to stay in the afternoons and evenings to teach the lowest caste girls from neighbouring slums, who would otherwise have no school at all. Dr. Urvashi Sahni, beginning with 80 girls from local slums, founded Prerna School in 2003. They recruited door to door and now have 650 students.

At Prerna, all graduating students are placed with jobs. The school currently has a staff of 20. Classes take place in the late afternoon hours, housed in the private school building, and use all its facilities. There is a very powerful rights-based program in the curriculum. It also has strong community involvement and interventions. Many of these take the form of drama in the streets. To date, Prerna has graduated three classes of Class 12 students, and by 2013 all the girls from the very first graduating class had graduated from a three-year degree program with a bachelor of arts degree. UNESCO's education and millennium development goals reported in 2010 that if all children in low-income countries left school knowing how to read, something that currently does not happen, then 171 million people could move out of poverty. Another way to think about this: a child born to a mother who can read is 50 per cent more likely to survive past age five. Education, quite literally, is a life-or-death issue.

In many developing countries, including India, live folk theatre has been a key tool for addressing social problems, raising awareness about issues, and mobilizing public support for change. This mode of theatre is necessarily participatory in nature, relying on a collective process of learning between community members. India, Lori McDougall writes (2003), has seen a mushrooming of community-based organizations in recent years. Many of these organizations have sought to use popular theatre as a tool for development education. They have sought to tie drama to specific social development objectives, such as raising awareness of domestic violence or the importance of female empowerment (p. 173). Empowerment, as a concept, has been critiqued by many post-structural feminists who object to a general lack of analysis of power when it is constructed as merely a psychological phenomenon. Such a use of "empowerment" often has the unintended effect of either pathologizing those seen to be in need of empowerment and/or reinforcing the often-unstated dominance of those who seek to empower. Exploring tensions in school-based participatory action research, Kohfeldt et al. (2011) define the term in a useful way as "a process through which individuals and groups gain increased control over access to the conditions and resources that affect their lives" (p. 29). Performance methodology may be more or less participatory in nature, depending on the supporting organization and the scale of the program. Grassroots organizations tend to undertake small-scale activities that give equal weight to the "means" (collective analysis) as well as the "ends" (community mobilization). Meanwhile, larger organizations such as government departments may conceive of folk theatre as a form of mass social advertising, in which drama is used to illustrate specific developmental themes and messages in a popular fashion (McDougall 2003, p. 173).

India has been reported to have experienced high rates of economic growth since 2008, but sharp inequalities and minimal effects on the reduction of poverty, it must be remembered, have accompanied this. The middle and upper-middle classes in India have overwhelmingly reaped the benefits of neoliberal globalization and the opportunities that have come with the new economy. However, families living in poverty continue to take their children out of school, or keep their older children in and take their younger children out. That girls' education has suffered in comparison to boys' is reflected in the observation that among families who had been involved in gem and jewellery work (the most highly integrated into the global market), 20 per cent have withdrawn their girl children from school (Hirway 2009).

As many as 300 million people in India are officially living in extreme poverty. Bhaduri (2008) points to neoliberal policies during the period of globalization (beginning in the early 1990s), the exploitive nature of the informal labour markets, and inadequate pro-poor policies that have sharply increased undernourished and illiterate children coexisting with billionaires created by this rapid growth.

On What Do We Base Our "Findings"?: Performative and Relational Methods and Modalities

A "finding," as a term, is inadequate for the kind of research we do. With its positivist reverberations, "findings" imagines researchers "discovering" static things that were always there, waiting for experts to uncover them, like needles in a haystack. In fact, we spent five years co-creating understandings about each other – researchers and young people and teachers and artists – and about our shared and our different contexts.

To the extent that we can enumerate, here is a picture of the methods and modalities we used to collect our extensive data sets. Data is yet another term that misleads the reader with its positive connotations of facts and figures. Our data, too, were relational, performative, and deeply embedded in broader social relations. At the end of year 1, between our 2 Toronto schools, we had filmed 16 classes (roughly 17.5 hours of footage) and 2 student theatre performances, and conducted 4 teacher interviews, 6 focus groups containing a total of 22 students, and 6 individual student interviews. At the end of the second year of the study, we had filmed one 8-hour day with our international collaborators at our Toronto meeting, 15 classes (23.5 hours of class time) at our Toronto schools, and 3 student theatre performances, and had conducted 3 focus groups containing a total of 8 students, and 9 individual interviews. By the end of year 3, we had accumulated another 13 filmed classes (17.5 hours) at our schools, 2 student theatre performances, 4 focus group interviews containing 10 students, 11 individual student interviews, 1 teacher interview. Also, in the third year, after performances of the production *The Middle Place* at both Theatre Passe Muraille and the Canadian Stage theatre in Toronto, we conducted a further 69 post-performance interviews (41 of which were with youth audience members – interviewing 77 youth in total). In the fourth year of the study, in India, we completed 3 teacher interviews, 2 principal interviews, and 1 focus group interview containing 4 students.

The following provides an example of our attempts, through transcriptions of videotape, to capture the dynamics of a lively classroom of students, their communication with their teachers, and the first tentative steps towards building a research relationship. Here is how it all began in Toronto:

> MS. S: OK,OK, so we're doing a couple of things today … ahhhh one is we're going to talk about the research project, and consent forms, and Professor Gallagher, who is right here (*door slams, student walks in*). So, so, ah, I ask that we have a better day today than we had yesterday, and not offend anyone by talking out of turn (*glances towards Fabian*) and not listening to each other –
>
> BELLA: Yesterday wasn't a bad day!
>
> MS. S: Well yesterday was a difficult day for me as a teacher, I felt. OK, because I didn't feel that the respect and listening was there (*looking at Fabian*). And so Fabian, so you're going to sit up so you look like you're listening.
>
> FABIAN: Ummmm, am I?
>
> MS. S: You're going to sit up, so you look like you're listening.
>
> FABIAN: Miss, how can I hear you differently when I'm lying down right beside you?
>
> MS. S: It appears, when you're lying down, that you're not, ahh (*trips over Fabian*) that you're not listening. (*Hands Kathleen over some things.*)
>
> FABIAN: I know you're mad Miss, but … (*Other students laugh.*)
>
> MS. S: All right. Kathleen?
>
> KATHLEEN: I'm just going to hand these out [consent forms], so that people can see just what it is. First of all, is anyone here under 18?

(Some students mumble, a few hands go up.)

> FABIAN: I'll be 18 in a week.
>
> KATHLEEN: OK, because if you're under 18 then you also need your parent to say that it's OK that you are part of this. A parent or guardian.
>
> CAT: Aren't these the same?
>
> FABIAN: One's for the parents.
>
> KATHLEEN: Ah, one is for the parent and one is for you. So you'll see that we tried to make it, um, a little more understandable, what we're doing. Although you still may have questions.
>
> FABIAN: I feel safe (*he inaudibly says "Dr Kathleen Gallagher"*).
>
> KATHLEEN: Did you just say my name?
>
> FABIAN: Yeah.
>
> KATHLEEN: (*touches him on the shoulder*) Well that was very nice, thank you.

(The classroom gets strangely quiet.)

KATHLEEN: So, you'll see there's just a brief description of what the study is about. This is about working in drama classrooms, in different places –. In Toronto, in Boston, in Taiwan, in India –. And looking at how students engage. There's a lot written about youth, but there isn't a lot of research that really um, that really addresses your concerns your, your perspectives on how school works for you or doesn't work for you. So the broad concept is this term that's used a lot in education, "student engagement," which really means "why do we care when we care? And why do we not care when we don't care about school, about what we're doing." So I want to look at that. Um, and also look at young people who might have really different concerns than you in different parts of the world, or who actually, despite our differences, share some common concerns about being who you are, at this historical moment in time. Yearbooks do this, right? It's a particular moment in history, it's a particular cultural moment, and when you are 35 and you pull out an old yearbook and you say "what was going on at that time? When I was that age? And how did it shape me, or how did I contribute to it? How did I even not connect at all with that part of my culture." It's a very interesting exercise so the thing for me is to, as much as we can by engaging with you, participate in the knowledge that you have and the meanings that you make in doing this. You become a special kind of, in research terms it's called an "Informant." Sounds a little criminal, but it's not. It's that you have special insights and we'll pursue that in interviews, if you're willing. It's called research on "human subjects," like, not lab rats, so when we're dealing with human beings they need to have choices, so you can say to me "yeah I don't mind being in the video, but I don't want to be interviewed" or "yes, I want to be interviewed but I don't want to be in the video." And if at some point, at any time, that we are working with you that you decide, "I said yes, but I don't want to do this anymore," that's also your right. You are free to participate with us, you are free not to participate and there will never be any consequences to people saying no to that. Um, but obviously, I hope that you do want to participate, and I totally respect if you, for whatever reasons, don't, on any given day. Umm, that's it. Are there any questions?

CAT: Miss, do you have a pen?

KATHLEEN: I do.

2 The Social and Pedagogical Context for Engagement

Spacialization of Affect

We know that important ideas and feelings are communicated through a space:

> MS. S: You see the school is so old and so run down. You never get anything done at that school in terms of – like the space, the actual physical space – all schools were pretty much built horribly. They're not ... They're not ... Happy places. They're very institutional ... Just, the light ... If I could make education better, I'd just tear down all the buildings and, you know, rebuild. With lots of light, and lots of wood, and lots of beautiful things to look at. I think it affects how they feel. If you're in a classroom where your curtains are all shredded, and your pipes are all leaking, and your blackboard is falling off the wall, and the plaster's falling – and even on your head sometimes, because that happens at our school too – you feel like your education environment is not being respected. And you stop respecting your environment too. I think the quality of the place itself, the actual physical plant affects the students. I think classrooms that are more in shape, and have proper blinds, and lots of light, lots of natural light, and plants, and pictures – I think those classrooms are actually better.
>
> (Interview, Ms. S, Middleview, December 3, 2008)

The obvious disinvestment in public schools helps us to understand the spatialization of affect, the relations of feeling within school spaces. Political economies and policy build possibilities for young people. Disintegrating school infrastructure communicates important ideas to students, to teachers, to a public. Add to this, conflict in the surrounding community and we often have decaying spaces fraught with strained social relations. Foucault believed that the anxiety of our era had to do fundamentally with space. Ms. C at Braeburn shares her perception of conflict beyond the school walls:

> So this was a girlfriend of a gang rival, or something. So I had paired two gang rivals together to do a very romantic, lyrical dance. And I – we went outside and we did that kind of wall thing. I said, "we're gonna walk in and we're just going to be without the borders of our communities, and you know, we're just going to do this as dancers and people sharing art. Can we just try this for me?" And all that history, it's there, and it's real, but let's just start again. Let's just make this space the "start again space."
>
> (Interview, Ms. C, Braeburn, December 11, 2008)

Teachers in both of our Toronto schools worked hard to reinvent the space socially. They both believed that drama gave them some kind of edge, some kind of bracketed-off space that might be able to alter social relations or negate the obvious signs of institutional negligence. The notion of a "start again space" is something teachers in all our sites believed in. It was relevant to their imagining of the intersection of lived experience, classroom interaction, and the difficult work of relationship building and cooperation.

Ms. C at Braeburn offered what is perhaps a common and certainly bleak picture of the larger social breakdown she holds responsible for the challenges she encounters at school:

> We get a lot of violence at school, we get emotional breakdown in the class. We get a kind of apathy ... they're sleeping, they're down, they don't care. And after five years we've realized that it really –I've realized that it's really about this connection to a lack of family on holidays, and a lack of joy on the holiday, and they're not going to get presents, and they're not going to have the family dinner. And they have to go home now for two weeks in their dark lives and deal with the abuse that they're getting, or their gang life, or whatever.
>
> (Interview, Ms. C, Braeburn, December 11, 2008)

Many students at Braeburn also mentioned in interviews their own sense of solitude and hardship. When I asked in a focus group what might prevent them from making it to school on any given day, Kemba replied simply:

> Sometimes, usually bus fare is why I can't, usually I don't have much bus fare. I went to the guidance office and asked, "is there any incentives, like what can I do, can I do some volunteer work, work hard," because I don't believe in getting things free. So what can I do to get a bus ticket? They've been doing so much already so I just asked, but they said there is nothing. Like sometimes I'm demotivated and like I could find fare, I could just ask the TTC driver and go, "look I don't have any fare, I need to go to school, I want to learn, can I have a ride please and a transfer?" and that would work. Sometimes.
>
> (Focus Group Interview, Kemba, Cherry, Max, Peanut, Braeburn, December 1, 2008)

Preserving dignity in the face of economic hardship is a common theme among socio-economically disadvantaged young people. The youth we spoke with do not believe they are owed anything. They have strong self-preservation instincts, but they have also internalized strong neo-liberal messages, taking responsibility for their social and economic struggles. This discourse of not wanting "handouts" is pervasive; an attempt at minimizing the humiliation and powerlessness that they feel. Poverty creates clear structural barriers. As McLoughlin (2013) demonstrates in her study of "couch surfing" among youth in Australia, young people who leave home during their school years and do not have access to parental support face significant barriers in negotiating labour and housing markets, let alone the demands of school. I realized I had been expecting the students to speak about their personal struggles getting to school, and their sense of disengagement with school perhaps. But it was obvious for some that basic economic barriers were in the foreground. Kemba's friend Cherry underscores the challenges:

> I'm just going home and at the end of the day it is only me, I have to depend on myself to go to school. No one is gonna give me what I want so I have to work hard for it.
>
> (Focus Group Interview, Cherry, Kemba, Max, Peanut, Braeburn, December 1, 2008)

Important national and international work has been carried out on the relationship between housing and the social determinants of health, though little work has been carried out on the relationship between stable housing, health, and educational achievement. Dunn et al.'s (2006) needs, gaps, and opportunities national assessment across Canada determined that stakeholders across the country were keenly interested in the impact of housing on the health of vulnerable subgroups, including Aboriginal peoples, immigrants, children/youth, and seniors. It would seem that as urban economic polarization continues, there will be a great need for drawing clear relationships between unstable housing and educational attainment.

Of course, as Giroux and many youth studies scholars suggest, neoliberalism has disabled this kind of social vision, exiling youth to a place of invisibility. In *The Abandoned Generation*, Giroux (2003) wrote that the socio-economic disinvestment in youth has left most children behind. In our experience, young people internalize this "failure"; the discourse of blame and individual responsibility is pervasive. In an interview at Middleview, Ashley offers:

> (*laughs*) No. The attitudes of – no because the people like, they come here or whatever and they always have a negative thing – like, "OK, we're going to do this and this today" and they choose "ooh, (*sighs*) but I'm so lazy, no that's so stupid." It's just the attitude; you have to change it somehow. You have to come there expecting to do work. You have to – that's what school's about. You come to class to do work and to learn so it gets you a better education and whatever and benefits you in your future. Not just to sit around and be lazy and try to get your credit. That's not gonna happen.
>
> (Individual Interview, Ashley, Middleview, November 28, 2008)

David Harvey (2005), an anthropologist at the Graduate Center of The City University of New York and leading critical voice on the contemporary condition of neoliberalism, defines neoliberalism as, "in the first instance a theory of political economic practices that proposes that human well-being can best be advanced by liberating individual entrepreneurial freedoms and skills within an institutional framework characterized by strong private property rights, free markets, and free trade" (p. 2). What is key to his analysis of the rise of the neoliberal state is the ways in which our most treasured cultural values and desires have become the unwitting foot soldiers of an unrelenting movement towards a neoliberalism that ill serves the majority. He explains:

> For any way of thought to become dominant, a conceptual apparatus has to be advanced that appeals to our institutions and instincts, to our values and desires, as well as to the possibilities inherent in the social world

we inhabit. If successful, this conceptual apparatus becomes so embedded in common sense as to be taken for granted and not open to question. The founding figures of neoliberal thought took political ideals of human dignity and individual freedom as fundamental, as the "central values of civilization." In so doing, they chose wisely for these are indeed compelling and seductive ideals. These values, they held, were threatened not only by fascism, dictatorships and communism, but by all forms of state intervention that substituted collective judgments for those of individuals free to choose. (p. 5)

Neoliberalism in education is the term most often used to describe education that is more concerned with producing workers who have acquired standardized skills and understood sanctioned information, focusing more on performance objectives than authentic forms of engagement. In neoliberal education, student-consumers are free to choose their paths, free to succeed or fail on their own terms, and individually responsible for their outcomes. The students we spoke with had internalized this common-sense view. No more notions of the collective, no more analysis of social conditions. Such neoliberal concepts of education are seen as a radical break from earlier paradigms in education that privileged original and critical forms of learning to serve democratic citizenship and the social good, as in the work of John Dewey and others. However, there are also students, like Aleesa, who still struggle with how things are the way they are, and how they have found themselves in such circumstances. These more critical student voices articulate their sense of being misunderstood and how the broader social culture does not appreciate the complexities of young people's lives:

> ALESSA: But there's probably a large amount of people that don't understand why students are here and don't see that it's not because, you know, they're from a ghetto area or they're not smart enough or they're in some sort of crime or something like that. I guess they don't see that there's other things that can happen along the way to set people back.
> (Individual Interview, Alessa, Braeburn, April 29, 2009)

There are two further conditions of schooling post 9/11 that play out in significant ways in urban North American classrooms. As I have argued elsewhere, the formation of new policies of security and surveillance have disproportionately affected the school experiences of socioeconomically marginalized and racialized youth (Gallagher, 2007;

Gallagher and Fusco 2006). Racism, though not a new phenomenon and one that has always been a force of social marginalization in schools, is accompanied by a newer form of xenophobia. Below, a response from Ms. S at Middleview, when I asked her about the place of cultural identity in her teaching:

KATHLEEN: Are students' cultural backgrounds important to how you teach?
MS. S: (*long pause*). Yes. It's part of the social fabric of the class. You can't – you can't ignore or not be sensitive to what's being said in the classroom in terms of culture. Because sometimes students can say things that are very flippant. Like there's this one kid in my class right now who's from Afghanistan and who all the other kids are calling Kumar, because of Harold and Kumar – because he's like the "Indian guy." Then, they also were asking if he was a terrorist recently. But then he had also been very insensitive to other people's culture in the class, too. So there's a constant intervention that I feel like I'm doing in terms of that. But you can't not address things like that. You can't just let them – And that's what happens sometimes, it's so frustrating in teaching that everything's happening all at once, and what do you stop and address? And what do you let go? And how do you – without having to just pounce on everything … but I feel like it's really important to address when somebody's culture is being … being dismissed, or denigrated in some way. And in terms of the work itself, I think … I think … I think sometimes students are just like – if we're doing collective creation, if we're doing writing pieces, there's students that are willing to explore their own culture and questions about their own culture, but you'd never push them to do that, because sometimes students just don't want to do that. So I think you have to be careful with that, that you're not going in saying, "OK, we're going to do a cultural exploration, we're going to ask you lots of personal questions about your culture." You can't assume that they're in a place where they want to be doing that. If the students feel that they can – that they're safe enough to explore those issues – then that's great, then you respect that. And I talk about being Jewish, and I talk about my religious framework and my cultural framework, and that often gets students talking about their own. It's really powerful when you, as a teacher, say things – we had a big discussion in one of my classes the other day about Judaism and Christianity and about God and they were asking tons of questions … So it's really interesting.

(Interview, Ms. S, Middleview, December 3, 2008)

It has long been the case that students seize on cultural difference as a marker of stigma. But this also signals to us how such fear and xenophobia translates into the cultural production of classroom spaces and interactions. The teacher's feeling of being overstretched in terms of being able to effectively deal with the issues of power and culture is also a familiar refrain as choices need to be made in the moment. The social fabric of school is saturated with these kinds of interactions and exchanges.

Attempts to understand race and racism also get worked out by students through their creative work. As we analysed their written and performed work, we were also struck but unsurprised by how often experiences of racism and sexism, and the policing of gender more broadly, make their way into the creative work. This is unsurprising in a class run by a teacher like Ms. S who encourages students to mine their own stories. Sasha performed a very poignant monologue that exorcised the "shadeism" she felt she had experienced in her life living in the Middle East, prior to moving to Canada. In his "black emancipatory action research," Antwi Akom talks about "pigmentocracy" that "refers to a system of advantages or disadvantages based on various phenotypes or skin pigmentation within a racialized hierarchical society" (Akom 2008 cited in Akom 2011, p. 127). Akom's work is to insert the construct of race more explicitly into critical ethnographic methodologies. In Sasha's case, she told of a Grade 5 experience where she was to do a class presentation and her peers told her to use makeup to lighten her face. The monologue goes on to describe her eating disorder that followed this experience wherein she writes about being "fat, ugly, dark people." It ends, however, with her moving out of the position of passive victim. This moment, and our reflections on it, point clearly to the challenge facing all research that attempts to account for the fact that while identity is discursively and performatively constituted, simultaneously, racist structures have real, material consequences.

Another student in her class, Bones McCoy, performed an elaborate monologue about social control and teasing endured by girls who step outside the gender expectations regarding fashion. A girl who likes to dress like a boy is an easy target. Relevant here is the concept of "performativity" and its theoretical elaboration in Judith Butler's *Gender Trouble* (1990) and *Bodies That Matter* (1993). Performativity conceptualizes the paradox of identity as apparently fixed but inherently unstable, revealing gender norms requiring continual maintenance. These texts and other subsequent writing contribute a new conceptual grammar in the interrelated concepts of performativity and citationality to denote a reading of gender neither as essence nor socialization, but as the consequence of the performative, recurring "citations" of gender.

The policing of gender normative behaviour is also explored in so many of the Prerna students' one-minute digital storytelling projects they shared with us. "If you had one minute to introduce yourself to the world, what would that minute look like?" the assignment asked of them. Preeti's video explored the burden of the dowry, Nishu's examined the "burden on the shoulders of families" when one more girl is born. Sunita's video showed a new, young bride facing the hostility of an older wife of the man she'd just married. Sadna's video presented her and her classmates in song, raising their voices against domestic violence and child marriage. Poonam's brief minute pondered the killing of baby girls all over the world. Moni's video was a playful exploration of fathers' attempts to suppress the dreams and desires of girls, in her case, her desire to dance. Priya's video uses humour to explore the differential treatment of boys and girls in the home, and Kushboo's, probably one of the more disturbing in the group, recounts her own story of having to live with her grandmother because her father threw her out of the home when she insisted on continuing her studies at school rather than marry at age16.

This digital storytelling work in India is consistent with others who have used this form in relationship to drama projects. Alrutz (2013) argues that as youth become "prosumers" (a term she borrows from Alvin Toffler 1981) of culture rather than passive "consumers," there is the potential for critique of dominant social meta-narratives. Alrutz lists collaboration and the critical reflection on self/identity, others, and society through embodied activities as central to this kind of work. To explore story and to generate material, Alrutz uses a critical practice of drama that focuses on "power hierarchies and inequities" (p. 47). She adapts the six steps outlined by Joe Lambert of the Berkeley Center for Digital Storytelling (to which the digital storytelling project at Prerna is also associated): "owning your insights; owning your emotions; finding the moment; seeing your story; assembling your story and sharing your story" (p. 47). All of the young women at Prerna, and those in Toronto, too, are acutely aware of the ways in which dominant discourses produce what is taken to be natural and true in any given culture.

Violence, Crime, and Well-Being

Another prevalent social stigma that provides important context for our examination of engagement and greatly shapes students', teachers', and the general public's perception of youth culture and the culture of urban schools is violence and crime. Furlong (2013) insists that the study of youth has always had a strong focus on crime and deviance. He suggests that while it is true that young people are responsible for a high proportion of recorded crimes, he also notes that illegal activities that involve large numbers of young people are both visible and targeted by the media, often creating moral panics. Most youth crime researchers find it difficult to get a clear picture of youth crime and schools because different sets of statistics, created by different groups, paint contradictory pictures. Crime survey statistics tend to paint young crime as largely involving "petty crimes" or minor assaults (Muncie 2009).

> ANNE: Now, what were your perceptions of Middleview before you came here? Did you know anything about it?
>
> RICHARD: Did I know anything about Middleview? I heard negative things about Middleview as well, not just positive (Anne: *Yeah*). Like, I heard there was a lot of conflict – a lot of fights and stuff which kind of was a push factor for me, but I did not let that get in my way and I still came to Middleview. And now it's not so bad as two years ago – there were lots of fights. But I guess they kicked out all the bad students and now it's just the good students.
>
> (Individual Interview, Richard, Middleview, January 14, 2010)

Later in the interview, Richard addresses crime in particular:

> RICHARD: I think the large world kind of – they judge youths. They think that youths are really bad in a certain way. That's not how it is. Even statistics doesn't show that I guess. Because there are criminals that are adults and there are criminals that are youth. I think there are more criminals that are adults most of the time. But I'm not going to say that because I could be wrong.
>
> (Individual Interview, Richard, Middleview, January 14, 2010)

And no matter what school our students went to, they easily imagined better schools and worse schools than their own. There was a comfort in imagining that others had it worse than them. Another common refrain:

> TAYLOR: I think it's changed here because when my mom used to come here she thought it was a really good school but as soon as I told my friends or somebody else that I was coming to this school, "oh, why are you going there, it's so bad. Fights, drugs." And I'm like, "well, isn't that at every school?"
>
> GOKU: My dad was like "they have metal detectors here."
>
> TAYLOR: Yeah, my dad said that too!
>
> ANNE: Do they?
>
> GOKU: I think they did a long time ago.
>
> ANNE: No, they don't.
>
> GOKU: Metal detectors? Like our school's not that bad. It's not like we're going to – what's that school at Jane and Finch?
>
> TAYLOR: Where that kid got shot?
>
> GOKU: That Jordan Manners …
>
> TAYLOR: CWJ.
>
> GOKU: That's a bad school. Like, Police have to roam the halls. Girls get, like, beaten up and raped and stuff. Like that guy got shot last year and there's fights all the time. That's a bad school. That's a school I wouldn't want to go to.
>
> (Focus Group Interview, Goku, Richard, Taylor,
> Middleview, January 5, 2010)

Despite high profile crimes such as the killing of a high school boy in Toronto, the first person to be killed "on school property" in that city, Furlong (2013) insists that criminal justice agendas are frequently driven by perceptions of patterns of criminality that do not reflect reality. He, and others, argue that young people are often the scapegoats for what is perceived to be wrong with contemporary society. Youth crime appears to be on the decline, according to most studies of youth in urban centres (see Furlong 2013 for a comprehensive set of statistics), yet activities that were once simply viewed as "immature" or "adolescent" are now increasingly interpreted as predictors of future criminality.

Students themselves are not immune to this ubiquitous cultural picture of their criminality. This has been the subject of much scholarly attention in the field of youth studies. How students see their own living and learning spaces and their identities as a reflection of those

negative cultural representations came up in almost every youth individual or focus group interview we held:

> PEANUT: I just think that the government uses the cops and the cops have
> the authority over us, you know? If you're walking down and you have
> baggy clothes or whatever, they stop you because they think that we
> have something in them. And I'm really opposed to the police and the
> government because I think that they have control over us, you know?
> And we really can never speak our minds, say what we want because
> they're always gonna be there, you know? And that affects us.
> KATHLEEN: So guilty until proven innocent.
> PEANUT: Yeah.
>
> (Focus Group Interview, Peanut, Kemba, Cherry,
> Max, Braeburn, December 1, 2008)

Although she does not name race or racism, the coded language of
"baggy clothes," like the word "urban" itself, stands in for the processes
of racialization young people of colour experience. Scot Wortley and
Akwasi Owusu-Bempah's work in Canada (2011; 2011a), and particularly in Toronto, substantiates Peanut's observations. Of the context in
Canada, they write:

> In recent years, racial bias with respect to police stop and search practices
> has emerged as a particularly controversial issue. Canada's growing black
> community has been especially vocal in their complaints about what has
> come to be known as "racial profiling." By contrast, allegations of racial
> bias have, in most cases, been vehemently denied by Canada's major
> police services. (see Tanovich 2006, Tator and Henry 2006)

Given the often expressed opinion of young people in urban schools
that they are largely criminalized by society and that youth of colour
are disproportionately affected by such negative stereotypes, the logi-
cal conclusion to be drawn from Wortley and Owusu-Bempah's (2011a)
research is the following: there is a direct relationship between how
closely people are monitored by the police and how likely they are to
get caught for breaking the law. Because Black people are systematically
stopped and searched more frequently than others, they are also more
likely to be to be detected and arrested for illegal activity than people
from other racial backgrounds who, they emphasize, are engaging in
exactly the same behaviour. "Thus, consistent with the major principles

of conflict criminology," they write, "racial differences in police stop and search activities directly contribute to the over representation of black people in the Canadian criminal justice system" (p. 403).

Akom (2008), researching in the United States, critiques the dominant discourse of the "culture of poverty" and how this constructs pathologies of people of colour. What he argues is missing from that discussion is "the availability of guns, differential sentencing, and the socio-political conditions that define the contours of United States racism" (p. 207). Young people are deeply affected and often angered by negative cultural representations of youth, as a group. In our early conversations about their own sense of space and context, we were struck by how the youth in our study had internalized negative stereotypes of youth and urban schools. I am not suggesting that young people have been duped by the media or prevalent cultural tropes, but only that those prevailing images of "tough urban schools" and violent student-thugs is an almost unquestioned set of images.

The idea of students' "emotional issues" seems also to pervade the social space. Teachers bemoan their lack of training and support for dealing with mental health issues:

> MS. C: We have no mental health support. So a lot of these issues that kids have just spiral into incredible depression, incredible addiction, you know, just from trying to deal with all this stuff ... anger. They have anger-management issues and never know how to deal with them.
> (Interview, Ms. C, Braeburn, December 11, 2008)

While anger management can be a kind of pathologizing discourse, we did find students forthcoming about their anger, although it was a difficult thing to pursue in discussions. We sensed how certain students felt especially stigmatized by their "anger":

> BURCU: What prevents you from coming to school?
> MAXX: Being sick.
> BURCU: When you get sick?
> ASHLEY: A boring class.
> BURCU: A boring class?
> MAXX: Angry? Angry.
> ASHLEY: Or a personal problem.
> MAXX: Extremely angry.
> BURCU: Maxx? You said anger.

MAXX: Oh no, it's just – sometimes if I'm late for class I walk around – walk around and just listen to music like, "man, I hate everyone" then I come back into class and I'm like, "OK, I'm fine now."

(Focus Group Interview, Maxx, Ashley, Stephanie, Carmen, Middleview, November 28, 2008)

Teachers, physicians, sociologists, psychologists, and those working closely with youth tend not to agree on the causes of declining well-being for young people, but most agree that mental health issues are seen as a growing problem and that many conditions of late modernity can be linked to this trend. West (2009) argues that young people feel more pressure with education playing a more significant role in their lives, and that the tightening bond between educational qualifications and labour market outcomes places considerable stress on them. Eckersley (2009) offers an analysis that is in line with the many conversations we had with young people regarding the uncertainty of their futures. The cost of individualism, he insists, is great. It includes: a heightened sense of risk; uncertainty and insecurity; a lack of clear frames of reference; and a rise in personal expectations coupled with an expectation that the onus of success lies with the young person, despite the obvious significance of social and economic disadvantage or privilege (p. 358). Here is how Twila, in the second year of our study, described it to us:

Like, we all grew up thinking we're gonna get married at 25, and we're gonna have kids at 30 and we're gonna have the perfect career and a big house with a white fence. Everybody thinks that when they are growing up. And then you realize that's not true. Like, times have changed, socially people have changed, like people go into shelters and I just realized that it's hard, life isn't easy, life isn't going to just hand you gold, you gotta work your way up.

(Individual Interview, Twila, Middleview, November 4, 2010)

There are many different kinds of analyses to bring to bear on the current state of well-being for young people. Students are searching for what is "real," acutely aware of cultural representations of youth in popular media and academic literatures. They cling to the idea of "the real" beneath the surfaces, behind the artifices. In examining their class-room work on Verbatim theatre, explored in chapter 5, this sense of "the real" will further come to light. But on the question of the social context of learning, Fisher's (2009) book, *Capitalist Realism,* offers important insight.

Fisher suggests that student apathy or anger today is a result of what is screened from view, that is, the social causation for our mental and emotional states of being. Drawing on Deleuze, Fisher argues that the older industrial disciplinary structures and subjectivities no longer hold; instead we have the consumer risk society where institutions become porous and agency is narrowed and depoliticized, sandwiched between the false autonomy promised by market forces/consumerism and the structured rigidity inhered in the extension of zero-tolerance culture and policing. The overarching point here is that students have little recourse to channel their private problems into common concerns and, thus, to link their emotional hardships to the larger economic and social forces that shape them. While it is obviously important that schools have access to social workers and counsellors, it is also obvious that we must deal with poverty, racism, homophobia, sexism, ableism, and other structural conditions that shape our social world to address the underlying causes that so often generate mental health concerns for students and diminish their sense of well-being in the everyday. The most recent UNICEF (2013) findings on the well-being of children and youth in the world's advanced economies discussed earlier illustrate the extent to which the contextual features of social life have conspired to create a very unhealthy and troubling experience for too many young people.

Fisher also points to the fragmentation and disorienting effects of postmodern culture as a contributing factor in the increase in mental illness. One of our researchers noted in his fieldnotes that the students appear numbed by the constant stimuli in the classroom, the unending distractions. He wondered if they had sophisticated filters for tuning out the noise we seem so attuned to? This calls to mind Fredric Jameson's (1991) ideas concerning the cultural logic of late capitalism, a postmodernism that makes it difficult to think coherently about identity and history in a world of consumer surfaces, digital noise, and depthlessness. Since drama requires listening, we often wondered whether this basic skill was helping to quiet the cultural noise and still the movement. We saw glimpses of small victories and great challenges in this regard. The pedagogy in drama classrooms that we observed illustrates clearly the gap between the noisy rhetoric of creativity and entrepreneurship, effectively co-opted by neoliberal policies, and the continued disenfranchisement of the arts in schools and communities.

Labour, Learning, and the Education Debt

The working lives of young people play significantly into the social and learning contexts of schools. The teachers in both Toronto schools spoke of the burden on young people of needing to work – often long hours – while in school, of never getting ahead financially, and the academic consequences of their working lives. They understood the poverty struggle and spoke very sympathetically about it, remembering the privilege they'd had to simply focus on school. For their students, they claimed, schoolwork, even when it was a priority, came second. In our focus groups with students, they regularly brought up the challenge of managing their school and work lives:

> STEPHANIE: And to be honest, work. I find work has a big effect on me not coming to school and my attendance. The reason is because it takes up a lot of my time because straight from school I have to go to work until about eleven and then I have to finish homework that I actually have and then I have to come back to school the next morning.
> ASHLEY: At that time you're all exhausted.
> CARMEN: I think it's hard to go to school when you're working.
> STEPHANIE: It's hard but it's like, you have no other way of making money. And I feel sorry for people that actually are on their own because they have to pay [rent and all that] by themselves. They have no other way of making money. They have to work.
> ASHLEY: That's one thing about my parents though that I love is that they'd rather me get a job in the summer. Like, I said that I wanted to get a job now but they were like, "no, focus on school and passing grades then in the summer you can get a job working in the summer." So it's like, I have that time to just focus on school and pass my classes and not fail.
> STEPHANIE: But [work] prevents me coming to school as much as I want to. I do want to be here, but it's hard. It's not easy all the time. And some teachers actually have to take that into consideration.
>
> (Focus Group Interview, Stephanie, Carmen, Maxx, Ashley, Middleview, November 28, 2008)

While students may have always held jobs and gone to school, and with the prevalence of this concern articulated by students, we wondered what has changed in a post-industrial, globalized, urban context. As in previous times, the challenge of balancing work and school is a class phenomenon. Those students with the least economic stability or parental/family support are the most likely to be working part- and full-time jobs to make ends meet or support the family. What happens, more and more systematically, is that avenues for social mobility for low-income students are limited, and the class structure becomes further entrenched. Though the Ministry of Education in Ontario is proud that the achievement gap between high- and low-income students is less than in many other OECD countries (PISA 2009), family income continues to have a powerful influence on children's chances for success in school. In 2011, more than 400,000 Ontario children and youth were living below the low-income cut-off (LICO), Statistics Canada's widely accepted measure of poverty. (Statistics Canada). That translates to one in six children. (Campaign 2000, 2010). And when, as data also suggest (see Metcalf Foundation 2012), those young people and their parents become what is commonly known now as "the working poor" – in other words those holding precarious jobs, earning low wages, and struggling with the high costs of living – we end up with an unsustainable cultural norm. This has also been evidenced by the latest UNICEF (2013) data noting clearly that Canada has lost its ground in measures for social mobility.

For immigrant and refugee students, the challenges are very complex. Asad, originally from Kenya, lived in a shelter in Toronto while working to support himself and go to school:

ASAD: Because I've seen Black people, I've seen White people; I've seen mad people in the Horizon for Youth. It's like a mad place when you go. I got a lot of hard time when I was in the Horizon. 'Cause sometimes I come from school, I'm tired, I want to read – I can't read. So I have to wait till 11 when people go to beds. I have to come out through the beds. Come and read. I have to wake up early to go to school. So it's kinda I have to read to stay here [in school] … 'cause I can't go to sleep, I have to wait till 11. And come out when the lights are down in the rooms.

KATHLEEN: Because you needed a quiet place. And you had to put the lights on.

(Individual Interview, Asad, Middleview, November 9, 2012)

These often-unbearable life conditions may or may not be known by schools. Their effects, though, are often felt in the teacher-student relationships. Even though teachers may understand the enormous challenges students face and students might understand that teaching can be hard work, inevitable miscommunications ensue as well as a basic inability of teachers to fully appreciate the life conditions of their students. I will speak about such dynamics of the classrooms later in the book, but as a contextual piece, I suggest that the school as a disciplined space, in the Foucauldian (1977) sense, creates untold problems for student-teacher relationships, pushing them both into roles they find intolerable. In a familiar tone of exasperation – part pity, part judgement – Ms. C describes the students she commonly meets:

> They were born into a very toxic family situation, or something devastating happened and they now live on their own. Or, they're disadvantaged because advantaged people get their basic footing in life, and these kids don't. Whether it's abuse, whether it's (*pause*). Well, it's usually abuse. Or they left early. Well their home life was terrible whether there was abuse or not. Neglect in many ways. And so they've tried to make their life on their own, so they've found abusive partners, or they're on welfare, or they've happened to get pregnant twice and they have two kids and now they're like 18 and trying to be in school and raising two kids. And they're at – at a disadvantage because life's so difficult now, and they're trying just to do something basic.
>
> (Interview, Ms. C, Braeburn, December 11, 2008)

Students, too, have their thoughts about the challenge that dealing with teachers every day presents:

> DEREK: Yeah, I think that that's a big part of why people skip as well. Um, first, for sure teachers.
>
> ANNE: To avoid certain teachers you mean?
>
> DEREK: To avoid certain teachers. I've had teachers that are good teachers in the end but they're really annoying or they're just way too strict and it discourages a lot of the – 'cause we have a lot of students who don't like attitude from teachers (*he smiles*). And when they get attitude from teachers, that just brings them that further – that much further away from wanting to go to class. And I have a teacher last period who (*pause*) I always consider not going to his class but if I didn't go to his class, he's like, there's only six kids, so he'd flip out. But I think, I think, that's a really big reason why some people don't go to class.
>
> K'THANIE ADDS: 'Cause my school wasn't semestered and all the teachers that I had – well most of them – were really rude. Like one teacher grabbed me on my arm one time and like threw me in a class and it

turned into this big thing and like the school wanted me out of that school even though I didn't really do anything. And, I don't know, they didn't make me want to go to school, like I was kind of failing most classes. Because I would go to class but I wouldn't act like I'm in class, like I would sleep in the back or something. 'Cause teachers do have that effect on you like if they don't help you or anything, you feel like you don't want to do anything and all that stuff. Like school's hard enough.

(Focus Group Interview, K'thanie, Bella, Derek,
Middleview, November 25, 2008)

Or from a focus group at Braeburn:

KEMBA: Well, you know what my mother used to tell me which was like an old saying, that the teacher doesn't make your marks. Obviously not, but you know, they don't have anything to do with the way you learn and what not but they do. Because I'm seeing them every day, they are a part of my life, they are teaching me something that I need to use in the future. Like this is not a joke thing, it's part of my being, it's something that I am accepting within myself to learn and to apply somewhere in the future ... And if they feel like they want to take off a few marks because of my attitude then they probably will just do that. And maybe I do deserve to get marks off if I'm giving them a certain attitude but maybe they need to talk to me and reason with me. Everything has two sides. So teachers do – they're like our second parents, like it's just like a household, you know what I mean? (*pause*) If they are teaching you in a boring way you probably have to force yourself, but it's how you communicate and reason with them and tell them, "look Miss/Sir, I don't really like the way you're teaching. You know it kind of makes me not really dig it really much. Would you try to help me out or motivate me just a little bit." Then they might have different teaching skills after I tell them that. They might try to ...

KATHLEEN: And do you think that a teacher would be accepting of that critique?

KEMBA: Well, some teachers might not. You have to scope out how they would take what. You – I might relate to a different way. I have to learn or feel out your energy, your vibes in a different way before I can comment – come to you and say whatever because all of us are different, so you can't go to someone the same way. Like you might – I might go to you and be like, "Yo, I don't like how you teach, OK Miss?" and you'll be like, "OK, fine" right? But then with him I'm like, "Sir, no hard feelings (*punches the air*) I'm telling you like, I really don't like the way you teach!" Add a little smile and be like (*winks*) you know? But you have to like do different stuff, you know what I mean? We're different people. We're not the same.

(Focus Group, Kemba, Cherry, Max, Peanut,
Braeburn, December 1, 2008)

All of the teachers we came to know over the course of five years talked about the toll their work takes, even when they love the work they do. There was a sense that "their students" were different from middle-class students and the proximity to their troubled lives was exhausting, even when they were obviously committed to what they do and clearly also enjoyed their students:

MS. C: Because I take it home a lot. Every – probably every day for the last five years I've had some kind of connection with a student that is going through the biggest nightmare you can imagine. And every time I think that is the biggest nightmare that someone can possibly experience, then there's another bigger nightmare next year. So as an emotional person ... I take on things, which I have to work on. And I'm much better now, five years later ... And I'll be honest; I was warned when I first took the job at this school that five years was the max. And after five – during five years or after five years you will burn out and you won't be able to teach any more. So you've got to actually go somewhere else. I was full on told that by many people. And I was so energized and passionate, I was like "Come on! I can do it, I can – no problem! I'll be fine, I'll be doing art and I'll be with the kids and ...!" Well I'll be honest, this year with the kids, I'm exhausted. Like I'm emotionally exhausted, and I'm physically exhausted, and like, I get it. Like, I've never really experienced real burnout in my life, I think as an artist you just manage to find a different project, different ways to inspire yourself. And I have, you know, I have projects at this school that are inspiring. I'm not saying my hands are up. But I am saying that I'm feeling the effect of five years.

(Interview, Ms. C, Braeburn, December 11, 2008)

And at Middleview, Ms. S explains:

There's a price. There's a real price to pay. I do get burnt out. It affects my personal life and my health. And I don't always know if it's worth it. But I do feel like it's worth it sometimes, because I do love to create art.

(Interview, Ms. S, Middleview, February 3, 2009)

There is, of course, much literature in the field of urban schooling, most notably from the United States, where the discourse of "achievement gaps," "opportunity gaps," and "low expectation and deficit mindsets" hold sway. For instance, Milner, in his 2013 editorial "Rethinking Achievement Gap Talk in Urban Education," in the journal *Urban Education*, deconstructs the discourse of the "achievement gap." He refers to Ladson-Billings, who at a meeting of the American Education Research Association in 2006 said that students of colour, English Language Learners, and those living in conditions of low Socio-Economic Status are not achieving at the same rate as other students in schools due to the "education debt" in the United States. "This education debt carries several important features, according to Ladson-Billings: historical debt, economic debt, socio-political debt, and moral debt" (p. 3). Milner goes on to discuss Irvine (2010), who suggests that there are other "gaps" worth considering.

> For Irvine, other gaps that shape our belief in (and consequently our discourse about) an achievement gap include: "the teacher quality gap; the teacher training gap; the challenging curriculum gap; the school funding gap; the digital divide gap; the wealth and income gap; the employment opportunity gap; the affordable housing gap; the health care gap; the nutrition gap; the school integration gap; and the quality childcare gap" (p. xii). From Irvine's perspective, when we address the many other gaps that structurally and systemically exist in educational practice, achievement results can improve. (p. 4)

Milner (2013) built on Ladson-Billings's work, arguing that we should focus on opportunity gaps (Darling-Hammond 2010) that exist in educational practices when attempting to make sense of, describe, or rationalize inequitable opportunities in some communities. He articulated a framework to assist researchers, theoreticians, and practitioners in explaining opportunity gaps: (1) Colourblindness; (2) Cultural Conflicts; (3) Myth of Meritocracy; (4) Low and Deficit Mindsets; and (5) Context-neutral Mindsets and Practices (p. 4).

His framework for understanding "urban problems" is not new, but it does refocus the argument away from particular cultural and racial groups and more on the institutions themselves, the values they espouse, and how these perpetuate inequities. This framing supports Hampton et al. (2008) who argue for an instruction-based approach to problems rather than framing educational problems as student-based.

Milner concludes his editorial drawing on Habermas and asserts that language is not innocent, and that the language we use to describe our perceptions and shape our discourse matters and influences the kinds of solutions we consider (p. 6). Teacher discourses, as I will illustrate in chapter 5, are at the very centre of the learning contexts for students.

Homelessness and Schools

In this chapter, I have attempted to introduce some of the intractable "educational problems" that students face in North American schools. But our thinking about educational problems evolved as we moved forward in the study and found ourselves, in year 3, outside school space and into theatre spaces with young and older audiences watching a play together, *The Middle Place*, about young people who live in a shelter for homeless youth in the northwest end of Toronto. It has been widely documented that youth underemployment in low-paid casual work prevents many young people without parental or state support from easily finding affordable housing (see Furlong and Cartmel 2007, McKee 2012). Seeing this play and interviewing 75 audience members following the performance gave us a very different kind of insight into public perceptions of "troubled" or "homeless" youth.

We followed the runs of the play at Theatre Passe Muraille and Canadian Stage, both professional theatres located in Toronto, and interviewed random adult and youth audience members, as well as youth audience members known to us who attended one of our school research sites. In the course of these interviews, we also interviewed a number of youth living in the shelter system, some attending and others not attending school. We did not collect social identity markers in these interviews so the participants below are numbered. These random interviews with young people echoed many of the discussions we'd had with the students in the schools. In the play, most of the shelter youth characters were no longer in school. We took the opportunity to ask some of the young people we interviewed why they thought that was the case. Again, the themes of mental health, violence, and family breakdown were echoed in most interviews:

ANNE: And what about you? What do you think about why school wasn't mentioned in the play?

1 : Honestly, a lot of kids were kicked out of school because of family issues. Personally, I wanted to go to school. I like school. I could escape a lot of

noise. But as I got older, and they became less strict on me, they became less structured. So I stopped going. And then I had a boyfriend when I was 15 years old, Bradley. He died of cancer. I had a literal mental breakdown because my family life was very circus freak, to say the least. So considering I didn't have structure at home, I didn't have structure at school, I couldn't trust my friends, 'cause they all did drugs. I was like at my breaking point, and I lit my school on fire. Once you do something like that, it's very hard to get back into other schools. Very hard.

> (Interview with two shelter youth, Theatre Passe Muraille, October 29, 2010)

This youth focus group with Middleview students following the play seemed in agreement about the causes of violence in youth culture:

> C SQUARE: I think it's like, basically on the news you hear about a lot of shooting, usually from youth. It's usually just like who you are and the way you act and who you are basically with. 'Cause, like honestly most of the youth are getting it from the adults because usually it follows somebody and that's where it all starts. It's not all the youths basically, I would say it's the adults.
>
> KANDY: They are not setting the right examples for the youths.
>
> PUPPY LOVE: Yeah, it depends on how you are raised. You know like if maybe it was rough and you had been abused and stuff and it's still inside you, and now you want to take it out on somebody. Like violence, maybe you saw maybe your parents are always fighting and it's getting in your head and mind and now you want to take it out on somebody else.
>
> C SQUARE: Yeah, like if you're a boy growing up and you see your dad hitting your mom you are going to think that it's OK to hit a woman because your dad does it.
>
> (Focus Group Interview with youth from Middleview, Theatre Passe Muraille, November 9, 2010)

A focus group of artist-educators who had come to the theatre also spoke about the endless cycle of misunderstanding, the barriers between home and school, the racial stereotypes, and the inability to focus on school when one feels displaced:

> 3: I'd like to address the school question. School isn't really addressed in depth, and I think it would be really powerful if, how, especially for the characters who play people of colour or youth of colour, how their

situation alone disengages them further from the education system, because teachers, students, don't necessarily know what's going on, they just see this kid who walks around with an attitude, or in the case of Khalia [a Black character in the play], she walks around with a wall, "this kind has behavioural issues, learning disability, this and that," all these labels get put on kids and then they disengage even more from the school system, you know what I mean? And then they get suspended –

2: Yeah.

3: Going through that entire system? And dealing with shelter life, and there is so much depth that could be had in that truth and I don't think it was kind of done justice.

1: Yeah, it's like, not having a home and having to go to school every day? That should have been, there should have been a bigger focus put on that most definitely.

HEATHER: And you said you have certain friends who …

1: I've experienced certain things of that nature. I have family; I have friends who have gone through it. And it's not even going through shelters. It's staying at Mom's house tonight and the next night staying at Dad's, whatever, you still feel displaced, but you don't feel you have a home, you live somewhere, but you don't have a home, and then you have to get up and go to school every day. And the teachers just want to know if you have your homework done. But you don't have a home.

(Focus Group, Canadian Stage Theatre, February 14, 2011)

One of my interviewees at the theatre, after the performance, was a 14-year-old girl who had been home-schooled all her life. She had just begun school for the first time in Grade 9. Her fresh insights seemed very much in line with others who had already spent the better part of their lives in school:

KATHLEEN: Do you think school can make any kind of difference in the lives of "troubled youth"? If so, how could it?

1: If school, like teachers, say yeah "don't do drugs, don't do this," but I don't think they really make, like they don't really say, if you see your friend doing drugs or something you could try and help. I have never really heard that before. It's always "contact a teacher, contact help, society will do something about it." But they never really say, why don't you walk up to the person, it's your friend even, say "hey, what's the matter? What is going on?" School is almost more dangerous to at-risk youth than it is helpful.

KATHLEEN: Say more. Why do you think that?

1: Well people are a lot judged in school, or that's what I see. And if you make a mistake, like do drugs, you're judged on that, or that's what I've seen. And I've been home-schooled my whole life and coming to school, like I watch movies and yeah, school's completely different, it's not at all like the movies.

KATHLEEN: When did you start coming to school?

1: Just last year. This is my first year in high school.

KATHLEEN: So you're in Grade 9?

1: Yeah.

KATHLEEN: Is it a culture shock for you?

1: It is. It's absolutely – and it's like the judgement that's put on people, and even my judgement that I put on people, even though no matter how hard I try not to judge people because I'm even judged for who I am. It's there and it's everywhere and it's painful to watch.

(Youth Interview, Canadian Stage, March 10, 2011)

Another important thing we learned in interviewing youth post-performance was that a few of our research participants from Middleview, who had come to see the play, told us that they lived in shelters. We came to understand that many young people in schools do not live at home, or have had periods of not living at home, and so this play had a particular poignancy for them:

SHASHAQE: Ya, what the actors did was like … I could relate to everything 'cause I've witnessed a lot of stuff that was talked about, like all the topics and it's very touching 'cause I'm a victim of a lot of issues that occur for many people. So, what was portrayed today was like, a very straightforward, like a very good point of view of everything that happens in a shelter. The drama – there's some people that you trust, some people that you don't trust. But, a lot of people like me go there to better yourself and I think that was the message because a lot of people judge people because they live there. Like sometimes, I feel afraid to tell people that I live in a shelter but now I'm not … 'cause I am doing the right thing. It's either that I live in a shelter or I do something else that would be bad, you understand? So, I like it. It's a good stepping point of being successful … I think … it's a very good play, 'cause actually, I was watching it and I'm like WOW … ya.

(Theatre Passe Muraille, Individual Post-performance
Interview, Middleview student, November 9, 2010)

A Canadian quantitative study (Hyman et al. 2011) on youth homelessness stresses the importance of looking at environmental, social, and economic conditions in youth homelessness and calls for a Canadian national policy that should tap youth for ideas. The study followed 82 youth who had been homeless for two years to identify predictors of school participation. While such studies are important and outline *individual* predictors of school engagement, the positive, supportive, and non-judgemental quality of school experiences, according to the youth of our study, seems to be an especially important consideration. Schools cannot control for students' lives outside school, but they can have a real impact on young people's sense of self-worth and horizons of possibility.

In her book, *The Dissonance of Democracy: Listening, Conflict and Citizenship*, Susan Bickford (1996) describes listening in a democracy as "that effort of building a pathway for deliberation which assumes – as I attend to the citizen other – that I could hear something about the world differently through the sounding of another's perspectives; we are able to be surprised by others and by our own selves" (p. 162). Most of our interviews with shelter youth, adults, and school students who came to the show were hugely positive. But there were two events that happened as a consequence of *The Middle Place* production wherein "real life" uncomfortably converged with the world of the theatre in the first incident and beautifully underscored the potentially affirming social relations of classrooms in the second. In the first instance, much light was shed on the challenges for youth when faced with public, cultural representations of them, and the second post-show episode back at the school, by contrast, helped us, as researchers, to see the relational engagements made possible through theatre.

Incident One

At one matinee performance, several factors converged to create a volatile confrontation. The youth at this performance were deeply offended by their theatre-going experience, and their upset came not only from the way they felt they had been treated by front-of-house staff at the theatre, but also from the content of the play, as the following fieldnote observes:

> The usher comes out of the theatre into the lobby saying that there was a "row of girls" who wouldn't be quiet. The house manager went in and

came out saying that they were "totally out of control." Then three audience members (older) leave the theatre and, as they get their coats on in the lobby where we are seated waiting for our interviews, they say that their experience of the play had been disrupted / ruined. One adult says that she was told to "fuck off" when she asked them to be quiet. She headed to the box office to ask for her money back.

As the front-of-house staff talk, we learn that the youth in question have used "Archangel tickets." We then realize that these are shelter youth.

Then the girls leave the theatre and come into the lobby. One is very pregnant. They are furious. The one girl had been texting her mother in the theatre because she was not feeling well – [that also explains why they may have been eating in the theatre]. Her friend, defending her, says, "Can't you see she's about to pop?"

They are asked to leave by the front-of-house staff and in the course of the conversation, one of the girls tells them to "fuck off." I overhear that they're from the Belleview Shelter [a shelter for homeless young women; we've used a pseudonym]. They are also angry with the play. They say things like, "I know shelters" and one says to us, catching my eye, that they shouldn't do plays about shootings – it's disrespectful – "it's important." I say in agreement, "it is important."

This is the clash that we thought might happen: the adults leave the theatre with their stereotypes reinforced about youth and the youth leave feeling alienated by an institution that has made them feel unwelcome. This seems like an engagement locked in power and the powerful win. I wonder what the pedagogy is here?

(Canadian Stage, Fieldnote, March 10, 2011)

In analysing these events, we reflected on our contrasting experience at Theatre Passe Muraille in the previous run of the show when shelter youth who stayed to the end of the play (but who were also eating chips and answering phone calls during the show), daringly stood up during the talkback to thank Project: Humanity for creating this play about their lives. They agreed to be interviewed and generously gave over an hour to our post-performance conversation.

When we recounted the conflict we had witnessed in the lobby to Project: Humanity company members, they were very disturbed. We decided to contact the Belleview Shelter to see if there could be any possibility to follow up with the girls who had come to the theatre that day. A shelter staff agreed that further conversation might be beneficial but asked that we consider sending someone of colour associated with the company because the girls who had seen the play were of colour. Antonio Cayonne (a biracial actor in *The Middle Place*) and Kathleen Gallagher (a White researcher) visited the shelter together. It was a difficult afternoon and our goal was to hear the girls out, to let them explain to us what had gone wrong for them and also to address whatever issues they may have had with the actual play. As we suspected, their major complaints had to do with their perception that they were unwelcome at the theatre and were mistreated by theatre employees and patrons. But they also reluctantly admitted that they found the idea of seeing homeless youth on stage offensive. What became clear was that the information sent to the shelter – about how the play was made, the goals and values of the company, and the free tickets – was never communicated to them. In fact, they came to the theatre that day with no prior knowledge of what they were seeing. This was exactly what Project: Humanity had requested not happen with the shelter youth and their free tickets. When Antonio explained that the show was not the company's invention but the Verbatim words of a group of shelter youth the company had worked closely with, this positively affected the girls' overall perception of the work. They began to ask questions about how the process had worked and seemed marginally more interested.

Despite this brief moment of interest, however, we realized that there would be a limit to the candour possible because of the constant intervention of the White shelter worker in the room. We sensed a strong animosity between her and the youth, which hindered our conversation. Antonio asked whether they would like to be involved in the kind of drama workshops he had conducted at the other shelter where the show had originated. They said they might like to do that. But we both left feeling unsatisfied with the experience.

Incident Two

Back at the school, after the viewing of *The Middle Place*, there was one unusual and very memorable day in the classroom. It is hard to render the feeling of this day without it sounding saccharine, but we experienced an unusual moment of unbridled kindness. Something about the "real" of *The Middle Place* production, the strife and hardship of living as a young person in socio-economically unstable times, had given birth to this pedagogical moment of taking account of the roles we play in the lives of others and how our communities come to matter. Ms. S lit a candle in the middle of the circle and began with the following:

MS. S: This is the anti-consumerist version of gift giving at holiday time. We are going to go around the class, and we are going to focus on one person at a time and we are going to – we are going to start with Hal and each person is going to say one thing, thanking Hal for a gift that he has given them this semester. OK?

NINA: Miss, can I go first? Hal, thank you for giving me that awesome massage when I was really stressed, working on my back when I had really bad knots and he took them away for me.

RAYNE: Thank you for all of those days when I was really down or whatever and you would do something really whacky, and you would make all of those silly sound effects and it brings me into a slightly decent mood – better than anyone else.

PUPPY LOVE: Um, thank you for letting me diss you. (class laughs)

VITAMIN N: Thank you for always making me laugh.

DAPHNEY EVANS: Thanks for making me laugh, even when I don't want to.

SHASHAQE: Thank you for those loving blue eyes – but I don't want them – but like, not in a sexual way (class "ooooos") man! He has a very nice colour blue in his eyes, like if you look at it!

POKE: Thank you for always making the class laugh.

MS. S: Thank you for all of your wonderful writing this semester. OK, so now Hal picks the next person who gets to go.

BONES MCCOY: Can't we just go around the circle?

[Everyone agrees. The following represents this movement, person-by-person, around the circle, as peers elaborated on what each individual student had brought to their lives or to the classroom. Although it is impossible to signal to the reader the name of each person being thanked as they were not named by their peers because they moved seamlessly around the circle, the following should give the sense of this accumulation of gratitude and the intimacy created in the classroom.]

RAYNE: Thank you for being like my Portuguese hilarious sister. You're like the hard-core version of me, so it's awesome and I love you for it!

PUPPY LOVE: uh yeah, thank you for doing that smile. (class "ooohhhh")

VITAMIN N: oh, your stories, your stories like every single day are very entertaining. Very good storyteller!

SINEAD CATIVA: Thanks for being eccentric.

SASHA: I just love your attitude … like as you are … never change.

DAPHNEY EVANS: Thank you for being just you, man.

MS. S: You're humble; you're a very humble person. You have huge talent and I thank you for sharing your writing and performances so bravely with the class.

NINA: Thank you for being so real and down to earth and acceptable.

SOPHIA: Thank you for not letting people, like, think something of you. Like, I don't know if you notice this but like when someone thinks a certain way about you and then you totally prove them wrong. One time, when Miss told us to get into partners and tell each other a story about one another and then we had to like tell it – and I was like no, change it – and you like totally covered for me and made up a whole new story.

RAYNE: Thank you for being like, you have this powerful essence to you. You're so inspiring, like how you want to follow through with everything you do and fulfil your dreams.

PUPPY LOVE: Thank you for your great attitude that you give to everybody, and I like especially that poem that you performed and shared with us, like, that was awesome.

MS. S: Thank you for sharing your writing with me this semester. It has been really inspiring for me to meet a student who is so interested in writing and who is like … you have so much intelligence that you are putting into your writing too, and I really appreciate that you have been sharing that with me.

BONES MCCOY: OK, don't take this weird or anything but, thank you for being like a brother to me.

(Everyone "awww"; someone: "that's cute!." The researchers join in.)

KATHLEEN: And I want to say thanks for, well, you didn't know you were doing this but I was watching you while you were watching *The Middle Place* and I was watching your engagement throughout that play, and it was really interesting to see your response to that play. You didn't know you were giving me that but …

BONES MCCOY: She watches you when you're not looking.

(Everyone laughs.)

SHASHAQE: One of the things that I admire about you is that, um, you're very outspoken – and, um, the way you cut your hair, like a lot of girls wouldn't cut their hair like that and like still feel beautiful and you rock it really well.

MS. S: Thank you for being a really fascinating person, who is also really helpful to other people in the class – like there have been a lot of times where you see people working on something or struggling with something and you're kinda there quietly helping people, and it's really lovely.

SOPHIA: Thank you for, I don't know, I don't think you realize sometimes how of value you are and, I don't know sometimes I look at you and I feel like you don't feel loved (*everyone laughs*). I know this is going to sound, it's going to be one of those things where you're like "Sophia, don't say it" but I just want you to know that if you were to drop dead right now I would miss you, a lot – I think we all would – because you always take in my hugs, even though we barely talk, I would miss you.

RAYNE: I say thank you because you are such an amazing person, like, you're so unique you'll say these things that you'll, like, tell, and I'll be, like, I don't even know … like you have the most amazing facts that I've never heard of; I don't know, they're awesome.

POKE: Thank you for your plum jacket.

KETH BROWN: Um, your heart.

MS. S: Thank you for your kindness and your intelligence that you always contribute to the class, like you're always listening – like, you're a great listener too.

ANNE: Thanks for being constantly friendly.

BONES MCCOY: You stole mine! Ugh, now I gotta think … uhh … thank you for two years of listening to my nonsense.

SASHA: It's been two years?

BONES MCCOY: It has!

(Everyone laughs.)

KATHLEEN: Something that I have noticed about you is, when Ms. S is trying to get students' attention you often help students pay attention to her – that is something that I have noticed about you.

(Someone: "Miss, are you getting sad?")

MS. S: No, it just nice to hear all of you say such nice things about one another.

This went on for just under an hour. And we watched these students find a way to relate that countered so much of the tone and discourse in schools. The cumulative effect of their appreciation of one another was overpowering. It was what Ms. S would call an aesthetic moment in the talk. It ended:

NINA: Guys, I think Miss S deserves a round of applause for everything.

(Everyone claps.)

NINA: On behalf of this class Miss, we all love this class.

MS. S: I just want to thank all of you. I have had lots of good classes, special classes throughout the years – I have been teaching for 10 years – but you know, this class has a very unique vibe, and you guys are all such individuals and it's very exciting for me to work with you, its been a huge gift for me to work with you and to get to know all of you and to just … It's a pleasure, every day to just come here; so thank you for that.

(Everyone claps.)

MS. S: Have a wonderful and safe holiday and I will see you in the new year! Happy 2011!

(Middleview class discussion, December 18, 2011)

These are rare moments of deep pleasure in classrooms. Such moments exist alongside the tribulations and the emotional burnout described by both teachers. Ms. S often referred to the "talk" of her classroom as powerful aesthetic experiences. In his study of new urban teachers and their capacity to transcend neoliberal reforms in education, such as standardized testing, Arthur Costigan (2013) found that teachers who embrace aesthetic education are embracing a kind of curriculum of political action. He extends the definition in much the same way that Ms. S does. An aesthetic approach to teaching, more than just evaluating a student's engagement with a text of literature or a dramatic performance, is understood here as the transaction a learner has with the broad intellectual "texts" of a discipline, the process by which, Costigan offers, a learner incorporates or resists incorporating new understandings into her ongoing narrative about the world. And, like the experience of seeing *The Middle Place*, there was a contagion of emotion that followed the classroom experience.

Here is where the work of affect theorist Sara Ahmed (2004; 2010) became very important to our understandings. Ahmed's conceptualizations of affect counter the social psychologists; she holds that emotion does not live in one person or the other but in the way people encounter one another. This was true both in the upsetting encounter in the theatre and in the positive classroom discussion. In each case, the emotion resided in the encounter. This classroom example, along with other many less happy though equally affective moments over the course of our years together, illustrate how important it is for a teacher to see both the individuals before her and the collective of which she is a part.

As I have previously noted (Gallagher and Wessels 2013), in Bruce McConachie's (2008) cognitive approach to spectating in the theatre, he argues that our emotional responsiveness to characters/actors is biological:

> Our muscular, chemical, and neurological responses to others' emotions are often so small that they escape conscious recognition, but they can have a significant impact on our behaviours. In other words, evolution has equipped us to attune our bodies to the emotions of other people. This basis for our sociality as a species is inherited and embodied. (p. 67)

Whether one ascribes to this more cognitive psychological view or not, what is clear is that the emotions of others produce emotions in us, whether these are in imagined or real situations. McConachie is extending the earlier work of Niedenthal, Barsalou, Ric, and Krauth-Gruber in the 1970s who, in their study on emotion and consciousness, demonstrate four major claims: "(1) individuals embody other people's emotional behaviour; (2) embodied emotions produce corresponding subjective emotional states in the individual; (3) imagining other people and events also produces embodied emotions and corresponding feelings; and (4) embodied emotions mediate cognitive responses" (in Barrett, Niedenthal and Winkielman 2005 cited in McConachie 2008, p. 66). That day in the classroom, as in many evenings in the theatre, we watched the contagion of emotion and the deep engagement of young people with each other.

Educational Supports: The Tangibles and Intangibles

As we worked to understand the complex educational problems and structural conditions in the schools where we conducted our research, we were also always trying to listen for the kinds of educational supports that existed in these sites. The supports were not always evident, particularly in cases where there was denial about the kinds of problems that existed. Sometimes, schools felt, or chose to feel, ineffectual in the face of the more personal and larger societal challenges faced by students. As we coded our data for educational and personal supports, we often found ourselves returning to the interpersonal relations between teachers, students, and families. Social bonds figured prominently in any discussions with students or observations we made in classrooms and hallways.

What is especially important to note is the fundamental contradiction that we ran into repeatedly with teachers and students. The buildings are run-down, the classrooms are under-resourced, the schools are stigmatized, but the students are fundamentally loyal to the place and generally hopeful about what might come out of their struggles there. This kind of thinking about urban schools is pervasive with teachers and students. It demonstrates one of the real tensions about school: school is a place of contradictions; it is supportive and antagonistic. It is a space that creates meaningful bonds and commitments *and* it is a space that always disappoints. Despite the negative perceptions of Middleview as a "ghetto school," the students' struggle for dignity and social advancement was palpable. Ms. S reflects in her first interview with us:

> A lot of the kids have a lot of pride in Middleview. They see it as a really interesting, diverse school; they have pride in the diversity of the student body; they have pride in the amount of programs that are available at Middleview.
>
> (Interview, Ms. S, Middleview, December 3, 2008)

The flexible programming at Braeburn was clearly something that students valued and needed. The school year is divided into nine-week quads that help students complete full credits in a much shorter period of time. When life is filled with such uncertainty, shorter commitments can sometimes make the difference. Supporting themselves, and sometimes their own children, financially required great program flexibility for students with complicated and burdensome living conditions:

> ALEESA: Yeah, but I was actually really thrilled to get that letter. Especially when I found out that you can, you know, do three classes in three months and, you know, it's so much faster to finish, so I was thrilled because I really wanted to finish my high school, and I was kind of really in a dilemma as to what to do, because I didn't know you could do it this fast so …
>
> (Individual Interview, Aleesa, Braeburn, April 29, 2009)

It is not only the flexible programming that helps many students; there are also financial incentives too. Of course this is a controversial idea, with many arguing that students should engage in their learning out of a sense of responsibility to their own futures. But in difficult economic times, with exploitive forms of capitalism on the rise (see Bauman 1998;

Bourdieu 1999; Bowles and Gintis 2011; Saltman and Gabbard 2010; Wacquant 2009; Means 2013), sometimes bus tickets can make the difference. We could not, however, get a clear answer from either students or administration about the details of possible financial incentives for students at Braeburn. Our sense was that it is a tacit understanding, negotiated on an as-needed basis. Although the details were elusive, the students clearly appreciated the effort the school was making to financially support their success. In one focus group, we got quite a strong sense of the importance of this aspect of the school:

MAX: I don't know, it seems like the school tries everything they do to make kids come here – they give out free lunches or whatever. I guess it just depends on you. They can't force you in the door, right?

KATHLEEN: Right. So they could go to a certain point and then it's up to you. OK.

CHERRY: And also I think to answer your question, because your question was what can we do or what can the school do to help you which is totally what I'm talking about off topic, I'm sorry but –

KATHLEEN: I love going off topic, that's where the good stuff is.

(Everyone laughs.)

MAX: I think they have an attendance thing here too. Like, if you get perfect attendance you get money.

KATHLEEN: Oh, is that right?

CHERRY: Yeah, that's good.

KEMBA: Yeah, like fifty dollars.

KATHLEEN: That's good motivation; you can get your registration back.

CHERRY: I'm trying!

KATHLEEN: That's really good.

KEMBA: I know. I messed up already.

(Focus Group Interview, Kemba, Cherry, Max, Peanut, Braeburn December 1, 2008)

And the next day in another focus group, the same sense of feeling supported was expressed and students seemed to be educating each other about possible institutional support:

FORTY-TWO MARKS: This school does so much. I love this school and the amount that they try. This is so far the best school I've ever been to because they try. They try, they try so much to get you here. They even – if you have perfect attendance, they give you a hundred dollars. Like that's, that's good. I don't have a perfect attendance any more. (*He shrugs.*) But it's like – no other school would ever …

SARAH: It's like …

SKEAM: What, they deposit it?

FORTY-TWO MARKS: No they give you one hundred dollars cash.

SKEAM: When did they tell you that?

SARAH: A long time ago.

SKEAM: I didn't know that. I would have not skipped at all. (*Laughter.*)

FORTY-TWO MARKS: See how much this school does to keep you here? This school is amazing. One of the reasons I'm here. You can make four hundred dollars a year.

SKEAM: So this is each quad?

FORTY-TWO MARKS: Yeah, each quad.

ZIGGY: It's not like you're going to show up to all your classes.

SKEAM: Oh, for four hundred bucks, why not?

SARAH: Of course.

FORTY-TWO MARKS: It's also …

SARAH: That's like it gives motivation to kids you know.

ZIGGY: Trust me on a Friday …

FORTY-TWO MARKS: These teachers don't even care if you're late. They don't even mark you late if you're late. They just – if you're there and you do the work they just mark you there and they don't even like care if you're there. It's more like college. It's an amazing school, like this school has got it almost perfect – this school almost has it perfectly. The only thing that I'll suggest that the school do is give out free metro passes to students who need it. That is the only …

SKEAM: Who need it.

SARAH: Not only here, too, but if you go to guidance, they give you bus tickets if you don't have any way to get home.

SKEAM: Yeah, once in a blue moon.

> (Focus Group, Skeam, Sarah, Ziggy, Gonzalez,
> Forty-two Marks, Braeburn, December 2, 2008)

Both Braeburn and Middleview are known informally as "second chance" schools. Ms. C at Braeburn describes:

> If they're on a section 20 – So if they've had to be suspended for violence, they come here. They go to a little program, and then they come here.

> They've been suspended from their school for whatever reason and they
> can't get back in, they come here. A lot of principals will say "You know
> we don't want you; go to Braeburn." They actually hear that. "We don't
> want you; go to Braeburn."
>
> (Interview, Ms. C, Braeburn December 11, 2008)

It is unsurprising then, that these schools are often personified as care-
givers, providing a kind of sanctuary for students. Sometimes students
point to the school or the teachers, and sometimes they point to their
peers. It's the people and the relationships that make them feel capable or inspired or motivated. The following two examples are repre-
sentative of something we regularly witnessed in our schools; social
resilience. Rather than the usual focus on individual character traits or
the ability of individual students to overcome challenges in their lives,
social resilience considers the sociality of spaces, attending to ourselves
and others in given contexts. In their study of socially and economically
disadvantaged Aboriginal populations in Australia, Gale and Bolzan
(2013) challenge neocolonialism and suggest that social resilience in
concept and practice has the potential to interrupt what they refer to as
the "circuit of dispossession" and arrive at something like "long-term
hope" (p. 269–70). Jackie Kennelly (2011), too, theorizes this phenomenon as sitting somewhere between Butler's and Bourdieu's notions of
agency, something she terms "relational agency," when young people
are compelled to act because of their social conditions and the human
community of which they are a part. Peanut, at Braeburn, describes
social resilience or relational agency in this way:

> Coming here has helped me to appreciate other people, look up to them
> even if they're my age, look up to them and be like, "wow, you know, I
> wanna be like them" you know? And school has helped me to do that,
> in this school. I didn't think I was gonna be happy here, and I am.
>
> (Focus Group Interview, Peanut, Cherry, Kemba,
> Max, Braeburn, December 1, 2008)

Then Cherry picks up on Kemba's thoughts:

> CHERRY: Sorry, I want to reflect on something Kemba said about how she's
> motivated by the people around here. I think that's also because everybody –
> we all know that each of us have our problems or had our problems
> or we're trying to come here to better ourselves so I think that you're not

just looking at other people and saying, "OK, this person is way more smarter than me and I can't do it." So, like, you see people go on to college or university and they started off with a bad situation or whatever and no matter what, they still went through it, so I think that that also helps us motivate each other. And I noticed that the majority of the teachers that work here they had their own problems from before or they either failed high school or something happened in their life and that's why they're here. Do you notice that?

(Focus Group, Cherry, Peanut, Max, Kemba, Braeburn, December 1, 2008)

I recall an interview with Ms. C at Braeburn:

I tell them as much about me as possible at the beginning. Breaks down barriers. So I say "Yeah, so I was a dancer and I had an eating disorder for two years when I was in Grade 9 and 10, and I was anorexic so I've dealt with a form of addiction. So if you've dealt with a form of addiction, I know how hard it is to get out of it." So I just throw it out like that. Or my dad was an addict, so I have to deal with my anger towards my father. I just say it, very nonchal – So eventually they start talking about their courage and their addiction.

(Interview, Ms. C., Braeburn, December 11, 2008)

We don't know if, as a group, the teachers in Braeburn could better empathize with students because of their personal histories, but what we do take from this student's insights is that teachers were not expecting less of them because they had challenges in their lives. There is a healthy body of educational research that has focused on teacher expectations, particularly as they relate to "urban" students' sense of self-efficacy. In one quantitative study (Tyler and Boelter 2008) conducted in a school population comprised of primarily low-income and Black middle-school students located in a city in the southeastern United States, the researchers inquired into the associations between student perceptions of their teachers' expectations and academic engagement and academic "efficacy" (p. 27). The authors differentiate self-efficacy from self-esteem and self-concept, and suggest that self-efficacy is the belief on the student's part that he/she can succeed at the academic task at hand. The authors define academic engagement as comprised of behavioural, cognitive, and emotional/affective factors. The findings of this study illustrate how the perceptions of teacher expectations were extremely relevant, rated above the mid-point on the measurement scale. One of the major contributions of this study is that:

> perceived teacher expectations were predictive of what the literature considers to be cognitive antecedents of student academic performance, namely academic engagement and academic efficacy. Middle-grade students' perceptions of their teachers' expectations were associated with a moderate level of cognitive engagement and high levels of behavioural and emotional engagement and academic efficacy. (p. 31)

Peanut, getting more personal, adds her thoughts, pointing to internal as well as external factors in finding a way to get to, and succeed at, school on a regular basis:

> For me – opening up now – I started with addiction when I was very young and I'm just starting to get myself together and that brings me down. Sometimes when I can't come here and all I can think about is "go to school! go to school!" you know? That's all I have and it's not always just about people talking about you or like your bus fare right? It's what's troubling within yourself like drugs and not being able to find that push, right? I found it here; I know I have it here … And I keep saying it but being a drug addict and stuff, I'm two years sober and being here is actually pushing me to try to get to nine years sober – you know I want to get there. I have my days where I'm like, "oh I wanna go and just do my thing" but seeing people like her (*points to Kemba*) and her (*points to Cherry*) I just like wanna be like them. I wanna have all this positivity in my life and – I know, my role models are here!
>
> (Focus Group Interview, Peanut, Cherry, Kemba,
> Max, Braeburn, December 1, 2008)

In so many of our focus groups and individual interviews, students said that they needed to rely on themselves in the end, although they were also quick to point out the influence of others, whether they be peers as above or family. We heard a lot about family, both positive and negative influences, but also the ways in which negative life circumstances were approached by friends and family and the ways in which resilience can be inspirational:

BONNIE: I wanna be a social worker first.
KATHLEEN: What kinds of groups would you want to work with?

BONNIE: Addiction worker. Well, that's what my Mom is because my Mom was actually an addict for a long while and she's been clean for two years and she went back to school because she wants to be an addiction worker. She works at a hospital. She volunteers with Children's Aid and I actually really admire my Mom so I'm kind of following in her footsteps.

KATHLEEN: That's amazing. What about you Bell?

BELL: What do I want to do? For me, honestly like, to be influenced on what I want to do – my brother has influenced me. Because we're both the middle child and so he wants to be a lawyer and stuff so I was always like "you know what, I wanna be a lawyer because you're doing it too." So he's kind of influenced me. He's the reason why I came to Middleview too. He doesn't know that and he and I don't really talk about this, but he's influenced me in a lot of ways. I wanna become a lawyer and be like a lawyer duo with him and like, yeah. Like, I'd wanna do it with him.

(Focus Group Interview, Bonnie, Bell, Mya,
Middleview, November 23, 2008)

In his seminal study of racial and ethnic segregation, student and family characteristics, and student achievement, *Equality of Educational Opportunity* (1966) researcher James Coleman found that family factors such as household composition, socio-economic status, and parents' level of education were stronger predictors of students' educational attainment than were direct school-related factors. This study gave rise to decades of research and writing, particularly in the 1970s and 1980s, on so-called "family effects" on students' academic achievement. For instance, two high-profile American reports by the William T. Grant Foundation, *The Forgotten Half: Non-College Youth in America* (1988a) and *The Forgotten Half: Pathways to Success for America's Youth and Young Families* (1988b), suggested that programs designed to produce school success would likely fail unless implemented along with family and community measures. Without this support around a child, motivation to perform well in school, as well as positive reinforcement to do so, may be absent. In particular, the adult-child, or more specifically the parent-child relationship, the reports argued, should be targeted to successfully advance academically at-risk teenagers (William T. Grant Foundation, 1988 a/b). These studies generally concluded that the factors Coleman identified do exert enormous influence on students' achievement, though they are not necessarily deterministic of it. For example, the home environment shapes a child's initial views of learning. What parents think about the importance (or unimportance) of doing well in school is often mirrored in student results.

In Canada, the Council of Ministers of Education report, *PIRLS 2011: Canada in Context*, analyses the *Progress in International Reading Literacy Study* 2011 and suggests that Canadians need to do more to make parents aware of how much they can influence their children's chances for success in school and in life. Academic achievement, according to several studies, is positively correlated with realistic and high parent expectations for children's school performance (Amato and Ochiltree, 1986). Entwisle and Hayduk (1988) found that parents' estimates of their children's ability had long-term effects on achievement. Scott-Jones (1984) found that realistic and accurate parent expectations were associated with children's superior performance on cognitive tasks.

Given their continued sway in educational understanding, such earlier normative conceptions of "family" need a serious rethinking, as some feminist and sexuality studies have begun to do. Increasingly, where transnational migration and diasporic experiences mark the daily lives and learning of so many young people, our sedimented understandings of family must be called into question. Juson, an English-language learner who had emigrated from China, helped us to understand the complexity of family and the role of "home" in learning:

> BURCU: What is it like to be a student? Because you were always attentive, you were here most of the time, you weren't absent and that is a big problem in this school.
>
> JUSON: It all depends. Like I guess mostly it depends on your family. Because like from China to Canada. I have lots of my friends in China, my grandparents; my grandfather and grandmother are in China ... My grandparents like love me so much. I haven't seen them in like 10 years or something like that since I came to Canada. So like they have a lot of hope on me. I can't fail them so – so I am pushing myself.
>
> (Individual Interview, Juson, Middleview, January 14, 2011)

The new realities for students perceived to be at risk of not succeeding in school in the early part of the 21st century, the students we have spent so much time talking to and working with, those who are supporting themselves financially – who are holding down jobs while in school or raising children of their own – are not adequately understood by more traditional forms of educational research, and yet students are struggling, in growing numbers, in mainstream institutions. There is no doubt that these realities continue to shape significantly how young people fare at school, but they do not begin to capture the complexities of students' lives, or the other external factors imposed on young people that affect their quality of life. Relationships with employers, with landlords or shelter workers, with dependents, correctional services, community centres, support groups, all play a significant role in the school experiences of young people today. We know this both from our ethnographic and our quantitative data.

India: The Intimacy between Problems and Supports

What must be said in this chapter, which aims to give readers a deep contextual picture of our research sites, is how key the relationship is between the educational and social problems experiences by youth and the educational and social supports available to them. Nowhere was the impact of school on quality of life more evident than in India. Much energy by educational and social activists in India has been put into the challenge of universal education, and in particular the education of young women, in developing countries. The problems in India are entrenched by legislation that legitimates deep structural inequities. Although in recent years there has been a significant reduction in the number of students out of school (an almost 60 per cent reduction), our collaborator Urvashi Sahni (2012) notes (*From Learning Outcomes to Life Outcomes*) that the highest percentage of children outside the school system are girls – 55 per cent drop out of primary school and 73 per cent drop out before year 10. Clearly, access to schooling is a significant problem but retention of girls in schools is also critical. Sahni points to the universally low cultural expectations for girls and that 75.37 per cent of girls in Lucknow were married by age 18. She asserts that for there to be gender parity there has to be explicit curriculum designed to meet that goal. At Prerna, through professional development as a school staff, they recognized that their early efforts were not sufficiently focused on "life outcomes" but on the simpler "learning outcomes" they espoused. With "life outcomes" in mind, Prerna offers many educational supports to address the multiple and overlapping problems the students face.

Sahni (2012), in her own research, writes about the undernourishment of girls as they receive less than their fair share of the food (particularly in poor families), which leads to health consequences that lead to absenteeism. Also at play are high levels of gender-based violence and child marriage. She writes:

> Plan International's nine-country study, which sought to identify the reasons why adolescent girls dropped out, summarizes its findings: "What emerges from the data is that girls are identified with their sexual and domestic roles, whereas boys are seen as providers and household heads. In our research, a girl as future wife and mother carries little value. She is a demeaned person not seen as worthy of rights. This demeaned identity remains a key barrier to girls accessing their right to education." (2012, p. 6)

In one of our first teacher interviews at the school, Ms. K expressed the kinds of concrete support that Prerna offers the students: food, books, and clothes. Although she acknowledges that the school cannot provide money or solve the conditions created by violent and incestuous fathers, they, as a school, do offer considerable support in response to the problems faced by the girls.

> KATHLEEN: So school here is not school. School is home, it's –
> MS. K: Yeah, it's more than a home even. Because at times these girls have found their homes to be most insecure places. There are girls who have faced incest problem, who have been facing, like Laxmi, it's very violent because of her father, Kushboo has the same problem, Prithiba has the same problem. Monetary problem is there. So though we are not able to support them with money and all, but you know the very support they require, we are there. If you require food, we are there, if you require books, we are there, if you require clothes, we are there, so I think that is a very good, big support that Prerna has built.
> (Interview, Ms. K, Prerna, January 20, 2012)

In Sahni's (2012) writing about Prerna, she also suggests that the school supports the students through making education "relevant to their lives and practicing Critical Feminist Pedagogy" (p. 24). We found, during our time at Prerna, that this pedagogical work creates a powerful counter-narrative to the cultural patriarchy and systemic disempowerment of girls. Sahni explains:

> The girls live in a world named and made by their fathers, brothers, and to some extent by their mothers. The social conditions lead them to expect to have a life named by their husbands and in-laws after they are married,

which they perceive as an inevitable condition of life, one over which they have no control. The critical dialogues and the other activities in the empowerment classes and the school calendar, help students become more critically aware of the gendered construction of the institutions in which they live their lives and in so doing they denaturalize and deconstruct their social and political structure. (p. 27)

Our most illuminating encounters with this community's critique of the ubiquity of patriarchy came from drama presentations made for us by the girls, and from the most extraordinary interview we had with one of the Prerna teachers. In the drama we witnessed, the girls showed us how patriarchy includes their fathers' control over their lives – over the way they dress, how and when they work, and especially how fathers always give preferential treatment and freedom to the boys in the family. In the scene we watched, the father was complaining about the quality of the food the daughter had prepared and gave his son money to go to a restaurant rather than eat what his sister had prepared. In this scene, we also watched the mother who was so economically dependent on her husband that she could not afford to speak up against the treatment she and her daughter receive. I was forcefully reminded during these scenes of Cahill's (2010) take on drama:

Firstly, drama is a medium that has the capacity to make the invisible visible, and thus can help us see and hear the discourses at play. Through stylised play we can embody, enact, exaggerate, sing or symbolise these discourses, and thus come to recognise them.

Secondly, the drama can be used to help us catch the discourse at play in orienting our desires and perceptions. We can pause the action, suspend time, and thus replay and re-examine instances of action or desire. We can move to other realities to demonstrate where else these desires may be at play. We can shift roles and perspectives and thus reveal the way that positioning can shape perception.

Thirdly, drama offers a communitarian form and a number of mechanisms for employing the imagination. Through collective enactment of the imagined we can create new possibilities, and taste new modes of being, thus engaging in the processes of re-writing, and re-storying. (p. 167)

What we also detected was the pleasure the young women took in sharing their performances with us, performances that exposed intolerable forms of oppression. There was a palpable delight in sharing this work. Seyla Benhabib (1992) asserts that "All struggles against oppression in the modern world begin by defining what had previously been considered private, non-public, and non-political as matters of public concern, issues of justice, and sites of power" (p. 100). Performance clearly gave these young women a forum for the public naming and shaming of previously private experiences of subjugation. Our role as researchers, then, both here and in Toronto, was to move our gaze from consumption to political and intellectual engagement, keeping in mind Julie Salverson's (2001) warning, which we share, that simple, naturalistic repetitions of trauma can be re-violating.

The following two lengthy excerpts come from the interview with our teacher, Ms. K, who makes clear that patriarchy is not just an issue for the poorest of the girls but is also an issue at all socio-economic levels of the society. I cite her here at length because we learned so much about the everyday experiences of young women in India from her detailed analyses:

MS. K: I think that the problems are universal; it's not only going to be with the Prerna girls. It can be with the Study Hall [middle-class] girls.

KATHLEEN, BURCU, ANNE: Of course.

MS. K: Because men are all over alike. Across all strata of the society, men are all alike. For them, they do not have any respect for females because they are socialized like that. So that is very important. And here in Study Hall we try and train the boys, also, to be respectful towards the girls, to be respectful towards females, how, probably not today, but say, 10, 15 years, when they become husbands, we will have some good husbands ... Their environment is like that. So I think that's very important on how well we are able to train them ... And I think every strata of the society needs that training. And training only the girls won't help us ... The person whose powerful politically, economically, physically, why should they give some for us? So we have to make the other party more powerful. And this is how we can make it ... I keep telling the Study Hall children, rather all the teachers keep on telling, the girls keep telling, first have a career for yourself. First become economically independent. Then, keep up with your relationships ... 'cause for boys, they understand that OK, I have to learn and look after my family. But how to look after, they are not told. So that is why there is wife beating, demand of dowry, killing of wives. Sometimes it's very abusive.

KATHLEEN: But what does that do to people's psyche to see that kind of violence against women. Does it desensitize you?

MS. K: The safest place called home is the most unsafe place for them. She's being burned to death for not bringing in enough dowry. She is burned to death because the husband is having an affair. These things, it's very sickening ... So I think the girls need to be trained to become selfish, to look for yourself first, and that training is important for all classes. Not only for Prerna girls, it's for all. Even my daughter needs to be trained in it. So it's like, every class needs that training. Recently, I think you must have been in India, but a gold medalist, he killed his wife who was earning 80,000 a month, because she said I want to continue my job. She was killed. It's terrible. Set her free, let her go, divorce her.

KATHLEEN: There's so much pride and –

MS. K: She'll do what I wish. She can't do what she wishes.

(Interview, Ms. K, Prerna, January 20, 2012)

Ms. K was a gracious woman with an exceptional warmth. We were very taken by her passion and her determination to resist what appeared to be socially entrenched.

MS. K: ... you'll find the police having that patriarchal state of mind. The judges sitting in court, they have that same state of mind. You know I've heard the judge telling the wife "oh, your husband has beaten you. Don't get annoyed, don't divorce him. Go and lie down. He'll come and love you." She's filing a suit for divorce that he's hitting me every day and he's saying this! ... So it's a total patriarchal mindset. So you literally have to train the females, you have to train the girls that this is the world where you're going to enter. So make yourself fit for it. It's like that. There's no need to be, you know, delicate. And lily-like flower. Don't be like a flower. It's your life ... Like these girls the first time they visited the village [where they had brought a theatre performance] there was a female who complained that the husband would hit her almost every day with the chain of the bicycle. So, they all told her, come out of the marriage. But it is very difficult for the women to come out of the marriage. Because parents won't accept the daughters back. They haven't given them any social and economical support. Even if she goes out of there she hasn't a place to live and she has to take the burden of the children also. So it's very difficult for them to come out. There is nothing like economic support for the females. The only thing they have is the jewellery that they get in the marriage. But how long will that continue? It's a very temporary phase. We have to train them that, that training ourselves to be economically independent, getting power, then get married. And

I think we are telling to almost to all classes, the same. And it's required, because it takes time for people to realize that this is the world. Especially for young females, you know, they carry so many symbols of marriage. Like the red powder on the forehead, the bindi, the bichhia, you know the rings on the feet, the finger ring, they all, the mangalsutra [necklace warn by married women] that they wear with the black thread, these all indicate that she's married, that she's a married woman … So it's very difficult. It's not only economically and all to come out of the marriage, it's physically, they can't, if they lose their identity, then who they are?

(Interview, Ms. K., Prerna, January 20, 2012)

We also held very informative focus group interviews with the young women themselves, who mainly spoke in Hindi, which was simultaneously translated for us by Dr. Sahni. We came to understand from our discussions the temporary nature of protection and support. One story relayed to us is intergenerational. A student had gone to stay with her grandmother to avoid the abuse she was receiving in the home by her alcoholic father. The grandmother recognized that the protection she could offer might last through high school but eventually the girl would have to obey her father and get married. Living with her grandmother was only a temporary respite. As Sahni points out in this exchange, even the girl's extended family and community did not show that they were there to support her in her commitment to continuing her education.

DR. SAHNI: So Grandma is also not letting you choose your own? Why?

(Kushboo speaks in Hindi with Urvashi.)

DR. SAHNI: So she says that my grandma that "listen, you're with me because your father has let you stay with me. And actually you have to do what he says because I might die tomorrow, so you have to do what he says. So her father 15 days ago said "I'm going to get her married" and so that the grandma says I'm going to make sure you go through Class 12, but after that, you know, you'll have to do what he says. So she says, but I don't want to get married even after Class 12. So she says, then that is up to you, and I don't think anyone can make you do what you don't want to do. But eventually you are his responsibility, not mine. OK.

KATHLEEN: That's difficult.

(Laxmi speaks in Hindi with Urvashi.)

DR. SAHNI: OK, so, we had a bit of a – she was saying even though my father – of course he's drunk most of the time – but my family, my folk in the village won't ever let me do this. I said I didn't know you had folks in the village. And she says, oh, you know, I do have a family. I have grandparents, etc. And they will not agree to let this happen, and they cast me out. So I was asking how much have they "cast you in" right now. I don't know that any of them have helped you at all. You've really done all of this [attaining an education] by yourself, and how do they have any authority at all to tell you what you want to do? People have authority over you if you are part of their family, if they do something for you, but in what way? I didn't see that they came to your rescue. Did they manage to save your mom? Do they manage to feed you? Do they manage to clothe you? She had no answer to that. So I was trying to point out that a lot of this is in your head.

(Classroom Discussion, 14 students present
at Prerna, January 21, 2012)

The students have extraordinarily candid and open relationships with their teachers because, in so many instances, they are their lifelines. We witnessed remarkable acts of trust. The girls saw them as teachers and guardians. In interviews with the girls, I engaged them in conversations about what we were observing:

KATHLEEN: And I have the impression that at the school as students you feel that there are a lot of adults who also help you and support you, so you can take some chances, and rely on the teachers that you have, and the principals, and that they are also a support system for you.

DR. SAHNI: (*translating for Laxmi*): She's saying that my life has completely changed. And, uh, she was saying I don't know how to say it, but, in the beginning I would never speak, and then I told my problems to Auntie [Dr. Sahni] and then she told me, and then (*turning to look at Dr. Sahni*), you took a lot of interest in my life, and then I felt if I kept talking about my issues then they do get solved ...

LAXMI: (*turning back to us, in English*) It was hard to see the dreams (*laughs*) become so real.

(Focus Group Interview, Sunita, Laxmi, Kushboo,
Moni, Preeti, Poonam, Prerna, January 21, 2012)

School is standardized in India and the Prerna students have to complete national exams as all students do. An insensitive and inflexible

Figure 3:   Prerna student studying before classes begin

evaluation system, oblivious to the gender constraints faced by girls from poor families, is an enormous hurdle in their transition from primary to upper-primary school and on to higher secondary levels. Home life, too, makes it nearly impossible to prepare for exams and so the students at Prerna did very poorly in their first attempts at national exams. Ms. K helped us understand why studying and completing school-work could almost never be accomplished at home:

MS. K: Academically, you know, they do not find a lot of time to invest in their studies. That is one of the biggest problems.

KATHLEEN: Right.

MS. K: If you come across children who are actually working from six o'clock in the morning until eleven o'clock, twelve o'clock [as domestic workers in others' homes] then they go back to their homes, finish off their own housework, chores, then they come to school. From school at six o'clock p.m. they are going back to their workplaces, and at nine o'clock, reaching back home. So after nine o'clock I think they hardly find time to study because they are too tired, so, whatever they are studying is within the school day. So, I think if they are attending classes and they give – attendance is good, healthy attendance here – so whatever their academic achievement, I think it's all because of their good attendance.

Because most of them are working as domestic workers. And it's all physical labour. So they get physically tired. So we can't expect them to, you know, read a lot and do a lot of homework. So, you know, we try to help them to study well in school, expecting that they will not find time at home. I think a few will find one hour; some will study for two hours, but not more than two hours study they can find at home. At times their parents do not allow them to study, they say why are you studying? Why don't you do the household work? So these types of problems they are facing at home.

(Interview, Ms. K., Prerna, January 20, 2012)

Given these broader conditions of living, Prerna makes particular efforts to engage with parents and families. In some cases, we learned, they make "house calls." One sees in these discussions how deeply interconnected the various social institutions are in the education of girls. Much progress is made in such a school, but it cannot be successful without the collaboration of other social institutions:

MS. K: Even here when they [mothers] come for parent-teacher meeting they are saying the same thing: that I want my daughter to do better than what I have done in life. So that feeling is there, but they do not have the power at home.

KATHLEEN: How else do you do parent education? How else do you – I know you show them concerts, and work with the students too, but what other things, as teachers, do you do that you think really have an effect on the parents?

MS. K: See we have these orientation programs. Shanti also interacts with the parents to tell them about not to let them get married at an early age, to leave the children, to give them time to study, have peace and loving environment in the family, so that these girls can grow. So these type of interaction we have with the parents. And if required, we have been visiting the places also. That is one thing we do. If required. The child is not coming and we come to know there has been some problem at home, so we go. And we are not bothered if it is a Sunday or not, we will visit the place, and see that the girl is safe and secure.

KATHLEEN: Have you done that in the past?

MS. K: Ah ha, we have visited Laxmi's place, Kushboo's place, the girl with the sexual abuse case, so we have visited them, we have taken them to the police, taken them to court, taken them to the child line. We do all these type of things.

KATHLEEN: Do you feel that these other institutions support you as a
  school? Like the police.

MS. K: We do get support from them, we do get support, but at times,
  especially, you know with the problems of child marriages, the mindset
  of the police is also.very patriarchal.

KATHLEEN: Yeah. That's right.

MS. K: They say, oh the parents must have got a good boy, let them get
  married. So that's a – then you feel really disgusted, but we have brought
  them till here, why can't they be punished? Why can't the law intervene and
  stop it? ... We have failed in two cases, we could not stop the child marriage.
  Because the parents say please let me let my child get married, because I
  have all the things ready, the guests have come, cards have been distributed,
  we have a social status, this and that, it's very difficult at times.

  (Interview, Ms. K., Prerna, January 20, 2012)

In her writing about the social and educational project of Prerna, Dr. Sahni
(2012) offers the following:

Prerna has made education relevant to their lives by including a very
strong rights-based empowerment component in the body of the curriculum from grade four onwards, where every week there are focused discussions on various issues that affect their lives closely, ranging from child
marriage, to domestic violence, sexual abuse, and health such as menstrua-
tion. The goal is to undo the inequitable mental constructs that the students have formed as a result of their gendered socialization at home. Uttar
Pradesh is well recognized as a state associated with some of the starkest
indicators of gender discrimination on the Indian subcontinent. (p. 24)

This philosophy was confirmed in our teacher interviews. The teachers
of Prerna believe themselves to be part of a powerful movement in the
education of girls. It was a humbling experience to be brought into their
world. And I close with Ms. K's understanding of relevant education
that was so clearly shared by our Toronto teachers:

MS. K: Like, they also know the word self-actualized. They have studied
  Maslow's theory. And they can put themselves where they are. They are
  able to relate what they are studying with themselves and others. So I think
  that is one of the best methods to study, that whatever I am studying I am
  able to apply it to my surroundings, my life, and my environment.

  (Interview, Ms. K., Prerna, January 20, 2012)

In India, as in North America, family is the single-most important outside-school influence on young people's success. In studies conducted on schooling in developing countries such as India, gender is a particularly salient factor. For example, Dreze and Kingdon (1999) and Glick (2008) found that when family resources are scarce and the cost of education becomes unaffordable, it is the girls' education that is sacrificed. Plan International's (2012) *Because I am a Girl: The State of the Worlds' Girls* and *Girls in the Global Economy: Adding it All Up*, found that in many countries, secondary education is not free, which is another reason why girls do not make the transition to post-primary education. Dr. Sahni finds that already reluctant parents are less inclined to send their daughters to school if they believe their daughters are unsafe there, likely to be abused physically or sexually in school or en route to school, are not learning anything or are disinterested in their studies because of poor quality, indifferent teaching, and irrelevant curricula (see also, Das 2010; Raina 2001; Reddy and Sinha 2010; NFHS 2007; National Sample Survey Organization of India 2005).

But irrelevant curricula or lack of safety are not issues at Prerna. When the girls went out into the community to interview elder women for their video projects on their lives, they began to place themselves in broader social histories and came to see such school projects as community development and critical consciousness as well as curriculum:

KATHLEEN: OK, so let me ask you, in some of your other video work you were interviewers, you were researchers, what was that like, with the microphone, interviewing people? What was that like as an interviewer or researcher, and you were also researching, in a sense your own lives, but talking to other people. So tell us about what that experience is like?

DR. SAHNI: (*translating for Kushboo*): She's saying that she also interviewed her grandmother. She's deaf, and she had to shout. She was married at 9, she told me; she was just a child. That when my grandfather would come she would actually run after him and chase him and she just had no clue what was happening. Then when my mother got married she was 17. A little shade better, but still. And so my grandmother told me that you know your life is very different. If you didn't have all this support and can say "no," otherwise you'd better be there too. So I learned from the interviews how things have changed over time.

(Focus Group Interview, Sunita, Laxmi, Kushboo, Moni, Preeti, Poonam, Prerna, January 21, 2012)

School, at Prerna, was the single most important avenue to social change. Their multi-tiered focus on support and family outreach, relevant curricula, intervention drama, made it an extraordinary place of learning. Such ethnographic accounts across our North American and Asian sites shaped our perceptions of the place called school, and its ability to identify implacable educational and social problems and think through potential supports often with very limited means. At a certain point, we wanted to take a step back from the stories we had been processing, to return again to our interests in self-other relations on a global scale, to see what such a panoramic view might yield. Our quantitative work helped us take that distance.

3 The Multidimensionality of Engagement: Academic Achievement, Academic Enthusiasm, Voluntary Initiative, and What the Numbers Tell Us

First, a word about the use of quantitative research nested inside our qualitative ethnography. In this chapter, I take a leaf out of the book of cultural geographer Michael Brown, whose quantitative work on the cultural geographies of sexuality and the body has been taken to task by critical, postmodern researchers who have read his turn to quantification as a betrayal of his critical scholarship. Brown (2007) defends his new appreciation of quantitative research as a "moment of honest troubling" (p. 211), a kind of scepticism. His view of postmodernism is not a rejection of meta-narrative but an acknowledgment of the plurality of it:

> A sense of scepticism, wonderment, unease and qualification towards science's premises, products and effects is how I have always conceptualized the term. That's not a rejection of science. To me, it is a call for a *very* difficult plurality of scholarship, where there is productive tension and debate ... (p. 211)

I appreciate Brown's attempts here to wrestle with the dichotomy of quantitative and qualitative epistemologies, putting forward instead the notion of a complex conversation about science – its premises, products, and effects – that aims to make something of its inherent tensions. With respect to my own turn to numbers, my view is simply that because the study of student engagement in the field of education has been largely a quantitative one, I needed to be conversant in that world and sit with the underlying assumptions of that science to be able to critique it, or to at least understand its premises or mitigate its effects in important ways. I needed to understand how that science has created a picture of engaged and disengaged students that continues to hold sway in both scholarly and popular discourses. I wanted to make my own "honest troubling" of the field, to use the master's tools to both learn from and undo some of the pervasive axioms of that work. Brown further claims that an internal critique of a scientific world is sometimes even more powerful than an external one, a view I happen to share. But, he submits, this of course demands a pluralizing of our epistemologies and methodologies. This chapter stands as my attempt to break inside a science, to understand the logic of its operations, and to make some space to question what I find there.

We learned a tremendous amount through our survey research about our students, the spaces in which they learn, the homes they come from, the community activities they engage in, the relationships they value, and how they come to engage in, or disengage from, school. It was obviously a very different kind of engagement with young people than our often intimate, face-to-face interactions. And it gave us much to think about in terms of the broader cross-site or global understandings we might glean from such data. Comparisons between sites was not feasible given the total number of students who participated in the survey. But working with the data across sites did give us a more global bird's-eye perspective that helped us to think through the local data differently.

In the broad sphere of social science research, countless different kinds of "outcomes" have been associated with the concept of student engagement. These include: fewer problem behaviours and feelings of alienation from school; fewer reports on experiences of depression and anxiety; fewer issues of substance abuse and teen pregnancy; improved academic achievement and attendance – as well as dropout and graduation rates – and healthier lifestyle behaviours (see summary of research by Waters, Cross, and Shaw 2010). For this reason, a comprehensive look at the more positivist conceptions of engagement as a phenomenon, and a close examination of the ways in which it has been studied, was necessary.

Historically, the study of student engagement and the very construct itself has been unidimensional and, politically speaking, rather conservative in nature. Very early on, student engagement was conceptualized as a causal relationship stemming from potentially static demographic variables. It has often created a kind of fatalism in education and used "predictive" factors to justify explanations that have systematically disregarded broader social contexts and left individuals without any agency. It is largely this reality that prompted us to reconsider quantitative tools,

and to simultaneously heed the criticisms of their underlying epistemologies in deploying them. Bloom, in 1980, was beginning to critique
the methodologies and concepts in the study of student learning and
outcomes, pointing to the overall paucity of qualitative and pedagogical
understandings of engagement, and the general lack of understanding
of potential interventions:

> In general, it has been found that learning in the schools is related to the
> education and occupation of the parents, to the social class and socio-
> economic status of the parents and to membership in particular ethnic
> groups and races … While such studies may be of some slight value for
> predicting levels of learning of groups of children, they offer no specific
> clues as to what the schools or parents can do to improve the learning of
> the children. (p. 346)

Student engagement, in more recent years, has been considered the
primary theoretical orientation for conceptualizing the dropout rate
and for promoting school completion (Christenson et al. 2008, as seen in
Reschly, Huebner, Appleton and Antaramian 2008). Given its presumed
pedagogical, curricular, and policy significance, student engagement
has received much more attention over the last several decades while
also becoming more complex and refined. Researchers, in an effort to
deepen and broaden our understanding of student outcomes as a stand-
alone variable, have gone on to consider a variety of variables that exist
outside school spaces, inside of schools, as well as those intrinsic to the
complex relationships between teachers and students.

   Our own quantitative work afforded just such an alternative perspective, that is, we examined school-based features, and a host of other
external factors, in our efforts to understand student engagement and
learning outcomes, rather than focusing solely on assumptions related
to family or community traits (Bloom 1980, in Kortering and Braziel
2008, p. 461). Bloom writes, "Researchers who were at one time concerned about providing *equality of educational opportunity for students*
now speak of the learning conditions that can bring about *equality of
educational outcomes* for students" (p. 337, original emphasis). Thus, an
important movement in the study of student engagement had been realized, as researchers began to focus on the *processes* that lead to learning.
And, if processes instead of characteristics were to be the new focus,
this movement also required a methodological shift in how engagement
and learning is measured:

... the movement from a study of characteristics of teachers and students to the direct observation of learning taking place in the interactions between teachers and students in the classroom ... it is a movement from the study of actors (teachers and students) to the study of teaching and learning as they take place under specific environmental conditions. (Bloom 1980, p. 338)

Bloom continues to briefly highlight in-school variables that can be controlled, altered, and measured (e.g., time on task, formative testing), as well as ones that occur within family homes, like parenting styles and practices (1980). The examination of student engagement was now in the position of focusing on the interactions and processes taking place in specific contexts. What remained to be determined was: (1) Which variables were relevant and important to consider for the construct of student engagement; (2) How these variables relate to specific types of student outcomes; and, (3) How the different contextual factors relate to one another. Our study addresses the first and third of these points as we identified and grouped relevant variables into measurable scales (e.g., Academic Enthusiasm, School Participation, Family and Caring Activities, etc.) and then correlated them within and across conceptual dimensions. Our scales were correlated with one another and then correlated with the Within School Space and Outside School Space scales that we developed. This move was a small intervention on our part that illustrates our attempts to capture the relational value we place on what were conceived formerly as discrete "factors" in the study of student engagement.

Other recent studies have also forged ahead with the view that student engagement, learning, and outcomes require a study of dynamic processes. Furlong and Christenson (2008) conclude: "There is a consensus that student engagement is a relevant multidimensional construct that integrates students' thoughts, feelings, and behaviours (Fredricks, Blumenfeld and Paris, 2004; Furlong and Christenson, 2008)" (p. 365). In other words, a single concept like "school connectedness" – which is the belief by students that adults in schools care about them as individuals, their learning, and their futures (Centers for Disease Control and Prevention 2009) – can be broken down and measured in a multitude of ways, all of which contain important insights for understanding student learning:

To date, most school connectedness research has focused on the measurement of the construct as well as the health, social, and academic outcomes with which it is associated. This research suggests connectedness is related to an individual's need to belong (Libbey 2004), and has been defined across a continuum for simply belonging (Anderman 2002) or participating (Fullarton 2002) in the school through to more complex definitions comprising behavioural, cognitive, and emotional domains. (Fredricks, Blumenfeld, and Paris 2004 in Waters, Cross, and Shaw 2010, p. 382)

Researchers in the field of student engagement have attempted to extend the complexity of this conceptual definition as they seek to identify ways of isolating or tracking outcomes for youth in schools. Furlong and Christenson (2008) summarize a series of papers that aimed to move the construct of student engagement from a three-part typology (affective, behavioural, and cognitive) to one that reflects a four-part typology (the former three plus "academic"; Furlong and Christenson 2008, p. 365). Each of these four parts is seen to be fluid, with the potential to change and develop under different circumstances. Furthermore, we can assume that there is an interaction level to these changes in that any change to one domain may impact the others. Furlong and Christenson (2008) summarize Brophy's work, which speaks to this point specifically:

Effective interventions address engagement comprehensively, not only focusing on academic or behavioral skill deficits, but also on the social, interpersonal aspects of schooling, particularly the need for supportive connections to other adults and peers and the explicit programming for motivation to address students' confidence and apathy. (Brophy 2004, p. 365)

Failing to see student engagement and subsequent outcomes as correlated or linked to one another in complex ways may prevent, as we now see it, the development of effective interventions to enhance learning for young people in schools. Wentzel (1998) conducted a study that helps to expand on this point as she found that student engagement was seen as a state that one exists in, though one that also fluctuates depending on interacting factors from home, school, and social contexts. Within her study of sixth-grade students, a questionnaire was used to gather information about the relationship between "supportive relationships with parents, teachers, and peers" and "motivation at school" (Wentzel 1998, p. 202). She found that the above variables were related to school motivation, but, more importantly, the "precise nature of these relations differed … depending on the type of relationship and the motivational outcome" (p. 207). For example:

• Peer support positively predicted prosocial goal pursuit;
• Teacher support positively predicted school – and class – related interest and social responsibility goals pursuit;
• Parent support positively predicted school-related interest and goal orientations. (p. 202)

By using a multidimensional model, specific causal relationships can be isolated to better understand how student outcomes come to be known as markers of the elusive concept we call engagement. Wentzel herself supports this view by cautioning readers not to limit themselves to oversimplified, narrow psychological constructs – like motivation – that fail to include contextual factors. Our study addresses this potential shortcoming by nesting our quantitative study (which in itself examines correlations within and across constructs) within our qualitative one. We were attempting to understand how the contexts, relationships, and processes of learning interact to create a complex picture of student engagement *and* disengagement. We also understood disengagement not simply as the absence of engagement, but also as a strategy and even, at times, a reasonable response to hostile school and societal conditions. Also, given our focus on contexts, relationships, and processes, we proposed a different way of conceptualizing student engagement by distinguishing three distinct but interrelated variables: Academic Enthusiasm, Academic Achievement, and Voluntary Initiative. We did this not only to add more complexity to the construct, but also because we had learned, in our qualitative work, that a student's achievement in school was related – albeit in a complicated way – to their enthusiasm about learning, their perceptions of barriers to that enthusiasm, and their sense of agency in achieving positive outcomes.

Finally, conducting our qualitative ethnographic work inside drama classrooms afforded us a particular kind of context. The drama classroom is a space that prizes the collective, a space that features students' abilities to draw connections between what they study in school and their broader social worlds – the culture of the school, and the social, academic, and artistic micro-worlds of their classroom. The sociality of the drama classroom provided a different backdrop for our move to an individualized online survey tool, which invited students to draw connections between this space and others in the school or in their communities and homes.

Understanding the Psychosocial Landscape: An Account of the Dynamics Relevant to Student Engagement within School Spaces

The learning context of schools serves a central function in engaging students. Again, Bloom (1980) identified several variables that can be altered within school learning contexts to shape student outcomes, such as choosing between summative or formative testing (p. 342). Other studies have looked at the relationship between the measurable variables found within schools, such as involvement in extra-curricular activities, attendance, grades, and credit accumulation, as well as more subjective variables like teacher and peer relationships, and sense of well-being in school. One study (McMahon, Parnes, and Keys 2008) attempted to explain the sense of transience and impermanence we have often felt in schools with high numbers of so-called disengaged students. In that study, researchers looked at a population of African American and Hispanic urban youth with disabilities after they had transferred to a new school context, and examined the relationship between positive school environments and "school belonging" with various student outcomes, including academic, social, and psychological outcomes. The variables they looked at were school-related stressors (interpersonal stressors with peers, teachers, and staff; contextual stressors such as witnessing victimization), social resources (support and empathy from staff), and school belonging (acceptance, inclusion, connection with peers and teachers) (p. 388–9). When these variables were compared to other academic and psychological outcome variables, the researchers found:

> students who have more school-related social resources and fewer school-related stressors experience higher levels of school belonging, which in turn predicts higher levels of academic self-efficacy and school satisfaction, and lower rates of depression. Anxiety … was primarily predicted by school stressors. (p. 394)

While still heavily focusing on isolated, psychological factors, we took this study as evidence of the importance that must be placed on program innovation that zeroes in on facilitating students' access to school-related resources like available bus tickets in the case of Braeburn, or food, clothing, textbooks, and school intervention in situations of domestic violence in the case of Prerna.

Active involvement within the school space, as well as the development of relationships with teachers and peers, are contextual factors that also played an important role in McMahon et al.'s study, and other studies support this finding. Sharkey, You, and Schnoebelen (2008) examined the relationship between school assets (relationships with teachers and peers), internal assets (perceived parental support, belief of the self, self-efficacy, goal orientation) and student engagement. They found that a positive, caring relationship with a teacher was a significant factor in predicting student engagement. In fact, they found this to be especially important for students from difficult home or family environments, as caring teacher relationships served as a mediator between the home and engagement variables (p. 414). They write: "Thus, school assets are not merely protective factors, but also important assets, or promotive factors. This result is meaningful in that it shows the importance of school assets for all students, not just those students who are at risk" (p. 414). Our study builds further on this study. Whereas they use a single measure of student engagement – school connectedness – one of the strengths of our study is that we broke down student engagement into practical and meaningful dimensions described to us by students in our qualitative interviews and our fieldwork (Academic Enthusiasm, Academic Achievement, and Voluntary Initiative). We then correlated each of these dimensions with different outcomes found within and outside school spaces.

There are a number of other studies that have attempted to understand the relationship between student engagement and variables found within school spaces, including extra-curricular activities. At the heart of many of these studies, as with our own, emerged the idea of school as a relational space – a context of and for relationships – intimately connected to all other positive outcomes and experiences for young people. When Waters, Cross, and Shaw (2010) looked at how school contexts shape various health outcomes for students, such as well-being, they summarized the importance of being physically present and active within school extra-curricular activities for the outcome measures of student health and well-being:

> … when appropriate school-level structures such as support for student autonomy and opportunities for involvement in school (Connell and

Wellborn 1991) are provided, young people are more likely to satisfy their
need to feel autonomous, competent, and related which, in turn, lead to
greater feelings of school connectedness. (p. 382)

What became increasingly obvious as we examined this literature,
however, was how these depictions of school seemed to evolve from
some imagined ideal world. And yet the worlds we were coming to
understand from our qualitative work with our research participants
were anything but ideal. For instance, Cooper, Valentine, Nye, and
Lindsay (1999) looked at the relationship between after-school activities
(homework, television viewing, extra-curricular activities, other types
of structured after-school groups, and jobs) and academic achievement (standardized test scores and grades). They found that there was
a positive relationship between after-school activities and academic
outcomes, even while controlling for factors such as gender, grade
level, and ethnicity. They also found a positive relationship between
extra-curricular activities and both academic outcomes and homework,
which were positively correlated with grades (p. 375). By simply providing opportunities for increased involvement in schools, teachers
can increase student success for various health (Waters et al. 2010) and
academic (Cooper at al. 1999) outcomes of students. This may be true
in relatively homogeneous middle-class settings, but how, we found
ourselves asking, does a young person who holds down two jobs and
must make enough to pay a monthly rent or is caring for dependents,
find the capacity to engage with the school beyond the school day? For
many of the North American students we met, the after-school world
was a place about which they knew very little. In the end, we would
argue that involvement in school-related activities does not necessarily
mean a student is academically engaged, but such involvement does
provide opportunities for greater peer-and-teacher relationships, and
potentially a greater sense of support from teachers, which has been
consistently shown to be related to positive student engagement.

Much depends on what we take the concept of engagement to mean
and the community value that is placed on school relationships. Sirin and
Rogers-Sirin (2004) looked at a sample of middle-class African American
adolescents and measured their level of school engagement, relationship
with their parent(s), educational expectations, and self-esteem. They
found that "educational expectations and school engagement have the
strongest relationship to academic performance" (p. 334). Patrick, Ryan,
and Kaplan (2007) provide an even more academic definition of student

engagement, one that emphasizes academic learning and classroom activities. In their study of fifth-grade students' perceptions of classroom social environment, student engagement, and personal motivational beliefs, they constructed student engagement from the concepts of self-regulation strategies (planning, monitoring, and regulating cognition) and task-related interaction (suggesting ideas, helping others, explaining thoughts or reasoning) (p. 86). The benefit to this approach is that they developed some interesting insights into how classroom practices and behaviours relate to student achievement:

> When students feel a sense of emotional support from their teacher, academic support from their peers, and encouragement from their teacher to discuss their work, they are more likely to use self-regulatory strategies and engage in task-related interaction. Students' personal motivational beliefs (mastery goals, academic and social efficacy) fully or partially mediated the relations between these perceptions of the social environment and students' engagement. Our results thus support the premise that adaptive classroom social environments enhance students' focus on mastery and feelings of efficacy and, in this way, facilitate engagement. (p. 93)

Our study expanded on this approach by looking at Academic Achievement and Voluntary Initiative as separate variables within the construct of student engagement, whereas Patrick et al. (2007) combined elements of these two. Our efforts to parse these ideas gave us a better understanding of the separate aspects of a student's desire to succeed and improve (Academic Achievement) and their ability or desire to work with others within the academic context (Voluntary Initiative); a notion that gained considerable prominence as we watched the necessarily collaborative aspects of drama work unfold.

Understanding the Relational-Spatial Landscape: An Account of the Dynamics Relevant to Student Engagement outside of School Spaces

As outlined above, families and communities were assumed to have, historically, the greatest role in predicting student engagement up until the focus began to shift towards school contextual factors (Bloom 1980). However, even though Bloom was accurate in his observation of this and in his suggestion to eliminate bias or prejudice from this field of study, more recent research is redirecting the focus back towards the family and community as being a primary predictor of student engagement. Given the greater critical, postcolonial, and class-conscious understandings in the field of education today, such "home" conditions are being examined with greater complexity than in the past. From a current reading in the psychosocial literature, it appears as though stereotypical characterizations of family, more often than not based on race and class, are no longer unquestioningly the focus. However, this shift in thinking itself reveals other normative and hegemonic assumptions about family that warrant a critical challenge. Sharkey et al. (2008) summarize the shift well as they dissect the various elements and characteristics of families and community lifestyles to better understand the role these spaces play in student engagement. First of all, they note a recent study that found "parenting behaviours and family relationships are strongly related to student engagement, which appears to be consistent across ethnic and socioeconomic groups" (Wentzel 1998, in Sharkey et al. 2008, p. 404). Interestingly, Sharkey et al. cite other studies (Glasgow, Dornbusch, Troyer, Steinberg, and Ritter 1997; Steinberg, Lamborn, Dornbusch, and Darling 1992) that identify an authoritative parenting style as the type of parenting important for positive student outcomes, including engagement:

> The authoritative parenting style is positively related to multiple dimensions of student engagement ... as indicated by improvements in school engagement (i.e., classroom engagement, school orientation, bonding to teachers, school conduct) ... Thus, parents who combine high levels of acceptance, supervision, consistent discipline, and democracy promote student engagement compared to those who do not exhibit these parenting behaviours. (Sharkey et al. 2008, p. 404)

Sirin and Rogers-Sirin (2004) completed a study on the psychological and parental factors related to academic performance with African American, middle-class students. In addition to their findings of the relationship between educational expectations, student engagement, and academic performance, they found that parent-adolescent relationships are positively correlated with student engagement and self-esteem (p. 333), and "that positive parent-adolescent relationships are related to better academic performance regardless of the individual factors involved" (p. 334). It is not only the fact that outside of school space factors, such as the quality of family relationships, impact student engagement, but that there is the possibility of a cumulative effect, or at least a necessary connectivity between outside and within school variables, which clearly impacts student outcomes.

But what of our many students who were neither living at home nor with parents, a growing phenomenon in North American schools. And what of our students in India who were caring for younger siblings, acting as parents, and heading their families? Poverty and social disinvestment in the world's advanced economies, as well as in the global south, have changed the face of "parenting"; and our research studies have not kept pace. The danger, then, is that certain kinds of families (Black families, poor families, "broken" families, migrant families, families with addictions, etc.) are blamed for parenting practices or familial relationships that deviate from these normative and hegemonic conceptions. In our study, we worked with our collaborators to ensure that our research questions and underlying assumptions were culturally appropriate, and that our analyses were not overly deterministic or outright disregarded other social and contextual dynamics. In Taiwan, for instance, we had to understand how students and schools in vocational streams were positioned within broader Taiwanese society and, as in North America, how these streams were indicative of larger class distinctions. In Toronto, we tried to understand how young people not living with parents articulated their relationships to parents. In India, we used our interviews to better understand how the students were often the heads of their families and how differently, therefore, ideas of parenting affected understandings of self. In our efforts to correlate scales, we consciously focused more on what students *actually do* at school and at home, rather than on who they are and what we think that means.

And yet, so important are these family and community relationships that they have even been found to have a greater impact on student-related health issues when compared to school contextual factors. One study found that family connectedness "was a stronger predictor than peers, school and adults at school for suicide prevention" (Kaminski, Puddy, Hall, Cashman, Crosby, and Ortega 2010). Even though this study did not look directly at student engagement, it suggests that the contextual factors from within school spaces believed to be integral for impacting student behaviours may not be as powerful as outside factors. In fact, it suggests that there is something very important about the dynamics or construct of families and communities for preventing the devastating outcome of suicide. It may not simply be the kind of family relationships that have an impact, but the mere presence of an adult figure in a student's life (a teacher, a caseworker, an employer, a youth worker) that makes a difference.

Waters et al.'s (2010) summary of research better grasps the student-school relationships of Prerna, for instance. In Lucknow, the school played such a caregiver role that some of these Western generalities simply do not to apply. Waters et al. summarize research showing that connecting with adults is positive for students, whether these are family members or not:

> Adolescents may also experience feelings of connectedness or belonging in settings other than schools. Blum and Mann Rinehart (1997) reported American adolescents who felt connected to their families were also protected from participating in antisocial behaviours. More recently, Grossman and Bulle (2006) described the importance of adolescents feeling connected to adults other than parents and teachers and found these positive relationships improve young people's health and well-being. (p. 382)

This interesting phenomenon relates strongly across all of our sites to positive responses to our survey items regarding religion. Religious involvement provides structured activity outside of school as well as connecting youth to other adults. In our study, structured activities outside of the school space appear to be a significant factor positively related to student engagement.

White and Gager (2007) conducted a study that examined the effect of economic status on youths' involvement in extra-curricular activities occurring within school spaces as well as in the community. They found that involvement in structured activities outside of school leads to greater participation in school. They summarized their findings as follows:

> Our findings also highlight the importance of examining youth time use across a variety of activities as other extracurricular activities, paid work, housework, and time spent watching television have a bearing on likelihood of participation. [Y]outh involved in extracurricular activities are more involved with housework, similar to findings by Gager and Hickes (2004) that "superkids" are highly involved across contexts. (p. 106)

This study highlights the idea of being "involved across contexts" (p. 106), which suggests that engagement or involvement in school may be a patterned behaviour that exists in the various facets of a young person's life. But what if this "involvement" includes domestic labour for young Indian girls or other forms of exploitive capitalist labour in Western democracies? The danger here is that such studies suggest that student engagement can be predicted simply by examining the number of hours students are involved in measurable, objective activities like housework or an organized club without examining the political conditions under which such "engagement" occurs. The more we delved into the literature, the clearer it became that a critical ethnographic practice, an "honest troubling," and a difficult plurality of epistemologies *and* methodologies was absolutely necessary to address the inconstant social conditions under which young people's "engagement" was being measured.

Lastly, several studies have also examined activities related to entertainment or employment, and have found an adverse relationship between these and connectedness with school. For instance, Eow, Wan Ali, Mahmud, and Baki (2009) conducted a study with secondary school students from Malaysia to look at computer game use and academic achievement. They state "computer games are found to have a weak negative association with students' academic achievement" (p. 1,090). What is even more interesting is that for the very high- and low- academically performing students in their study, time spent playing computer games did not necessarily "affect their inclination to perform better or worse academically" (p. 1,090). These results are consistent with our own because the Entertainment measure of our survey was not negatively correlated with many of our engagement scales. Cooper et al. (1999) found that the more time spent watching television or being involved in a paid job resulted in lower academic achievement as measured by standardized test scores and class grades (p. 375). The point here is that engagement can be predicted to some degree simply by understanding how students are using their time outside of school, but it is misrepresentative to assume "entertainment" means one kind of predictable activity for youth across socio-economic and cultural differences. I would further suggest that when entertainment satisfies an urge for autonomy and agency in the face of multiple forms of oppression, or inequities of labour and shifting cultural norms about youth labour globally, we end up with a decontextualized and politically naive picture of the value of "entertainment" in young lives. Our own study did not examine in fine detail the multiple meanings of entertaining behaviour for young people, so it remains of limited use. But we did experience, qualitatively, the outside school stories of our research participants enough to know that much more nuanced and critical readings and quantitative measures of the idea of "out of school" or "organized" entertainment is necessary.

While all of these quantitative studies represent important contextual features of an expansive terrain, we were constantly struck by the ways in which the lives of the young people we came to know in Toronto and Boston and in our Asian sites, Taipei and Lucknow, were of a very different order. Some aspects of our work could be understood within the context of the studies we read, but other aspects were so far outside the presumed assumptions about parenting and family life embedded in this literature that we knew our own quantitative work would only make sense if tempered by our extended ethnographic experiences and our socio-cultural perspectives. We were not looking at a homogenous group of students but rather a group of students in parallel universes, using drama to explore their broader family and social contexts, unfolding in a time of advanced capitalism and adverse processes of globalization and neoliberal incursions. Our measures, however innovative, were also bound up in a literature based in generalities and assumptions, some of which were obviously disconnected from the lives and worlds we were encountering in four diverse cities, a decade in to the new millennium. The value of our mixed methods work, however, was that we could make explicit some of the suppositions and disciplinary foci embedded in the world of engagement research that would ask us to finely attune our contextual sensitivities, to make explicit our critical dispositions, and to push beyond the platitudes of a field well-trod.

What We Did and What It Might Mean

A total of 118 secondary school students across our four cities participated in our quantitative survey. Nine participants were removed from the final analysis, as they did not complete the entire online survey, leaving a total of 109 (Female = 55). Our survey participants were drawn from our participating drama classrooms from the four urban sites in their respective countries: Canada (n = 20), India (n = 14), Taiwan (n = 36), and United States of America (n = 39). The age of participants ranged from 13 to 19 with one person reporting their age to be older than 21. Of these participants, 17 self-identified as being from Aboriginal descent in their respective cultures and 38 self-identified as minorities based on either their ethnicity (n = 32), gender (n = 9), sexuality, (n = 4), economic status (n = 6), age (n = 8), disability (n = 3), or another reason not listed in the online survey (n = 14). Participants could select multiple categories when self-identifying as a minority.

Student Engagement Scales

The Student Engagement scales were developed by adapting items from existing surveys on student engagement and motivation (Guay et al. 2010; Sharkey et al. 2008; Sirin and Rogers-Sirin 2004) and from reviewing relevant literature on factors associated with this topic (e.g., Furlong and Christenson 2008). Our research team developed potential survey items and engaged in discussions to narrow and focus the final lists (survey items are listed in Table 1). We attempted to build upon existing tools and literature to further expand current notions of student engagement so that it more closely reflected the breadth of psychological and social factors attributed to this concept (see Appleton et al. 2008), as well as to develop categories that reflected the broader philosophical and theoretical constructs of our research. The first scale, Academic Enthusiasm, consists of 8 items that reflect several concepts: Intrinsic Motivation (3 items), Identified Regulation (2 item), and Affective Connection (3 items). The second scale, Academic Achievement, also consists of 8 items and is based on several sub-factors: Identified Regulation (3 items), External Regulation (2 items), and Imagined Achievement (3 items). The third and final scale, Voluntary Initiative, consists of 3 items that reflect a general level of involvement in various dimensions of the school community: Extra-curricular (2 items) and Assisting others (1 item). All items were rated on a 5-point Likert scale, ranging from 1 (*Strongly Disagree*) to 5 (*Strongly Agree*). Each of the scales was validated using the Chronbach's alpha test for internal consistency. Essentially, it provides an indication of whether the scale being tested is a single construct by correlating all of the items within the respective scale and providing a score between 0 and 1.00, with the latter reflecting the strongest possible correlation. Generally, any correlation above .700 is considered acceptable. All three scales passed this threshold with scores of .850 for Academic Enthusiasm, .879 for Academic Achievement, and .801 for Voluntary Initiative.

Within School Space Scales

Two scales were developed by our research team based on our initial ethnographic experiences to measure behaviours that occur within various school spaces. Behaviour was the focus of these measures as we were interested in what students *do* while at school to explore whether our conceptual measures of student engagement were related to the actual actions and involvements of students during the academic day. These would be observable, concrete activities for which students can roughly gauge the frequency or amount of time they engage in them. We divided the items into two scales: Academic Participation Scale and School Participation Scale. The former consists of 9 items related to how often students engage in academic-related activities while at school, which were organized into 3 categories: Classroom Involvement (1 item), Task Completion (4 items), and Academic Discussions (4 items; a list of all items is available in Table 1). These activities were measured using a 4-point modified Likert scale that had participants indicate how often they engaged in them during a typical school day (*Never, Sometimes, Frequently,* and *Always*).

The School Participation Scale measures a participant's estimation of how many hours per week they spend engaged in various in-school activities. The scale consists of 6 items designed to reflect the breadth of opportunities and activities available to students, such as clubs or organizations, school governance, volunteering, mentoring, school events, or studying (for a complete list, see Table 1). Estimation of total number of hours per week spent on each activity ranged from *Less than 1 hour* to *5 or more hours* with half-hour intervals in-between for participants to select. For the analysis, the first and last categories remained the same, but the hourly categories were grouped with their respective half-hour option (e.g., *1.0* hours was grouped with *1.5* hours). Chronbach's alpha scores were as follows: .802 for Academic Participation and .745 for School Participation.

Outside School Space Scales

Three scales with a total of 21 survey items were created that reflected various behaviours or activities participants may engage in outside of the school space (e.g., in their homes, communities, etc.; for the complete list, see Table 1). The items were grouped conceptually into scales that reflected three areas: Family and Caring Activities (6 items), Academics and Studies (5 items), and Entertainment (10 items). Participants were asked to estimate how many hours they devote to each activity in the course of a typical week. Similar to the Within School Space Scales, the items being measured were observable activities or behaviours. Possible responses were identical to that of the School Participation Scale and the response categories were regrouped for analysis in the same manner as well (see above). The scales received the following Chronbach's alpha scores: .817 for Family and Caring Activities, .761 for Academics and Studies, and .714 for Entertainment.

Demographics

A series of demographic questions were presented to the participants, which included the following: gender, age, years in school, Aboriginal status (relative to their respective cultures), minority status, whether they live with their parents, number of residents in home, how many jobs they currently have, and how many jobs they have had over the last 5 years. Gender, Aboriginal status, minority status, and whether they lived with their parents were all measured by asking the participants to select the correct alternative (e.g., 1 = female; 2 = male). For age, students were presented with a list of options, which ranged from *Less than 10 years* to *More than 21 years*. A similar method was used for the number of years in school (*Less than 5 years* to *More than 14 years*), number of residents in their home (*1* to *More than 8 people*), and how many jobs they currently have (*I do not have a job* to *More than 5 jobs*) or have had over the last 5 years (*I have never had a job* to *More than 5 jobs*).

Translation and Administration of Surveys

To increase test equivalency and maintain meaning across the cultural and linguistic differences of the sites, we used a combination of "blind-back translation" and expert review (see Peña 2007 for a description of this process and potential conceptual and methodological considerations). Three versions of the survey were created: English, Hindi, and Mandarin. The survey was first developed in English with feedback from research teams from the sites in Taiwan and India to reduce cultural bias as well as to increase relevance across the sites. Two Canadian graduate students with no previous involvement in the study, were hired to assist with the translations: one was fluent in Hindi and the other in Mandarin. Surveys were then returned to the research team and forwarded to the India and Taiwan sites to ensure translations were culturally appropriate and accurate when compared to the English version. Instructions for students on how to complete the surveys were also translated into the respective language spoken at each site.

The survey was delivered using the online tool, Survey Monkey. During the 2009–10 school year, each investigator from the four countries collaborated with the research team in Toronto to coordinate the completion of the online survey in their respective school sites. All student surveys were completed at the midpoint of the study, between March and April of 2010 and then analysed using the software SPSS (IBM Corp., 2012).

Correlations of Scales

We wanted to understand how a quantitative measure of student engagement relates to the activities and behaviours youth engage in. So we correlated our three student engagement scales with how often students were involved in various behaviours, actions, or activities that occur within a school space (such as programs, participating in classroom discussions, etc.), and outside the school space (in their neighbourhoods, homes, communities, etc.). Table 2 shows the numerical data for the correlations outlined below. Information pertaining to the mean and standard deviations for each scale, gender differences, and other survey items can be found in Table 6.

Student Engagement Scales

First, we compared the Student Engagement scales with one another: Academic Enthusiasm, Academic Achievement, and Voluntary Initiative. As these are considered subsets of the larger construct of Student Engagement, we were not surprised to find that all were significantly, positively correlated with one another. Academic Enthusiasm was compared to Academic Achievement and Voluntary Initiative, and a significant, positive correlation was found in both cases. Academic Achievement also showed a significant positive correlation with Voluntary Initiative. Given that other studies conceptualize student engagement as a multidimensional construct (e.g., Fredricks, Blumenfeld, and Paris 2004; Furlong and Christenson 2008, we fully expected to find that these scales had a positive relationship with one another. With all scales being correlated, we can assume that as one of these measures increases for a student, so does their score on the other two measures. Therefore, our findings indicate that the subcomponents of student engagement, specifically enthusiasm, achievement, and voluntary initiative, are interdependent. The question remained as to whether these components would show individualized relationships with non-student engagement scales (e.g., Within and Outside School Space Scales) or be significantly correlated with all of the other scales.

Within School Space Scales

Next we correlated each of the Within School Space scales with one another and found a similar pattern. Academic Participation and School Participation showed a significant, positive correlation. Our measure of School Participation required participants to estimate how many hours a week they spend engaged in a variety of school-based activities (student council, clubs, etc.). It is important to note that the distribution of scores was heavily skewed towards the low end of participation: 54.6% of participants contribute less than an hour a week in this area, 26.0% of participants spend 1 hour participating at school-related events, and only 1.8% spend 4 hours or more a week (see Table 3 for distribution of responses across time intervals for each scale). Therefore, even though both scales are correlated with one another, it appears as though this does not translate into a great number of hours being committed to activities within the school space. What we have, then, is the general idea that the more you participate in academics in school, the more likely you are to spend time involved in school-related activities or initiatives that occur at school as well. But just how much more time one contributes, as his/her score for Academic Participation increases, is difficult to state with any accuracy. The quantitative part of our study could not easily consider the factors within these school sites that help to foster or facilitate classroom or school participation. These variables could have included school-related social resources, like support and empathy from teachers and staff (McMahon, Parnes, and Keys 2008); positive, caring relationships with teachers (Sharkey et al. 2008); and access to extra-curricular activities (Connell and Wellborn 1991, in Waters et al. 2010). In order to better understand the large skew in the School Participation data, we needed to consider how schools were or were not encouraging students to increase their participation in school, which according to our qualitative work varied immensely across sites.

Outside School Space Scales

The Outside School Space scales were also correlated with one another. Once again, we found that each of these three scales was significantly, positively correlated: the Family and Caring Activities Scale was compared to the Academics and Studies Scale and the Entertainment Scale, and a significant, positive correlation was found in both cases. The Academics and Studies Scale showed a significant positive correlation with the Entertainment Scale. Though each of these is related to one another, it does not mean that the contribution of hours to each category is the same. An interesting trend emerged as we looked at the distribution of responses within each of these measures. First, for the Family and Caring Activities Scale, we saw a distribution of responses similar to the School Participation Scale discussed earlier: 48.0% of participants contribute less than an hour per week in this area, 30.0% of participants spend an hour participating in family or caring activities, and 4.0% spend 4 hours or more a week (see Table 3). However, we see a different trend for the other two scales. For the Academics and Studies scale: 27.0% of participants contribute less than an hour a week in this area, 28.0% of participants spend an hour a week, and 8.8% spend 4 hours or more a week (see Table 3). For the Entertainment Scale: 8.0% of participants contribute less than an hour in this area, 28.0% of participants spend an hour participating in entertainment activities, and 6.0% spend 4 hours or more a week (see Table 3). Essentially, the trend for these last two scales is one where responses are less skewed towards the low end of the scale and more evenly distributed across the range of possible categories. This trend suggests that there is something inherently different about the Academics and Studies and Entertainment scales. What is perhaps even more counter-intuitive, but clearly demonstrated in our data, is the fact that the number of hours a student puts into studies outside school is positively co-related with voluntary initiative within school and not with either the scales of Academic Enthusiasm or Academic Achievement. This tells us that this particular dimension of student engagement – taking up voluntary activities and initiatives in the school – is quite distinct from the other two dimensions of academic engagement (enthusiasm and achievement) and quite important to a student's overall sense of engagement with school.

Correlations of Scales across Categories

STUDENT ENGAGEMENT SCALES WITHIN
SCHOOL SPACE SCALES

When we examine correlations across the different categories of scales – Student Engagement, Within School Space, and Outside School Space scales – we see many expected results, but also a few surprises. When we compared the Student Engagement scales (Academic Enthusiasm,

Academic Participation, and Voluntary Initiative) to the Within School Space scales (Academic Participation and School Participation), we found that all three of the Student Engagement scales showed a significant positive correlation with the Within School Space scales (see Table 2). This was to be expected as student engagement as a multidimensional construct has been linked to classroom behaviours and relationships (Patrick et al. 2007) as well as extra-curricular participation (Waters et al. 2010). Thus, the greater the level of student engagement, the more likely students are to participate in classroom environments as well as get involved in school-related, extra-curricular activities.

Student Engagement vs Outside School Space Scales

Our findings become more complex when the Student Engagement scales are compared against the Outside School Space scales (Family and Caring Activities, Academics and Studies, and Entertainment). First, Academic Enthusiasm showed a significant, positive correlation with the Family and Caring Activities Scale but no correlation with the Academics and Studies Scale and a significant, negative correlation with the Entertainment Scale. Interestingly, how enthusiastic a student is seems to increase as involvement in family activities increases, decreases when one spends more time engaged in activities related to entertainment, but has no impact on how much time one spends doing academic tasks outside of school. Next, Academic Achievement showed a significant, positive correlation with the Family and Caring Activities Scale but no correlations were found with the Academics and Studies and Entertainment scales. Finally, when the Voluntary Initiative Scale was compared against the other three, we found a significant, positive correlation with the Family and Caring Activities Scale and the Academics and Studies Scale but not with the Entertainment Scale. Consistent across all three of the student engagement scales is the significant, positive correlation with the Family and Caring Activities Scale. However, we were surprised to find that the Voluntary Initiative Scale was the only one from the student engagement category to be positively related with how much time students spend on academic-related tasks, like studying (Academics and Studies Scale). We fully anticipated that all three of the Student Engagement scales would have a significant relationship with how much time students spend working on learning at home or in their community. The explanation for this may have less to do with the affective and cognitive components of student engagement and more to do with family life and caring relationships with other adults. To fully understand this, our analysis required further deconstruction.

As one's score increases for any of the three Student Engagement Scales (Academic Enthusiasm, Academic Achievement, and Voluntary Initiative), the student is likely to be spending more hours engaged in activities related to their families or caring for others (Family and Caring Activities Scale). Student engagement and family and caring activities, then, have a positive connection, which is a finding mirrored in studies of parenting and family relationships (Wentzel 2008) and family routines (Taylor and Lopez 2005, both seen in Sharkey et al. 2008). What's more, this result has been consistently found with students from more challenging socio-economic backgrounds (Connell, Spencer, and Aber 1994), suggesting that the levels of student engagement for students from these circumstances – including our sample of students – are not necessarily determined by economic factors alone, but at least in part by more complex family, home, and community relationships.

The number of hours one spends each week engaged in academic-related activities outside of the school space (i.e., Academics and Studies Scale) only correlates with Voluntary Initiative, whereas there was no relationship found with Academic Enthusiasm or Academic Achievement. Therefore, those who are able to make time for studying outside of school are more likely to have a greater need to participate in things like extra-curricular activities (or conversely, those with a greater sense of academic involvement are also more able to commit time each week to academics outside of school). Our Voluntary Initiative Scale is positively correlated with how often one participates in classroom and other academic-related activities at school (Academic Participation), as well as the number of hours spent involved in school events or clubs that take place in the school space (School Participation). It makes intuitive sense, then, that this phenomenon would apply to hours committed to academics outside of school too. This is further supported by the fact that Academic Participation and School Participation are both positively correlated with the Academic Studies Scale, meaning the more time one is able to put into academics in one space, the more likely he/she will do the same in another space.

If we compare these findings to the research on structured activities for students that occur outside of school spaces, which found that students who were highly involved in school activities were also participating in structured tasks and activities in their communities (Bartko and Eccles

2003; White and Gager 2007), we may, in our study, be seeing an extension of these earlier findings to academic studying. It is possible that students who are highly involved within structured school and out-of-school programs may apply these same practices to their studies and work habits at home. Another theory might be that high involvement both within and outside of school may be an indication of high achievement or future-oriented goals as these experiences could be used to support post-secondary applications, which are only strengthened by good grades. However, the fact that we found no correlation between the Academics and Studies and the Academic Achievement scales suggests that the former may be more accurate in that dedication of time and committing to one's responsibilities or tasks is a learned, practised, behaviour that translates into more time studying and learning outside of school. We also had extra survey items from the outside school space category that did not fit into any scales. We correlated these items with the various scales to gain any insights that might emerge.

Interestingly, we also found correlations between how much time was spent engaged in religious activities both within and outside of the home. The survey item regarding religious activities within the home was significantly positively related to all of the scales except for the Entertainment Scale, and a similar trend was seen with the survey item about religious activities outside the home (positive correlation with 4 of 8 scales; see Table 4 for complete list of correlations). There was a further significant, positive relationship between how many hours students' spent in a week visiting family members they did not live with (4 of 8 scales), earning money (4 of 8 scales), and attending a community centre (6 of 8 scales; see Table 4). When you look at how these correlations are distributed across the three categories of scales, it is interesting that even though all of these extra survey items are outside of school space items, they are all positively correlated with at least one (but usually both) scales from the within school space category. Furthermore, the high number of them that are correlated with the Family and Caring Activities Scale strengthens the work of Bartko and Eccles (2003) and White and Gager (2007) even more: Highly structured activities that are varied across contexts show a positive relationship with involvement in school-based activities.

Academic Enthusiasm and hours spent engaged in entertainment-related activities are negatively correlated. This means that the more enthusiastically one engages in academics, the fewer hours per week will be spent engaging in entertainment-related activities outside of school. Conversely, students who dedicate more hours each week to entertainment-related activities have a lower level of academic enthusiasm. It is interesting that this relationship does not hold true between Entertainment activities and Academic Achievement and Voluntary Initiative. At the very least, it may suggest that when considering the paradigm of Student Engagement, one's enthusiasm for academics is related to, and influenced by, time spent on Entertainment activities, but the sense of achievement and voluntary participation within activities related to academics remains unaffected. The question remains: Why? The study by Eow et al. (2009) found that achievement was negatively correlated with entertainment strategies, though they describe this as a weak relationship. This finding was attributed to the fact that the very high and low achievers' academic performance in their study was not affected by entertainment. Instead, the results suggest that achievement is a more internalized construct. Our findings support this analysis, as we found no relationship between Academic Achievement and Entertainment, suggesting that the construct of achievement is consistently independent of the influence of Entertainment activities. One might ask then what would happen to one's level of Academic Achievement and Voluntary Initiative over time if Academic Enthusiasm increased or decreased as a result of time spent each week on Entertainment activities? All three categories of Student Engagement are correlated with one another; a change to one effectively means a change to all three.

Within School Space Scales vs Outside School Space Scales

The Academic Participation Scale showed a significant, positive correlation with the Family and Caring Activities Scale and the Academics and Studies Scale, but no correlation was found with the Entertainment Scale. The School Participation score showed a significant, positive correlation with the Family and Caring Activities Scale and the Academics and Studies Scale, but no correlation was found with the Entertainment Scale. Essentially, the more often a student participates in academics or academic-related activities within the school space, the more likely he is to commit a greater number of hours each week to activities related to his family, caring for others, and even academics outside of the school space. Time spent on Entertainment activities outside of school had no influence on tasks completed within the school. Of course, we cannot determine causality from these correlations and it is just as likely that the opposite is true. But why would this be? If Entertainment was

·shown to have a significant, negative correlation with Academic Enthusiasm, how can it have no impact on how often students participate
in academic-related tasks or events within the school space? Perhaps
entertainment-related activities are necessary avenues of release for
both highly engaged and less engaged students. Why wouldn't a student who participates in class, studies with his peers, and joins clubs
and other extra-curricular activities take time to explore different forms
of media or visit friends? Maybe entertainment is, simply put, a
necessity for youth. Its negative relationship with a student's enthusiasm may be comparative – exposure to more highly entertaining
activities makes academic ones seem less enjoyable and more laborious.
Thus, constructs like achievement and sense of initiative are unaffected
because they are more goal-directed and less affective when compared
to the enthusiasm scale.

Gender Differences in Responses to Scales

There were differences between females and males in the scores for
some of the scales (see Table 5). There was a significant effect for sex in
the Academic Enthusiasm Scale as girls had higher scores than boys. A
significant effect for sex was also observed in the School Participation
Scale as girls spent more hours in a week participating in school events
or extra-curricular activities compared to boys. The outside of school
space category showed a similar pattern to the above findings. In the
Family and Caring Activities Scale, there was a significant effect for sex
as girls contributed more time each week to these activities compared to
boys. The Academic and Studies Scale also revealed a significant effect
for sex; once again, girls completed more hours in a week in this area
. compared to male students. A significant effect was also observed when
students estimated how many hours a week they spend engaged in
religious activities within the home as girls reported more hours in a
week than boys. The only reverse seen with sex was when a significant
effect was found for how many hours a week students played sports.
In this case, boys estimated spending more hours a week participating
in sports compared to girls.

These findings are interesting but perhaps not terribly surprising.
However, they are not meant to reinforce the idea that differences in sex
and gender exist as mutually exclusive hierarchical categories. We are
not meaning to legitimize a heteronormative sex-gender-sexuality system. The gender binary has been socially constructed through normalizing

discourses and material practices that frame certain ways of thinking and doing as common sense and thus unassailable. Our qualitative data, for instance, include the thoughts and ideas of many students whose self-concepts, behaviours, and ideas do not conform to such a system. But here, we are taking note of the ways in which gender roles in families and gender behaviours among peer groups might play out. Again, Butler's (1990) idea of the performative has complicated our reading of the discursive and material conditions of the processes of gender identification that is not easily captured in this analysis. It is challenging to read into quantitative data the social and cultural forces that have already gone into producing and reinforcing normative gender scripts. But such readings have importantly influenced our ethnographic imaginary.

Summarizing Thoughts

Community spaces or practices that increase participation outside school (clubs, religion, traditions) appear to have a very strong correlation with student engagement. There is a real effect: As more time is spent engaged in religious activities within or outside the home, visiting family members, and attending community centres, student engagement and participation generally increase too. Second, student engagement increases as the number of hours per week spent caring for family and friends increases. This begs many questions: What kinds of dialogues occur within those family, social, or communal spaces that influence a student's sense of engagement with education? Why is it that the number of hours spent caring for someone who is sick is positively correlated with student engagement? What is occurring during those interactions? How is identity shaped by these caring or altruistic activities? What does this tell us about the place of community in learning? How then do we need to broaden our understanding of the function of communal activity and its significant role in academic engagement? Drama has always been preoccupied with the relationship between the individual and the collective, and between the world of the classroom and the "real world" from which young people draw inspiration for their creative work. Now, it appears, we have a definite measure of the academic boost it offers by being engaged in communal activities and relationships beyond school. This measure affects how we should think about pedagogy and the real role that drama has to play in processes of democratic citizenship. Freire's (1970; 1973; 1976) early ideas about autonomy and learning, about the desire to have an impact on one's social conditions as a significant component of education as a practice of freedom, is one compelling explanation for the relationships we have seen between one's broader community engagement and positive attachments to formal education.

Contributing to the Broad Field of Student Engagement

Our study looked at the *overt/low* inference subtypes of student engagement, mainly behavioural indicators and extra-curricular involvement, as well as *higher inference* levels of student engagement, including student self-perceptions of participation, enthusiasm, motivation, and preference towards school elements (Reschly et al. 2008). Our study also incorporated the four-part typology presented in Furlong and Christenson (2008) as our survey items for student engagement reflected academic, behavioural, cognitive, and affective engagement. But probably most significantly, our quantitative work attempted to address some of the criticisms of this kind of work, the very criticisms we found ourselves making as we became more familiar with the field.

In particular, White and Gager (2007) emphasize the fact that many studies do not use student or child self-reports (p. 76). Marsh and Kleitman (2003) and Bartko and Eccles (2003) also point out that extra-curriculars at school are the main focus of studies and that not enough out-of-school activities have been considered when understanding school satisfaction. Curiously, the Toronto District School Board's 2012 student experience survey has included, for the first time, questions about out-of-school activities and students' caregiver activities; clearly, these other spaces and more complex notions of young people as actors in their social worlds are coming to the fore. Further, Bartko and Eccles (2003, in White and Gager 2007, p. 81) argue that not nearly enough attention has been paid to race and sex. We have made strides towards redressing some of these criticisms.

Our study further contextualized the link between different spaces that students live in, both inside and outside schools. It accented the relationship between student engagement and behaviour as measured by time spent engaged in various activities (family and community activities, school involvement, etc.) instead of merely examining outcome variables (grades, dropout rates, credit accumulation) (White and Gager 2007, p. 80). We prized self-reports from students, not parents or teachers (White and Gager 2007, p. 76), which is, in our view and the view of others, the most valid and reliable way to measure cognitive and affective engagement (Furlong and Christenson, 2008). We further nuanced these data with self-reports of estimates of the number of hours doing activities inside and outside the school, on a weekly basis, to provide an idea of how much time young people are committing to various activities and not just that they are or are not involved in something (e.g., how many hours do you play sport vs play sports or not).

We also confirmed previous research indicating that family activities and greater involvement outside of school are both related to involvement inside the school, by adding insight into how different subsets of student engagement (Academic Enthusiasm, Academic Achievement, and Voluntary Initiative) correlate with inside and outside school variables. In fact, we found that Voluntary Initiative was positively correlated with academic activities and studying outside of school. This further strengthens and expands the inside-outside involvement link by highlighting how involvement in school-based activities outside of the classroom is related to more studying outside of school, providing the potential to improve outcome variables like grades and credit accumulation.

In addition, we have confirmed previous research indicating that involvement outside of the school space leads to greater involvement inside the school space, and we were able to link it to a specific facet of student engagement: Voluntary Initiative. Voluntary Initiative was positively correlated with hours spent per week doing a multitude of outside-school space activities (attending community centres, playing sports, artistic pursuits, religion in the home, religion outside the home), whereas the frequency of correlations between these variables and the other two Student Engagement scales was smaller. The greater a young person's motivation to get involved and make connections with others, the more likely she is to be involved inside school space and outside school space, which only serves to strengthen a student's overall engagement in school.

Other studies have found a negative correlation with Entertainment activities. We found that Entertainment is negatively correlated with Academic Enthusiasm, but it is actually positively correlated with the Outside School Space scales and has no correlation with the other two measures of Student Engagement and the Inside School Space scales. Thus, even though particular facets of entertainment, like TV time and computer gaming, have negative effects on academic achievement (Eow et al. 2009; Cooper et al. 1999), our more global measure of

Entertainment suggests that it is a positive part of activities conducted outside of the school space and may, in fact, have less of an impact on student engagement (specifically achievement and voluntary initiative) than some of the literature currently suggests.

One of the strengths of our study is that we imagined student engagement as comprised of different elements instead of seeing it as one thing, such as "school connectedness" (see Sharkey et al. 2008). This made it possible for us to see how different aspects of student engagement related to various outcome variables inside and outside school spaces. It also added an important complexity to the current theories of student engagement by providing a practical and lived model, rather than the more normative academic, behavioural, affective, and psychological freestanding elements. One obvious limitation of our work is that we were not processing thousands of surveys nor did we look at academic outcomes for individual students within our study; therefore, we could not determine how the correlations we examined combined to have an effect on individual student outcomes. Our focus instead was to look at the relationship between our measures of engagement and more comprehensive ways of measuring outcomes related to in – and out-of-school spaces. Taking this more global view became significant the more time we spent with our research participants, coming to see how their complex lives, as well as the changing social, political, and economic global realities, were significantly impacting on their ability and desire to connect with the place called school.

4 Social Performances: Students and Teachers Inhabit Their Roles

It is probably no mere historical accident that the word person, in its first meaning, is a mask. It is rather a recognition of the fact that everyone is always everywhere, more or less consciously, playing a role ... It is in these roles that we know each other; it is in these roles that we know ourselves. (Park, 1950, p. 249)

A tremendous amount of time was spent thinking about the everyday performances taken up by students and teachers in their school meeting place. School prescribes certain roles, to be sure, but the idea of young people inhabiting the role of student and teachers performing the social expectations of teacher, remained a point of general interest throughout the study. This involved thinking intentionally about the dramatic roles students took on, in light of the social roles they were always in the process of performing. In what ways do the roles of the social actor (the student) and the dramatic actor (the person involved in dramatic activity) interact to give access to a range of representational resources? Here again, Massey (2005) makes a major contribution to our conceptualizing of this phenomenon, writing

> what we might have called representation is no longer a process of fixing, but an element in a continuous production, a part of it all, and itself constantly becoming. This is a position which rejects a strict separation between world and text and which understands scientific activity as being just that – an activity, a practice, an embedded engagement *in* the world of which it is a part. Not representation but experimentation. (p. 28)

This dual focus, as it were, allowed us to also see how youth is lived as a theoretical and an aesthetic condition, as well as a set of social relations and material circumstances. The greatest conclusion to be drawn from our work is this: The failings of individuals, rather than the outcomes of inequality, have permeated our social discourses and imaginaries, and dangerously skewed our perceptions of the social world.

Identity and the Pedagogy of Possibility

There was a tacit understanding of the rules of social engagement in the classroom. There were also moments of the students' guard coming down in interviews and exchanges, where they told us they were revealing their "true" selves, as opposed to those selves they performed daily and effortlessly for their fellow peers, teachers, and us, presumably abandoning in these stolen moments the kind of performative norming they are accustomed to. While my postmodern sensibilities continue to make me uneasy with notions of a "core" or "true" self, I knew what they meant.

So we began to pay close attention to those everyday performances, as one does in ethnographic work, but also in relation to those intentional dramatic performances that were more apt to be understood as contrived and constructed. We paid attention to the processes of developing identities and relationships so we could begin to draw lines of understanding between the social and the artistic performances in school that young people engage in. What is fascinating about drama spaces is that broader and more intransigent social relations can be reproduced, disrupted, or temporarily suspended within them. In John O'Toole's (2009) historical account of drama in schools, he highlights an early period wherein the contribution of process drama is made explicit as follows: "in terms of the structures of status and power that underlie and drive curriculum in real school contexts, process drama has a quite exceptional potential to allow these structures to be suspended, altered and renegotiated, just for the purposes of the students' learning" (p. 113). It is also a space that can be porous, where different aspects of subjectivity can come to the fore, a space where the social relations and terms of engagement in the broader culture of the school come under scrutiny by those students and teachers who habitually engage in them. Our sets of data of social performances illustrate broader processes of the negotiation of student identity within the political and educational context of our urban schools.

The work of Canadian feminist philosopher Lorraine Code (2006) offers particular insight. Her notion of "ecological thinking," or ideal co-habitation, relies heavily on the social imaginary. In our work, we attempted to delve into the relationship between a social imaginary and a theatrical one. This relationship is central to the question of whether, or how, dramatic and improvisational work bears a significant relationship to the development of a social imaginary that might challenge the oppressive material social order lived by so many of the young people in our study.

The term performance, as I am using it here, includes notions of discourse and embodiment. Taking, in essence, a Foucauldian (1978) perspective, we understood discourse as bodies of knowledge that construct ways of being. Daniel Yon's ethnographic work has been especially useful in helping us see, in our own data, how discourse is orchestrated by institutions and sociocultural forces creating "networks of meaning" that structure the possibilities for thinking and talking about the world around us (Yon 2000).

There is a terrible thirst, we found, for students to find a "real" space in schools, or what they *call* a "real" space; a space where the intransigence of social norms can withstand some challenge. In our many interviews, the students favoured the drama space because it held out some possibility for this kind of freedom. The danger here is thinking that we, and our data, make a utopia of drama classrooms. This would be a mistake. Drama classrooms, in our experience, are messy, chaotic, unpredictable spaces that seem to offer some possibility for different kinds of engagements in the performance moments and the "real" relations of the classroom. These possibilities are sometimes explored, sometimes left unrealized, and can also seriously backfire and reinforce the fear and vulnerability that persists for many young people in schools. They are what Foucault (1984) has called "heterotopias" in the sense that they are real, unlike utopias, but that they simultaneously represent, contest, and invert other real spaces. This hoped-for space of the drama classroom is similar to Foucault's description of a space that is both a representation of the real but also a contestation of it.

It would be a further mistake to imagine that we are promoting drama spaces as rarefied or unique kinds of classrooms in and of themselves. While they may look different from other more regimented and disciplined environments in schools, they matter as much for how they fail as for how they succeed. Students need to learn in spaces where things can be attempted and failure can be overcome. The social and academic stakes are always high, even in so-called low-performing schools;

identities and relationships are always on the line. What matters about many drama classrooms is that the ideal of an inclusive, respectful space is held out as a possibility, even if it falls short or remains unrealized. Henry Giroux (1990) put it well when he wrote:

> A language of possibility does not have to dissolve into a reified utopianism, instead it can be developed as a precondition for nourishing convictions that summon up the courage to imagine a different and more just world and to struggle for it. (p. 41)

This sense of a counter-discursive pedagogy of possibility was also clearly articulated by my friend Roger Simon (1992) when he insisted on the term "pedagogy" rather than "teaching" to, as he said, "introduce suppressed or forgotten issues back into the conversation" (p. 56) about teaching. And what he meant here was that educational practice is a power relation that enables and constrains what is understood as knowledge and truth:

> When we teach, we are always implicated in the construction of the horizon of possibility for ourselves, our students, our community. Remembering such a perspective in our conversations about practice means finding a way of discussing practices that reference not only what we, as educators, might actually do but as well the social visions our practices support. (p. 56)

Giroux and Simon recall what earlier thinkers like Paolo Freire and John Dewey understood to be the main purpose of education. Freire (1998) argues for a pedagogy of exploration when he writes:

> The kind of knowledge that becomes solidarity, becomes a "being with." In that context, the future is seen, not as inexorable, but as something that is constructed by people engaged together in life, in history. It's the knowledge that sees history as possibility and not as already determined. The world is not finished. It is always in the process of becoming. (p. 72)

Drawing from Freire, as many drama researchers have done, Neelands (2009) argues that drama has a unique and important contribution to make to children's social and political development, in particular, and that this is at the heart not only of school drama but drama in a democratic society. Students in many drama classrooms strongly feel the call to engage in a potentially transformative critique of what they experience as their everyday lives. That such a possibility exists, in schools, is already a victory. Having the impulse to disturb the usual relations of power in classrooms and create something as yet unimaginable is no small feat.

Simon imagined three dimensions as essential to the creation of a pedagogy of possibility: communicative openness, recognition of partiality, and a sense of collective venture. Rather than the usual Western, liberal focus on personal development and academic growth, this kind of pedagogy is calling on an engagement with the world and its givens to provoke something new. Simon advocates a "community of solidarity" (p. 65) as the form of sociality ideally suited to a pedagogy of possibility. So, our attention to the social relations in drama classrooms was driven by a desire to understand the possible, as much as the real, terms of engagement in a collective venture that is theatre making.

In a focus group with Bertham, Fabian, Chrysanthemum, and Erica at Middleview, they spoke of how the performative dimensions of the drama classroom often work to create an environment where the typical divisions between students can break down. They talk about this as creating a "tighter bond" among students where "even if you don't like them you still – you have a better bond with them." We get the sense from them that the drama classroom holds the potential for pedagogical and social engagements that push outside the official discourses and expectations of schooling:

> FABIAN: Yeah, I agree with Erica. The thing about Drama class is you feel like you have a tighter bond with people in your Drama class than you do in any of your other classes. I don't know why it is but when you're in that Drama class you feel almost like, I don't know how to say it, but when you're in your Math class there is kids you don't talk to during the whole class but Drama class you talk to everyone. Even if you don't like them you still find a way to relate.
>
> (Focus Group Interview, Fabian, Erica, Bertham, Chrysanthemum, Middleview, November 24, 2008)

The danger with much of this work is that students, teachers, and researchers begin to adopt the narrative of "authentic selfhood" as though students wear social masks for most of school but somehow find a vulnerability that makes them less concealed in certain places. But that is not what I think the sense of possibility is about. Even though the social masks of schooling can be constraining and difficult

for students, what they enjoy about drama is the play between so-
called fiction and reality, the play between an intentional performance
and a social one. In these spaces, one often finds ways of being or
identities that challenge the regulatory social norms in schools and
this, students find, quite satisfying and unexpected. Finding the complexity, Chrysanthemum adds:

> And I really love it because it's a place to be yourself without being your-
> self. Like, you can act in any way because you're taking on the role of
> somebody else. But then you're acting the way you would wanna act if
> you were that person, so you're acting like yourself without acting like
> yourself.
>
> (Focus Group Interview, Chrysanthemum, Fabian,
> Erika, Bertham, Middleview, November 24, 2008)

My sense is that many students appreciate the possibility of playing with identity, experimenting with what they know, what is socially
acceptable, and what may be desirable. But this playing with identity
and social performativity has a dark side too. As we learned over and
over, the notion of engagement in school is a highly changeable one,
and it is a moment-by-moment negotiation for students and teachers.
Engagement often sits uneasily beside disengagement, and the sense of
connection we imagine engagement to contain is a tenuous and tran-
sient thing. In drama class, students feel and perform engagement and
disengagement, and sometimes perform their disengagement through
disruption. These moments force us to reconsider the very meaning of
engagement. If one of our key observations about drama classrooms
and curriculum is that they can give students a more flexible space for
working through and discovering their own sense of self in relation to
others, then perhaps there is room for thinking about productive disruptions. This might refer to the pedagogical possibilities that exist when
things go askew or when students are presented with opportunities
to reflect upon their own thoughts and actions in ways that might not
only bring them back into the curriculum but also enrich that very curriculum in the process. The idea of "productive disengagement" relates
to the rich area of educational sociology that has traditionally described
the dynamics of student disruption as resistance, which can of course
have both emancipatory and oppressive consequences and effects.

One of the more obvious kinds of disruptions we witnessed involved
humour, which can be both playful and distracting. But the students

used humour, often in its derogatory forms, to make connections, to create affective encounters, to practise solidarity. The students often felt that teachers misunderstood their humour, and that putting each other down was one of the important ways that they communicated, perhaps even creating solidarity against the adult world. There was a constant refrain that the adults did not understand their humour, that they took it too seriously. For instance, Bella explained in the focus group: And people in the class just can't see that and they need to like get around that. And they're like, "oh no, Bella's rude." I'm not rude, that's just like how I am. Derek replies: I think it's just like that's the modern humour among youth. It's like dissing each other and putting each other down but we all know that we don't mean it but to Ms. S, she thinks we're not getting along or we're arguing but we're actually really getting along (*he laughs*). Following the humour in the room was difficult precisely because it was so woven into the social fabric of the classroom and sometimes aggression masqueraded as humour; we found the teacher to be very alert to this more insidious form of social breakdown.

Upon coding several of our fieldnotes, we discovered many instances in which students' behaviours upon entering the space, for instance, intentionally disrupted the space, as in, "Fabian shows up late and begins with distracting comments right away: 'Miss, I like your sweater' in the middle of her attempts to give instructions." In another instance, it was Derek, who had been absent the previous week and was having trouble contributing, so instead he made several jokes to various members of the class and then highjacked the whole class by throwing his journal across the room. Ms. S responds: "Derek, focus. Because when you go off it's frustrating, and it throws other people off." These antics were key to our reading of how the temperature of the room was highly changeable. This very space that offered a kind of authorship to students and dispersed leadership, in its shadow side left the room open to countless distractions and individual tirades. We did not read these as the teacher's lack of control but rather as the resistance many students have to the more democratic ways of working that some drama classrooms provide. Ms. S's classroom rules, on view on the blackboard, were brief and clear:

Be on time. If you arrive late, enter quietly and don't interrupt.
    Spit out gum before class.
    Think before you speak. Be aware of how your words may hurt or offend others.

Don't criticize, whine or complain about an activity. Offer a solution to
Ms. S after class if you want something to change.
Focus on the drama, not the "drama."

For some, this is a space of unexpected freedom, but for others, at certain points, this sense of freedom and looser structure makes it impossible to stay focused. iPhones, iPods, nail polish, and other distractions
were recorded throughout our fieldnotes because they challenged the
focus of the room. The teacher was constantly reminding the students
to resist these distractions. Were she more authoritarian and made rules
with harsher consequences about their presence in the room or con-
fiscated the offending items, we may have seen fewer interruptions.
But these forms of distraction signalled to us when engagement was
waning and prompted us to be more attentive to the social, academic,
artistic, and relational shifts in the room.

Ms. S was attempting to be a counterpoint to an otherwise highly
regulated day, which left very little room for self-motivation. She
wanted students to have more ownership over the processes of their
learning, and over their academic experience and labour in general. It
was a tenuous contract at best. Ms. C at Braeburn governed her classroom with less flexibility but there was a lot of talk about professionalism and what it takes to be a professional. This was also a school
where students tended to be older and had already lost opportunities
at other schools. They were reading Braeburn as a last chance. In our
focus group with Cherry, Peanut, Max, and Kemba, two of the students
speak eloquently about their understandings of what motivates and
demotivates them:

KEMBA: At the end of the day it is only me. I have to depend on myself to go to
school. No one is gonna give me what I want so I have to work hard for it.
So even the teachers at school are not gonna help me with that. All I have to
do is just, like, motivate myself. I have my friend and she helps me with the
bus fare. If she doesn't have, I ask someone, I ask people in the school I don't
know. It is just the bus fare, you know what I mean? Sometimes getting up
early because I have work after. I live on my own – I can share that with
you – and I work after and then I go home late and I have to study, do my
homework, I have to study, get up early in the morning at six because I live
so far, travel to school, and it goes over and over again. But I have to just sit
properly and just smile and, you know, be here and always up your energy
because if you don't up your energy no one is going to do it for you at the

end of the day. Like, she can try, he can try, you all can try, but if it doesn't come from inside; you have to be intrinsically motivated. If I'm not, then how is it gonna work? That's what I do for myself. I have to motivate myself like from the day before. You know what I mean, think about today but also motivate yourself for tomorrow 'cause you don't know how you are going to feel. So yeah, that's what I do.

(Focus Group Interview, Kemba, Cherry, Max,
Peanut, Braeburn, December 2, 2008)

Cherry, too, picks up on the independence, the social performance of self-governance that is required for success:

CHERRY: And plus, like also if people bring you down in your day you have to be able to think about that in the morning like, "OK, I'm going to go to school happy." Whatever problems are gonna be out the door 'cause I'm here for myself. Because a lot of times if you think like – the way I used to be in like Grade 9 and 10 – that's basically why I'm here because I didn't get that many credits – so at that time I was like, everything that affected me at home I would take that out at school. And after, I've been pretty good for three years now, but I've noticed that if I start off my day like, "OK, I'm happy all the time and nothing's going to bring me down" I think that's what keeps me going every single day.

KATHLEEN: Your own motivation …

CHERRY: Yeah. Because everybody's going to bring you down. Everybody's going to say, "you can't do it." But you just have to prove them wrong. And if somebody – girls have this thing, I know it's not usually a guy thing but, that a lot of people are like "I'm not going to go to school because this person's chatty or that person's chatty" you know? You have to take that other door because we're older now so you can't focus on those kinds of things anymore right?

(Focus Group Interview, Kemba, Cherry, Max,
Peanut, Braeburn, December 2, 2008)

These kinds of conversations always call to mind the ongoing tensions between the disciplinary model of education with its rationalized structure of high-stakes individual competition and the neoliberal call, also individualized, for creative thinkers and problem-solvers. Where does this position arts spaces in the discourse on educational models? How can we understand the familiar attempts in these spaces to "create a community" and build "camaraderie"? The performance of solidarity, even if a thin veneer, marks it as different according to many teachers. Ms. C explains:

> You know, I try to create a culture where people cheer each other on all the time for any work, even if it's a work in progress, it doesn't matter, let's just try it. So there's all these baby steps of huge achievements. And that kind of camaraderie, let's just do it. I've had English class discussions, and they're interesting and everyone says an idea, but no one got up on the desk and started clapping, and no one said "Dude that was awesome!"
>
> (Interview, Ms. C., Braeburn, December 11, 2008)

Class, Race, Risk and Neocolonial Salvation Narratives

One of the other aspects of identity worth thinking about is the social performance of "toughness" for working-class and racialized urban youth. The idea of gangs, youth violence, and criminality has entered the cultural imagination in very disturbing ways. Confusion about what constitutes a gang, or gang behaviour, even among researchers of youth gangs, often causes moral panic when things like race, fashion, demeanour, and music are conflated with violence. These "images" become inseparable from perceptions of threat and before long youth, rather than criminal behaviour, become indistinguishable from criminality with identities saturated and over-determined by negative cultural readings. Several studies have signalled the importance of social performances to our perceptions of gang culture. In Gunter's (2010) recent study of young Black males in East London, he points to the performativity of criminality and the ways in which it adheres to particular bodies that may, themselves, be performing strategies for basic survival. He writes:

> The road to culture and fashion … is very much influenced by the hyper-masculine and style conscious attitudes and personas of the "rude boys." Therefore the majority of young males involved in road life will tend to walk around in small groups, wearing designer sportswear … When walking, these young black males will tend to "hog the pavement" by walking in small groups oblivious to other pavement users' needs. They also will adopt a "screw face" in order to warn potential male foes that they are "not to be messed with." In short these young males are putting out a message that they are not victims (weak or "pussies") rather they are victimizers. (pp. 99–100)

What Furlong (2013) concludes is that statistics on youth crime are problematic and vary depending on how they are collected and by whom. Crime reporting is also affected by media interpretations and a large number of crimes remain unreported. An accurate picture, under these circumstances, is difficult. But he also concludes that most crimes committed by young people are "trivial" and many involve no victims. This is, of course, a very different picture from the one most commonly circulating in popular culture and in the public imagination. Most significantly, Furlong notes, is that such a focus on young people as perpetrators of crime "detracts from the extent to which they are overrepresented among victims of crime" (p. 207).

In schools, and in popular culture more broadly, the proliferation of salvation narratives where youth and crime are concerned continues: Schools save troubled youth from a life of criminality and violence and steer them in the right direction. Nowhere is this more evident than in arts classrooms or on the sports field, where popular movie culture has also sanctified the heroic drama teacher or the tough-loving coach. Ms. S was equivocal about such narratives but Ms. C introduced early on in our conversations the idea of youth and gang crime:

> When I first got here, there was a lot of gang kids from different gangs, which I didn't really realize. And I had this thing where we would have to sit in a circle, because that's how I start my drama classes. And I didn't know why – You know, out of teacher's college, yay, let's sit in a circle! – and no one would sit in a circle because that would mean eye contact, and you can't make eye contact with other gang members, or you've broken down some of your respect issue and territory issue. So you know, I had to work on just the circle. It took me a week, not too long, just allowing them to make eye contact, or be safe about making eye contact. I had this thing where they'd touch the wall when they walked in, and they left their life outside the room outside. And they came into this totally safe space.
>
> (Interview, Ms. C., Braeburn, December 11, 2008)

I have reflected elsewhere (2007; 2011a; 2011b) that I think the goal of safety in high school classrooms is a very important one, but that safety for all students is an elusive, if impossible, goal. We may work towards safety but there is no way we can know, from moment to moment, how each student, differently socially located as they are, is feeling. Safety, in my view, is a constant negotiation and as soon as we think we've arrived, it will slip away again. The boundaries of safety are not static;

what feels safe one day is dangerous the next. Social dynamics are in flux. One's sense of safety is in a continual dialogue with the changing social performances in the room and the broader cultural narratives beyond it. Ms. C, by way of example, shares a story worthy of further consideration:

> I did a Kiwanis festival and two kids came and said "We want to do Kiwanis," which is like a dance competition, well not really a competition, they get feedback about their work, which is why I like it. And two kids came to me separately – a male and a female – and said "I really wanna do Kiwanis, so if you want to put a choreography for me ..." "Well there's two of you," so I said "Meet me at lunch." So they came at lunch and they both looked at each other and they turned around and went to leave, and I said "Where are you going? Come back?" He's like "No, Miss." So this was a girlfriend of a gang rival, or something. So I had paired two gang rivals together to do a very romantic, lyrical dance. And I – we went outside and we did that kind of wall thing. I said, "we're gonna walk in and we're just going to be without the borders of our communities, and you know, we're just going to do this as dancers and people sharing art. Can we just try this for me?" And all that history, it's there, and it's real, but let's just start again. Let's just make this space the "start again space." And so they came in. I didn't even tell them we're doing lyrical. I think they assumed we were doing hip hop. So they came in and they sat down; there was a kind of tension. So we kind of worked through that a bit. And then I put on this – I think it was "Braveheart" or something, it was this very lyrical, beautiful music – and they're like "Miss, what's this?" And I said "we're going to do lyrical jazz." "No, no, we're gonna do hip hop, right miss?" Because that's what we were doing in the class at the time. I said "No, no, no, we're gonna do lyrical jazz, because really, it's about stretching you, right? You can do hip hop. You can do hip hop better than me, so let's do lyrical." So, and then it became – and actually it became about the dance form. And they got together on the fact that they wanted to do hip hop. So now they're kind of communicating in tandem, and it wasn't about that. And I said "All right, all right, just, do you know that hip hop came from a form of lyrical dance, that hip hop is after all of these genres." And I was explaining – and all of a sudden, we're dancing. And all that crap from the real world ... And they won. They won the Kiwanis thing, they got a scholarship, they got money to take dance classes, and that guy is now in dance at York [University]. Never took a dance class before he came to Braeburn. And he went to a

university, and he's dancing. So anything's possible with art. I think it just
breaks down – It just breaks down walls.
(Interview, Ms. C., Braeburn, December 11, 2008)

As arts researchers, we have heard this story, or versions of it, many
times. As consumers of popular culture, we've seen this movie, heard
this song, and hold onto it with all our liberal humanist, enlightenment
being. It's a victory story. It is also about, in this case and in many others, a White teacher "caring" and "saving" Black youth; a school as safe
haven; art making as the social leveller; and aesthetic engagement as
social cohesion. It is also about a dominant Western ideology that fixes
social differences through its colonization of cultural and artistic traditions. It is hard, we found, for teachers to not dream in this way, to not
want this much from art, from school, from themselves. I wish we had
been able to follow up with the two students described in this story, but
that was not possible. If we had been able to, we might have looked
with them into the ways in which notions of "care" are bound up in
power relations inherent in Whiteness and teaching (Pennington, Brock,
and Nadura 2012). From a 2008 qualitative study of pre-service teachers'
perceptions of urban schools, Hampton, Peng, and Ann suggest one of
the main findings of the study is the pervasive perception of the urban
teacher as a "noble savior" (p. 285). The researchers consequently recom-
mend more research into media representations of urban schools and
urban youth, and more critical media literacy for pre-service teachers. Their work also reiterates what much research in the area of urban
schooling reveals, that is, that strong and effective instruction is the most
powerful factor in student motivation and student achievement.

There is a body of research that has begun to focus more consistently on
the relationships encountered by students in school and student achievement, although these larger scale studies tend to leave out relations of
power in favour of attention to such psychological concepts as intrinsic
and extrinsic motivation, or positive and negative emotionality. But in
our experience, relations of race and power in the classroom figured in
every relationship and determined the extent to which students felt able to
take up the support being offered, whatever that support looked like. For
instance, a study conducted by Klem and Connell (2004), *Relationships Matter: Linking Teacher Support to Student Engagement and Achievement*, examined conditions contributing to student success beyond the usual nods to
"high standards" and "quality curriculum and pedagogy" and found, of
course, that for students to take advantage of high expectations and more
advanced curricula, they need support from the people with whom they

interact in school. These researchers specifically highlight the experience of support from teachers as well as "student autonomy." They write:

> First, students need to feel teachers are involved with them – that adults in school know and care about them. Students also need to feel they can make important decisions for themselves, and the work they are assigned has relevance to their present or future lives. Some researchers refer to this as autonomy support." (p. 262)

Autonomy, according to Reeve et al. (2004):

> is the experience of being the author and origin of one's behaviour – the subjective sense that one's moment-to-moment activity authentically expresses the self and its inner motivation. Behaviour is autonomous when students freely endorse what they are doing in the classroom, and this inner endorsement of one's actions is most likely to happen when students' inner motivational resources (e.g., needs, interests, preferences) guide their on-going classroom engagement. Given this understanding of the nature of student autonomy, a definition of teacher-provided autonomy support can be offered. Autonomy support is the interpersonal behaviour teachers provide during instruction to identify, nurture, and build students' inner motivational resources (Reeve, Deci, and Ryan 2004, p. 149)

Citing several other similar studies, Reeve et al. (2004, p. 152) go on to explain the benefits of an autonomy-supportive motivating style:

> Compared to students in classrooms managed by controlling teachers, students with autonomy-supportive teachers experience a wide range of educationally and developmentally important benefits. These benefits include not only greater perceived autonomy and greater psychological need satisfaction during learning activities but also greater classroom engagement, more positive emotionality, higher mastery motivation, greater intrinsic motivation, a preference for optimal challenge over easy success, higher creativity, enhanced psychological well-being, active and deeper information processing, greater conceptual understanding, higher academic achievement, and greater persistence in school versus dropping out. (Black and Deci 2000; Koestner, Ryan, Bernieri, and Holt 1984; Reeve, Jang, Carrell, Barch, and Jeon 2004; Vallerand, Fortier, and Guay 1997)

All of these studies attempt to define and describe engagement in a way that I appreciate, but what became clear through our ethnographic research is that engagement is an evanescent experience, something to be negotiated moment by moment between people; the "between-us" as Luce Irigaray has named it. If we take test scores or self-reporting data as evidence of engagement, as many of the above-cited studies do, we miss in my view, the precariousness of engagement and the fact that engagement is earned moment by moment in a classroom, is contingent upon the social relations in the room and the historical ones that precede them, and is enhanced or diminished by teacher and student actions. Later, I will pay attention to some key episodes in the classroom, and offer a further analysis of the impermanence of engagement and its intimate relationship to broader social and historical relations. Engagement must be earned 10,000 times a day by a teacher and freely given equally as often by a student. That is why studies of motivation and positive emotionality, although useful, create the illusion of permanence, which, we have observed, is not how school or school relationships really work.

Many critical arts scholars have challenged the rhetoric of transformation through the arts, especially prevalent in Western traditions of arts education. There is a slippery move from anecdote to rhetoric, noted in Neelands's (2004) important article on drama education in which he troubles the term "miracles," as "accounts of events which claim some profound and new change in a student" (p. 47) – as we heard above in the story of rival gang members turned award-winning artists. I am not attempting here to discredit the story. There are many such stories of transformation in the arts and education literature. They do happen. But it is often far more complicated than such neorealist narratives would have us believe. As postcolonial scholarship teaches us, the naturalizing of such pedagogies and experiences mask complex histories of struggle and domination. And the mythologizing of such contemporary arts pedagogies come as a result of endless pressure to justify so-called frill subjects in a "back-to-basics" educational landscape, through empirically demonstrating their power to transform. But, as Neelands points out, these stories – when traded locally and experienced by those closest to the social contexts under scrutiny – can still be powerful. For instance, Perry (2012), another theatre practitioner working in Canada, analyses Boalian theatre practices in community and school contexts suggesting that this work addresses colonialism in both its overt, cultural, and subtle manifestations. He regards theatre as a site for decolonization owing to people's ability to re-imagine and re-articulate individual and group identities through the cultural practice of theatre in postcolonial contexts.

It is not, as Neelands and many others have argued, however, that the arts or drama is DOING any of this, but it is what we do with drama that matters. And what we do with drama has everything to do with political, pedagogical, and aesthetic prejudices, and with the power relations of given contexts. Social and economic disadvantage, which so clearly mark the students in the schools we worked in, illustrate the effects of colonial policies, institutionalized discrimination, and contemporary racism. The story of such spaces reproduces pervasive notions of "risk," which regularly conflate identity with life histories and trajectories.

As I suggested in the introduction, I have seen repeated many times an interesting desire for "the real" as well as a resistance to it from young people. Nowhere is this more obvious than in their relationship to social identity categories. This ambivalence surfaces often as both a rejection of, and attraction to, fixed categories of identity. They both lay claim to certain identities and wish to unlearn them, to not be determined by them but to also emphasize the many ways in which material and symbolic relations of domination and oppression are manifest through the social effects of race and class. That social categories are also constructed and incomplete does not change the fact that their salience in determining educational advantage continues to give the lie to liberal multicultural discourse. When we asked students to identify themselves in terms of social class, their challenge to the static nature of social identity and their critique of language as always inadequate, became obvious:

> KEMBA: Well, the word class to me – I don't fit myself into a category, you know what I mean? I don't categorize people or group them into anything because I know what I am, you know, and you could not look at me and perceive me to be something that – you don't even know what I am because I didn't tell you that and share that. It's what's in my head, my heart, and my mind. And there's definitions that you see in the dictionary and that our parents grew us up or that we are socialized into the world to be a certain way, so these words are here and we see them and we fit ourselves into this definition and we act it out, just like the word embarrassment. Like I was telling my friend one time that never feel embarrassed because like, if you don't care what people say then you don't have to feel embarrassed, like, where did that word come from, you know? So you just have to look at certain words and unlearn them. That's what I feel, that is my opinion, you know?
>
> (Focus Group Interview, Kemba, Cherry, Max, Peanut, Braeburn, December 2, 2008).

Kemba is asking questions that many young people ask, and resisting the idea of class as a fixed and overdetermined category, pointing, instead, to its constructedness. Social status both determines their lives and is powerless in the face of their dreams. I have wrestled with this tension over the last decade, trying to understand the ways in which Marxist understandings of class and class struggle do not fully capture the complexity of youth experiences of class and status. Today, young people experience class disadvantage alongside ubiquitous liberal discourses about meritocracy and neoliberal discourses about individuality, progress and the market, that make it impossible to separate out socio-economic disadvantage from the other pervasive cultural discourse of individual weakness and failure. Instead, young people opt for defining themselves in terms of dreams and future aspirations, or the strength of their moral character, which will surely spare them a life of socio-economic disadvantage. It is not simply the case that young people are living with false consciousness regarding class and educational opportunity or life chances. How class is lived has changed significantly, as social safety nets disappear and narratives of impoverished children succeeding in both popular culture and professional sport proliferate. It makes understanding class as a lifelong trajectory very difficult for young people. And as a researcher, trying hard to listen to young people speak the complexities of their classed lives, hearing how their economic status has been conflated with moral character, I struggle with the inadequacies of earlier analyses:

KEMBA: Well class is like, please (*waves hand dismissively*) it only makes people feel either lower or higher or in- between. Like where are you gonna put me? Like I have to define myself for me, I have to say where I fit and for the most of it I don't fit anywhere. I'm just everywhere, you know what I mean?

KATHLEEN: Yeah, and the other thing you said that struck me was that there are so many circumstances that we don't control.

KEMBA: Exactly. There are so many things that we – that could make us be whatever classes are defined a certain way. But we are more complex than class, and that's why we don't fit anywhere into class. Some people they have money so some people say, "well, OK, that's class" but some people have like dignity and respect for themselves and they don't have a lot of money. They have manners and they love. And to me that would be a higher class than someone who has money and they are very snobbish. So where does class fit in? How do you define class? How do I define class? Is class based on how you define it or how I define it or what the dictionary defined it as. What is it, you know?

(Focus Group Interview, Kemba, Cherry, Max, Peanut, Braeburn, December 2, 2008)

Dillabough and Kennelly (2010) found, in their ethnographic research with youth in the cities of Toronto and Vancouver in Canada, that unlike earlier British youth working-class cultural studies research, the youth of their study did not carry working-class pride but instead expressed a strong desire to "break their own class ranks" (p. 150). In their work on class, culture, and the urban imaginary with increasingly marginalized youth in the "global city," they argue that urban development has not served working-class communities and has reinforced inequalities, revealing the "sheer power of symbolic and moral distinctions to shape young people's place and self-making projects [and] wider questions about who can be a good citizen in the new global city (p. 207). With the youth of our study, our learning about their understandings and critiques of class, and about fantasies of escaping class disadvantage, resonates with Dillabough and Kennelly's empirical work.

There are, of course, other social categories that pull focus in our interviews with students. The contradictions persist in terms of how social categories define ideas, feelings, and behaviours but also how they are regularly overturned by the messy social relations of schools and by the individual and unbridled imaginaries of young people. In discussions of race, or "bad schools," we very quickly find ourselves again in the terrain of identity, Blackness, and criminality. I often began focus group discussions with the open question, "Tell me what your school is like." Watch how easily a school's reputation elides into discussions of social identity and threat:

DEREK: Very. Lots of, um, extra-curricular activities. And also the classes, the teachers are great.
BELLA: Not every teacher's great, Derek. Most of the teachers that we have are great. Some of them can be stuck up but yeah, it's teachers. That's just how they are, I guess.
DEREK: But yeah. There's so much offered at this school. And it's usually looked at as like a thug school and because we've got all the homies on the front step. (*Bella laughs.*) But it's not – that's like –
BELLA: That's like a stereotype.
DEREK: Judging a book by – (*at the same time as Bella*) its cover –

BELLA: its cover. 'Cause like my aunt, won't let my cousin come to this school 'cause she thinks, "oh my God, like there's so much Blacks at the school." Not everyone's bad. Like every school has Black kids and every school has –

K'THANIE: So?

BELLA: She doesn't want her to come here. Like my cousin's gonna go to Rosedale. So I'm like, "you're going to Rosedale. I'm at Middleview and your cousin went to Bloor and he's at Central Comm." The three worst schools in Toronto, like not really the worst but they're rated the worst. And she goes like, "OK." It's kinda – I don't know, the school's good. I love it. Although it's kind of dirty, I still like it.

(K'Thanie is tapping her knees and playing with her earrings through this. Listening but not saying anything.)

(Focus Group Interview, K'Thanie, Bella, Derek, Middleview, November 25, 2008)

In a different focus group at the same school, race and ethnicity appear again with the open question of what the school is like. Social categories give meaning to the school, both explicitly and implicitly, and the liberal multicultural discourse lives easily alongside the equally pervasive discourse of race and risk:

BELL: Our school is very multicultural.

KATHLEEN: What does that mean to you?

BELL: There is a lot of rich ethnic backgrounds. It's like – it's very different coming here [as opposed to] my other home schools – it's very different to come here. And I guess it's a warmer feeling. Because, when I was back at my old school [name of school] it was basically – like everyone looked the same. There was no diversity really. We had like the one or two odd students but everybody else was the same and like coming here –

KATHLEEN: And by that you mean White?

BELL: White, yes. But coming here it's very different. It's very multicultural and I like it. It's much more fun I guess, to be engaged with different ethnics, for me.

KATHLEEN: And what do you guys think?

MYA: I feel the same thing. I see like, different people with different opinions and different viewpoint, which is good 'cause you get to meet different people who are speaking the same thing and yeah. And I believe people come here for their future career, like they know exactly what they want to do so they have a very specific thing in this school so that helps a lot, yeah.

KATHLEEN: Any other thoughts?

BONNIE: Our school is old (*everyone laughs*). Our school is known, that's why a lot of kids come here 'cause everyone knows about Middleview.

(Focus Group Interview, Bell, Bonnie, Mya, November 23, 2008)

Regarding "race," there is also a clear desire on the part of many students to not have their social world so clearly demarcated by race. Students of all racial backgrounds tend towards colour-blind notions of social relations. Here is Joe, recently emigrated from Mexico, in an individual interview at Middleview:

JOE: This generation I think is like, again freedom. I think maybe it is more difficult for us, but who can say? Maybe the old times were more difficult because of the racism – all that stuff and we're like, "yeah, whatever." I play soccer and it's really, really multicultural. An African guy pass me the ball, and I pass the ball to an Italian. I don't know, that's beautiful. Like, here in Canada and maybe to old people that didn't happen.

ANNE: So you think that that's been a change here in Canada?

JOE: I think in most part of the world.

(Individual Interview, Joe, Middleview, January 12, 2010)

Or Twila, a self-described "mixed-race" student at Middleview, offers:

Like, walking down the hallways. If there's all these Black girls they just look down on me. Like I don't have weave in my hair, my hair grows – and I don't dress with the typical ghetto girls with the tight sweaters and the tight jeans and the gold earrings. I don't dress like a White girl. Some people say, "you dress like a White girl" but how does a White girl dress? I go to the store and I pick what I like. It's not a preference as to White or Black, it's a preference to what I like. I don't know.

(Individual Interview, Twila, Middleview, January 14, 2010)

It is perhaps important at this point to remind readers of the ubiquitous discourse of "family" in many drama classrooms. It shapes, in significant ways in my view, how students perceive others and how they believe they are being perceived. I press Twila on this point:

KATHLEEN: Lots of students are comparing their drama class to a family in our discussions so I am trying to figure out what that means because it looks to me, you know, like people still have conflicts and there are still glances and looks and things you would expect in high school. So tell me more about what you mean by family.

TWILA: Even with family by blood, like, I go to dinner and I try talking to everybody but you just – I think naturally in the mind you tend to just talk to that one person that you have so much in common that you hang around with that one cousin or one aunt or one niece or nephew more than any other niece or nephew. Like, if they're shyer than you then you just can't talk to them as much. It's the same thing with the drama class. Like maybe you and someone else in the class get along really well. But like, me and Mave, we just like having fun and joking around and she's friends with some of my friends, and I'm friends with some of her friends, so I knew of her before I came to this class. So we just have a lot of similarities; we just talk to each other. Then other people, like Joe, like he's not – sometimes I can't understand him properly, like I know he's new to Canada but I still don't let that put up a wall between us – it's not like I don't talk to him, I still talk to him. I think that's how it's similar to a family because you're closer than people in another class so you're closer like a family, but –

KATHLEEN: You still have preferences.

TWILA: You still have preferences – same thing in a family, in my opinion.

(Individual Interview, Twila, Middleview, January 14, 2010)

This explanation of the drama classroom stands in contrast to how Twila describes social cohesion or segregation in the school at large when I ask her about the atmosphere of the school. And Twila is someone who describes herself as capable of "talking to anybody":

TWILA: Yeah. Out in the front. Then you walk out a little bit by the art building. It's like the Italian and the Portuguese that sit there and always hang out with each other. And if you keep on walking straight and you pass by the field and if you go by the front stairs right there you see a lot of the gangsters, if that's what you call them, and they stay by the stairs right there and they look down on you and they're like, "we're better than you" and honestly I don't even go up there. I sneak to the school because I don't like the looks that everybody gives and so, I don't know. In the cafeteria there is all the shy people; the shy people stay inside. Like when I was in Grade 9, I would stay in the cafeteria because I was shy and it was my first year there. But then it started getting warm and I was like, "why am I still inside?" so when the winter ended I was like, "go outside" ...

(Individual Interview, Twila, Middleview, January 14, 2010)

The students clearly speak of a kind of ownership of the space of the drama classroom. Discussions about the way that classroom operates illustrate how students feel they impact the space and how much it determines who they feel they are in that space. Many claim there is more freedom in the space to express identity. Doreen Massey argues that spaces "are processes" (1994, p. 155), and in the process of identity articulation that we are talking about with students, the drama space looms large. Many students also regularly underscore how difference is accepted. This seems to be a feature of drama spaces in their view:

TWILA: Like in drama class everybody just accepts everybody like we are lucky that in our class everybody in our class accepts everybody for their religion and what they like and what they don't like. Maybe not in every school in every drama class everybody gets along. Like, we're lucky that we have that.

(Individual Interview, Twila, Middleview, January 14, 2010)

Comments about race, diversity, language, gender, and sexual orientation are persistent, as are fashion and music choices, or behaviours like smoking or comments about spaces where students congregate. All of these seemingly discrete factors, as the comments highlighted above, pertain to the performance of power in social space. Some conversations and descriptions of social performances related to turf, or fights; others pertained to how adults understand (or don't understand) young people; and some were about ways to gain control of the future and the social spaces where young people dwell.

What was unmistakable, nonetheless, was how an overall "positive" feeling seemed to infect the interview discussions. One might attribute this to the students' perceptions of us, the research team (people interested in youth), or our obvious sense of gratitude that they had decided to speak with us at all. It is notable, although difficult to say exactly why so many of our interviewees often felt "hopeful," affectively speaking. Even students like Carl who admits to getting sent to the school office for certain behaviours, or Goku, whose behaviours got him kicked out of school, still chose to spin their own self-descriptions as positive or "becoming better." Some students, like Anastasia, focused on their skills and actions when they described themselves, even if past behaviours point to life and school challenges:

> ANASTASIA: Like me, I have a lot of really good talents and stuff ... I would say I was really good at acting and I could draw really well but I didn't get the right motivation, right? ... I know I can be somebody.
> (Individual Interview, Anastasia, Braeburn, June 17, 2010)

Or, Marbles:

> MARBLES: I don't know. I try at – I can only try when I'm motivated at something.
> KATHLEEN: Tell me about motivation for you then.
> MARBLES: Like, if I like it basically; if I'm completely disinterested it's really hard to get me to do something. Like, I'm not gonna lie and be like "I'm good at everything!"
> KATHLEEN: Right.
> MARBLES: But like, if I'm interested, even if I suck at it I will try really hard to, you know, get better or at least put an effort in and try to learn and understand what I'm doing. And like, I've – I don't know how I can explain this but like, I make goals for myself and I try to follow them and everything else is just kind of like half and half.
> KATHLEEN: Right. Where did you learn to do that, to make goals for yourself.
> MARBLES: My Mom.
> KATHLEEN: Your Mom.
> MARBLES: (nods head) She's also huge on goals but she also like – say for example like you have three courses and to do what you want you only need two of them. Me, I'd try really hard in the two and in the third one I'd just be like "whatever" and my Mom is just like, "you need to do all three because in case those two don't work the third one's gonna save you!"
> (Focus Group Interview, Marbles, Twila, Joe, Middleview, December 11, 2009)

Many students place a very high premium on "being themselves" and not being forced into some kind of mould. Joe, who emigrated from Mexico, was particularly strong on this point:

> ANNE: How important is belonging to you?
> JOE: For me it's not important.
> ANNE: No?

JOE: I have asked for it, in Mexico. In Mexico, I don't care. I was like that, I am like that. I don't care to belong to something, I am comfortable with myself.

... and later ...

JOE: I am always comfortable with myself. I am the same to myself. I don't know what I think to myself but I am always feel like the same.
ANNE: So you don't feel this need to become something else to fit into a group or to fit into Canada or something like that?
JOE: Nope. Just like the problem with the language and yeah.
(Focus Group, Joe, Twila, Marbles, Middleview, December 11, 2009)

And this of course goes hand in hand with a common youth perception of the adult world. Many youth, especially those who feel marginalized by the kind of school they are in, or their race or fashion choices, feel misunderstood by the broader culture. They often feel that others do not see them (or other young people) for who they are, and that they make hasty, often false assumptions about them. Anastasia suggests that people outside her school make negative assumptions about all the young people there:

ANASTASIA: So by doing this [Verbatim piece] it shows how much successful people are at this school.
KATHLEEN: So you think that out there in the world, people don't really have that impression?
ANASTASIA: They don't. They don't get that impression ... People probably think because it's an adult school and we never got their credits in other schools that, "oh they don't have a future and stuff" but there's actually a lot of talents.
(Individual Interview, Anastasia, Braeburn, June 17, 2010)

Likewise at Middleview, Twila explains, in several parts of her interview, how her mixed heritage, music, and fashion choices belie stereotypes, complicate her identity, and demonstrate how "others" make assumptions about her because of lack of information, and perhaps because she does not fit neatly into the social spaces associated with particular cliques:

KATHLEEN: And do you feel that way? Do you feel equally identified with both races? You said, "oh, people just assume I'm Black."

TWILA: No one thinks that. People are like "oh you're light-skinned. Oh you're Black" this and that. I have a White boyfriend and everybody looks down on me. "You're going away from your race." And this and that. I don't listen to reggae, I listen to pop. I listen to Miley Cyrus and Hannah Montana. I don't listen to my cultural music. I still like it, I just don't listen to it as much; it's not my preference. And people think, "oh, you're going to be this highly educated this and that and you're going away from your race." And that's how people have looked at it since I was 10. And I'm just like, "you know what, I'm me; I'm not everybody else. I'm my own individual person. I'm different. I'm not like every other Black girl." Everybody's different. So I just – if anybody stares down I'm like, "I'm not that stereotype, get over it." I don't know, I'm so used to that mixed-race thing that I'm just like, people have to realize that racism has to stop – in schools, and everywhere. Especially in schools, because racism occurs all the time.

(Individual Interview, Twila, Middleview, January 14, 2010)

What's Obama Got to Do with It?

In ethnographic research, there are sometimes discussions that fill the space so powerfully, unfolding discussions that leave research-ers stunned by the reflections and knowledge they become privy to. I close this chapter on social performances with one such videotaped and transcribed conversation, presented here to give the sense of the free-fall that can characterize high school classroom discussions, and the powerful place of hope and the concomitant fear of disappointment in the minds of new millennium youth. It is also revealing of the ways in which categories of social identity shape readings of the world and intersect with historical, cultural, and subcultural understandings. The conversation says a great deal about American imposition in Canadian social and political life and it also marks a moment in time saturated with implications for the lives and futures of young people. We read it now, at the start of Obama's second term when the election campaign promise for a universal health care package has not been fully realized, Guantanamo remains open, and the economy remains weakened. We now know all of this, which imbues the following retrospective with new questions about the place of hope, cynicism, and the politics of difference in contemporary conceptions of democracy. The discussion came on the day following Barack Obama's first election victory and it remained with us for the next five years because it revealed so vividly how the intersection of race, class, gender, sexuality, and nation would challenge our thinking about the seemingly monolithic social category of "youth." The date is November 5, 2008:

CLASS DISCUSSION AFTER OBAMA VICTORY

Location: CTS drama room

Present: Kathleen, Barry, Burcu, Anne [researchers], Ms. S, Ms. M [student teacher] and students of first semester Grade 11 class.

Date: November 5, 2008

DEREK: Obama's sincere and, like, stands fully behind what he is talking about.
KATHLEEN: Did anyone think of Martin Luther King when he got into his speech and the refrain of "Yes, we can"?
VARIOUS STUDENTS: Yeah, yeah, that's what I thought of.
KATHLEEN: I kept thinking, "I have a dream, I have a dream," and you kept hearing it like a cadence. It was the same intonation every time "yes we can, yes we can" and then everyone was chanting it back. I thought that was the moment that kind of defined –
MS. S: He is a great orator.
KATHLEEN: Oh, he is a great orator.
MS. S: Maxx, did you want to?
MAXX: No.
ASHLEY: Ms. M wants to say something.
BONNIE: Who?
MS. S: Ms. M, OK. Can I just say one thing? I think it is important to remember Obama is White, and has a White heritage as well as Black.
BONNIE: As soon as there's Black in there, it's different.
FABIAN: Yeah!
MS. S: I know … it's very interesting. Because we haven't mentioned that.
MS. M: [student teacher] It's OK. It's off topic now.

(Ms. S doesn't hear her. She passes the talking pumpkin [acting as a talking stick for turn taking in the conversation] to Ms. M.).

MS. S: Do you want to say …?
MS. M: No, that's OK. It's fine.

(Maxx has his hand up.)

KATHLEEN: But Maxx was going to say something.

MS. S: Yeah, Maxx.

MAXX: I want to go to the bathroom.

(Everybody laughs. OHHHHH! OHHH!)

KATHLEEN: What a let down.

CAT: That was boring.

MAXX: I never go to the bathroom.

MS. S: Are we ready to move on? Okay so Cat … so this was very –

CAT: Oh Miss, I have one question.

MS. S: Yes?

CAT: Do you think there might be any Black prime ministers?

MS. S: Yes, absolutely.

CAT: Why does it take, why does it take America for the world to start changing?

ERICA: 'Cause they are … huge.

BELL: Everyone knows America.

KATHLEEN: You know what? I mean that's a good question, Cat. Maybe because we think it is so much "better" here, that kind of statement doesn't have to be made. It is a historic day in the US. But everything is so cool here compared to that. [This is said with irony]

MS. S: No it's not!

KATHLEEN: Exactly. Exactly.

MS. S: So are there significant barriers for a Black person to become a prime minister in Canada?

FABIAN: I don't think so.

ERICA: Excuse me? *(incredulous)*

FABIAN: A gay person will never be a prime minister.

KATHLEEN: Why is that?

ASHLEY: So many people are against it.

[OVERLAPPING] MS. S: Yes, yes there are. Are there significant barriers for a woman becoming –

KATHLEEN: Oh yes.

MS. S: Yes there are. Are there significant barriers for a gay person to become the prime minister?

FABIAN: A gay person would never become a prime minister. I don't think too many people would accept them. I would vote for them if they had, if they had whatever, but I just don't think a gay prime minister or president will happen.

KATHLEEN: So you don't think that the policies that are –

DEREK: Especially in the States, cause in the States the big thing is about the religion.

KATHLEEN: It is hard there, you're right. There's a lot of fundamentalism.

ERICA: OK, can I, can I? (*Erica asks for the pumpkin. Bonnie passes it without speaking herself.*) I don't wear my, like, sexual orientation on my skin, right? So for instance, if I get to be prime minister or whatever one day and I do all these great things for people and they don't even know that I'm gay, and then I come out about it, what are they gonna do? Are they gonna hate me even though I helped the whole country. Like –

STEPHANIE: They'll change their view.

ERICA: Yes, they might change their view but because I've done so much for them, why because I'm gay is that gonna make any difference?

STEPHANIE: It's still gonna make a difference.

ERICA: I don't think so. You'll be surprised.

CAT: We're in a society where gay just has started to show itself, like you know.

STEPHANIE: Especially in Canada.

ERICA: But it's moving so fast though.

CAT: In Canada, yes, we understand that, but in America where it's too big, way too big.

ERICA: Yeah, but in Canada …

DEREK: If Obama was smart …

MS. S: Even Obama doesn't endorse gay marriage –

KATHLEEN: He even said –

MS. S: He said, "No."

DEREK: He said he was opposed to it and like if he was smart, he would have not said that and he would have got so many more votes.

KATHLEEN: But what about in his speech? He said, "gays" and "straights," right?

MS. S: Yeah.

KATHLEEN: Even for a straight guy [politician], to say "gays and straights" is significant in the US.

DEREK: True.

MS. S: Bonnie?

BONNIE: Um, I forgot what I was gonna say.

MS. S: Bell?

BONNIE: Oh yeah, I remember what I was gonna say. For the Prime Minister of Canada, I think we need a person that's not like rich and ugly. Because everyone who gets voted is rich, so they always go for like the upper-class people. So we don't get anywhere, 'cause we need a person, that lives a normal life and went to public school, shop at like a normal store, to be like a president or prime minister.

CAT: Miss, do you know how much the Prime Minister of Canada makes?

FABIAN: True.

ASHLEY: I think it's not capable for someone of the lower class to be prime minister.

CAT: He makes $200,000 dollars.

KATHLEEN: That's right. It's not a lot of money.

CAT: Obama makes $400,000.

KATHLEEN: Which in the scheme of things, it's not a lot of money.

CAT: The president of Hydro Ontario makes 2. 3 million dollars.

KATHLEEN: That's right

MS. S: Wow! That tells you where power is located.

KATHLEEN: That's exactly right … that's exactly right.

FABIAN: I'll become a hydro person.

CAT: So, for someone who just runs the energy around the city compared to someone that runs the city …

FABIAN: Or the country.

CAT: This is why I'm lost.

KATHLEEN: Yeah, I know.

FABIAN: Very good point.

MS. S: Very good point!

KATHLEEN: Because we live in a corporate world, that's why.

MS. S: It is very interesting that you bring … Bonnie brings this other issue up, which is about class. And the really interesting thing is that in this campaign, like, both Obama and McCain were appealing to the working class. That was like the big coveted prize was to get the working-class vote, Joe the plumber, all that stuff right, and yet both of them are really privileged. Like to become – talk about a major barrier towards becoming, um, the prime minister or the president is class, right, that in itself, you know, they were trying to appeal to the "folks," right, but they are not the folks, right? I don't know if people realize that but it is complex, right? It is complex.

BELL: I agree with like Bonnie that we need someone from the working class, who knows what it's like, from like personal experience. But then again, how do we get that, like, foot in the door? How do we get people to listen to us even though they are like high, like they're more privileged. How do we do it? How do we get people to listen to us? How do we get people to help us. How do we know to go to that person, how do we know they are trustworthy?

KATHLEEN: We have these imitations of real things. In this election we had an imitation of working classness in Sarah Palin. Even her speech was meant to emulate you know, dropping the g's "I'm goin' to the store." She was supposed to sound working class. But we know, like reality TV, which is not reality and is totally staged and fake, she was totally staged and fake as well. Because there is no way you are the governor of anywhere and basically working class and uneducated. Even though that's how she came off.

DEREK: She's so dumb.

BONNIE: That's so dumb.

MS. S: It was a performance. It was a performance of working class.

KATHLEEN: So your question was a really good one because how we actually – I hate the word empower, but I'm going to use it – how we actually empower people who are in reality living those lives and not just performing those lives, is a question that has not been addressed. Not here, not there. So, it's back to my comment. Is everyone going to have health care? It is so basic; it is really basic. So unless you have the policies that allow people to live lives where they have full access in a democratic way to most things, then essentially we'll only have performances of people breaking through those barriers. And that's what we have now.

CAT: I have a question? You know how Bonnie was saying that we should have a certain class; how do you choose a class? How do you go from an unwealthy person to a wealthy person and choose which one? Everyone has different points, you know and if an unwealthy person, you know, they work hard, they have to, you know, 'cause money is not there. This wealthy person, it comes like this (*he snaps his fingers*) 'cause money is there and they can just throw money out and go to school and all that stuff. I don't …

MS. S: So, what is the question? Like … how –

CAT: I'm lost.

MS. S: No, no but it's a very interesting one, how do you –

CAT: It's how do you choose a class? She said that you can choose a class that should lead the country, right? How do you choose a class?

BONNIE: I never said choose a class. Like we need someone that knows 'cause my Mom was telling me, how like welfare, they cut like some kind of cheque, like how are you doing that, like welfare you don't even get a lot. So how are you cutting that little small cheque.

CAT: 'Cause women are going out and using children just to, just to, claim –

BONNIE: But still, I know other people that aren't.

CAT: In the society that we live in, you can't even say that. You can't even say that. You cannot say that. There is pros and there is cons about every situation.

(Derek raises his hand.)

BONNIE: They shouldn't do that.

(Cat throws the pumpkin to Derek.)

BONNIE: There are people who do take advantage and they do need it.
DEREK: The reason they put with money and power is 'cause money kind of equals intelligence and so they don't want some Joe Blow off the street.
KATHLEEN: Does it? Does it?
DEREK: It doesn't. It doesn't but that's what society looks at.
KATHLEEN: [You're saying] It doesn't. That's the perception. OK.
MS. S: That's what society perceives. OK. Erica and then you.
ERICA: It is pretty much like he is saying. Like you can't get some working-class person all of a sudden and be the prime minister. They need to have, like elections and all that stuff. They have to have money to do that. Like, you know what I mean? They can't get just like all of a sudden pull it out of your ass, like that's not gonna happen. So, I don't know, the thing is you can have somebody who, like, maybe grew up in Regent Park [public housing complex] like me, and then, like you know, and I go through schooling and get all that done and then I can represent people of a working class. But that's about all you can do.
STEPHANIE: Yeah, that's what I mean.
KATHLEEN: You never lose your roots.
CAT: And then you are destroyed knowing that you lived in that area. Then it's gone. You grew up in a neighbourhood where shit, but shit's not right. Shit's hard. You know you have to do certain shit to survive but you think you're gonna go up and tell the world, yeah, I grew up in one of the worst neighbourhoods in Toronto. And they're gonna want you?
ERICA: That could get you a lot of votes right there.
MS. S: Obama got a lot of credibility from doing his activism work in Chicago's south side, so, he, that gave him a lot of credibility, yet he did not come from that area. But the fact that he'd worked there. Carmen?

CARMEN: I want to say that some – the politicians they don't really care about the crowd; they will say anything. They promise and then when they get to office, they throw all their vows away. They don't care about the poor. Just care about their own self. They don't really understand how is that to go from poor to go for rich. Someone understands, someone who goes from poor to rich, they will understand their roots, where they come from.

MS. S: I just wanted to say something in answer to your question about how you change things or how you create a society where somebody who's poor and then that's Bell's question, I think, can move up. One thing is, vote. Like, you have to vote. You have to convince your friends, your family to vote; young people have to vote. Because they collect statistics, right, about who is voting. And the more people that vote from any part of the population the more power that group of people has. Like senior citizens are taken very seriously by candidates – their needs – because senior citizens, by and large, vote. So they have a lot of power as a group of people. They are listened to. So the more people that vote from a certain community or from a certain background especially young people, because they don't look at young people, young people's needs as much, because young people tend not to vote. So the more power you want as a group, you have to vote.

CAT: Miss, what was – sorry what was the percentage of people that voted in American cities?

BARRY: I don't think it's known yet. It's takes a while to figure that out. It's unprecedentedly high. Like it's never been so high.

ANNE: Highest ever.

CAT: It's never been so high. (*The classroom phone rings.*) I thought it was pretty bad. I heard it was 68%. (*Class phone rings. Sirens outside the window.*)

BARRY: That's very, very high for the US.

KATHLEEN: It's often less than 50%.

BARRY: Exactly.

KATHLEEN: So 68 is unbelievable.

BARRY: And Ms. S makes a good point. Because we just had an election ourselves – which so much of it went by – I'm sorry I don't have the pumpkin – (*laughter*) – so much of it went by without really any kind of – look at the public discussion we're having about this. It's amazing. I think, I'm like biting my tongue I want to say so many things. But our own election – (*Barry runs into the circle from the sidelines to get the pumpkin. Laughter.*) Our own election went by and did you guys talk about it in any of your classes?

OTHERS: No.

ERICA: No! See.

BARRY: It's crazy our own voter turnout was like less than 60% – which for us is the worst ever. It was horrible, And they're lots of reasons for that. Like that's a very complicated issue, right. There were not very inspired leaders. I mean you guys probably have your own ideas about why that happened.

ERICA: It was a boring election.

BARRY: It was, relative to this one. This one was spectacular.

KATHLEEN: How much of it was boring and how much was our endless fascination with all things American?

ERICA: That's the thing. Like that was all on our minds.

KATHLEEN: That's our steady diet, right? That's television. That's everything. That's everything we consume from morning to night.

CAT: But in like America's situation where there was a Black male and a female. That's what drew attention.

KATHLEEN: Right, more than ever. The drama.

MS. S: More than ever.

CAT: That was like the key to the next – you know? But here it's just the same old, same old. We don't know if there's going to be a female or an African American.

KATHLEEN: Right. And what difference would it make.

CAT: Exactly. Yeah.

MS. S: I think the American election will change that around. I think there will be more candidates that will be recruited.

CAT: That's if Obama doesn't …

MS. S: Yeah. Bonnie and then Maxx.

BONNIE: I think when you're trying to be elected as prime minister and all the promises you make, I think they should have like a law where when you say you're going to do something you have to do it.

MS. S: Or you're taken to court.

BONNIE: Yeah, or you just don't get elected, like you just get dropped.

BARRY: But doesn't the world change sometimes?

OTHERS: Yeah. Exactly.

BONNIE: Other than that. But like I mean like –

BARRY: I mean that's hard to determine.

BONNIE: Other than that. But I mean like I mean if you say, "Oh, I'll give you guys more money for welfare," or something, then you should be able to do it. That's never going to change. That part. 'Cause not everyone is rich. So that's never going to change and stuff.

KATHLEEN: But what he's going to say is that the economy has changed. And so I can't make good on that promise.

ERICA: Yeah, people don't have money for that.

KATHLEEN: Because I inherited this deficit.

BARRY: That just happened with the environmental issue in our own election. It started out – it became, "well, Sir, the economy is getting kind of bad, maybe this isn't the best time for us to be talking about the environment."

KATHLEEN: They're related when it matters, but it's convenient to separate them.

MS. S: Maxx, it's Maxx. Yes? No?

MAXX: What?

MS. S: You had your hand up, I'm coming to you. No?

MAXX: No.

MS. S: OK, are you sure?

MAXX: Yes.

MS. S: What were you going to say?

CAT: Tell her.

MS. S: OK, all right, ah OK, so could we – are we OK to go on?

FABIAN: Yeah.

MS. S: It is a really good discussion.

ERICA: I don't know it's just this day like – we just have a friggin' Black president voted in. We should talk about it.

MS. S: Yeah. But is there anyone that hasn't said something that wants to say something?

ASHLEY: Chrysanthemum.

STEPHANIE: I like this class because there are so many opinions.

CAT: You've been quiet today.

CHRYSANTHEMUM: I like to hear everybody's opinion. It's more interesting. I prefer to hear everyone else's opinions. 'Cause it's interesting. And then you …

KATHLEEN: You learn stuff.

CHRYSANTHEMUM: Yeah, exactly.

ERICA: But everyone wants to hear your's. Because it's the best.

CHRYSANTHEMUM: No mine's not the best. No it's not at all. Well, like personally, I wasn't really informed.

CAT: All right, your's is not the best but we want to hear all opinions. So that we can, you know …

CHRYSANTHEMUM: I wasn't paying attention to the election or anything like that. I wasn't really into the news for this past little while. So that's why I'm not voicing my opinion 'cause I don't really know. I think it's amazing it's a Black president, of course, because it's really true (*class telephone rings again and Ms. S has to leave the circle to answer it*), it truly is history. Like when I came home last night, I ran to the living room and I'm like, "who won? Who won?" Just for the fact of knowing if it's Black or not. That's why I didn't want to say anything because I didn't know if it was possible. And I said that plenty – a million times – that's why I didn't really say, "I want Obama to win, I don't want McCain to win." I personally didn't really know a lot of it – about the election – it was Black and White and from what I've seen that's why I don't have a big opinion on the whole situation. That's why I was quiet.

MS. S: Carmen, do you want to say something?

CARMEN: I just want to say one thing. I'm just fearful for Obama's life. I don't want …

MS. S: Yeah.

CARMEN: I fear for his life.

CHRYSANTHEMUM: I think he's going to have to go around in a bullet-proof box or something.

CARMEN: Some people in America – no offence, but some are very crazy. They are.

BONNIE: Barack is taking a risk. Like he knows that there's a possibility that he won't be alive in two months. He knows, obviously he knows. That's how you know he loves his country 'cause he's willing, obviously he's willing to be assassinated for his country.

ERICA: I'll do this quickly. Look at the way, like, the situation in the States is right now. It's not very good, like, they're financially in debt and all that. And he's got to kind of pull them up. That's like a problem alone.

FABIAN: What is their debt right now?

ERICA: And worrying about his life. Like he's got a – a whole new situation right now.

CAT: Maybe him dying might just change the world. Might just bring the world to its senses and say …

MAXX: Just like Tupaq and Martin Luther King? (*a note of sarcasm*)

ASHLEY: That's two different situations.

BELL: No, he's in a reign of power.

CAT: Do you guys understand what I'm saying, though? Maybe this is what the world needs, you know – you know, I think it would help African Americans you know, it would be like …

KATHLEEN: And you know what? Someone would immediately say, "but a White president was assassinated too, this isn't about race" and boom, up in smoke.

DEREK: But honestly, the more people who think like that, like Obama's going to be assassinated, the more it's going to bring it on to him. Because, like, we just got to think positive.

STEPHANIE: The world will end.

KATHLEEN: I had this thought this morning because many years ago, I was teaching in a high school drama classroom and we had a huge debate like this on the day that O.J. Simpson was not convicted. Do you remember that day? Or maybe I should ask how old were you when that happened?

BONNIE: I don't know, I read the book.

MS. S: You guys were like two, right?

KATHLEEN: Two years old? So I was with sixteen/seventeen-year-olds in a high school classroom in another school in this city having a debate and it totally divided along racial lines. And basically all of the Black students said, "We all go down with O.J."

BONNIE: Why?

KATHLEEN: They were desperate for him not to be convicted even though most of them thought that he was guilty because of the symbolic message that that sends. (*Fabian's hand raises from his lying position on the floor.*) So this morning I was thinking this is the flip side of the symbolic message. Do "we" all rise up with Obama? Is it the opposite of O.J. Simpson?

MS. S: Yes!

CAT: It has to be.

KATHLEEN: So, it's the opposite, but will it – will you have to swallow your cynicism the way the Black students did who believed O.J. Simpson was guilty but desperately wanted him to be found innocent? They had to swallow their cynicism in order to be in solidarity with their race. So that's a question I'm asking, do you feel you have to swallow your cynicism –

MS. S: Yes.

KATHLEEN: about what Obama might not accomplish in order to be in solidarity with your race?

CAT: Do you think the O.J. trial would have been something different if he had killed an African American?

KATHLEEN: Yes.

CAT: Do you think it would have been so like big like, you know?

KATHLEEN: No.

BARRY: It would have changed the story altogether.

CAT: No one would have wanted to be for him because he killed his own kind. Like it doesn't make any sense. But, since she – they weren't African American and they were White, we felt like he was being picked on, you know? I think he did it, to tell you the truth.

DEREK: I think it still would have been like pretty big. 'Cause like celebrities get more like than others. And like he kills his wife, like it doesn't really matter, he killed his wife. Black or White I don't think it really matters.

KATHLEEN: Because of sexism too?

MS. S: Right.

DEREK: Sure.

FABIAN: I think people need to stop putting all the focus on the race, you know? Like who cares if he's a Black president. What if a Black person assassinates him? You know? All these people are putting on this Black president just because he's Black. With O.J. Simpson, like you know what, if he was White, if O.J. Simpson was White, would he get all that attention? I think people need to stop putting focus on something just because someone's White like he killed White people or Black people –

CHRYSANTHEMUM: It's true.

FABIAN: Like what would happen if a Black person kills Obama?

CHRYSANTHEMUM: It's society.

FABIAN: No one thought of that. Everyone thinks about him getting killed – they're assuming it's White people.

CAT: What if we live in a society where this Black person who kills Obama doesn't like his own kind?

FABIAN: What if he is a like a person who loves Black people and does good things for his community, supports him, what if he kills Obama?

CAT: But you don't know that, you know.

MAXX: Why would he do that? Why would you do that?

CAT: Why would you kill someone who is trying to help?

FABIAN: I'm just saying if a Black person kills Obama – you have to think of that. Not 'cause of racism but because of policies or something like that.

MS. S: I think what Fabian is saying is interesting because it's, it's talking about how we can't just group all peoples together by their race or the colour of their skin, that they have the same opinions and it brings to mind for me an historical event where a prime minister in Israel, when he was signing the peace accord with the Palestinians, was shot by a

Jewish person and that really shook things up and made people realize that not all Jews in Israel are united in terms of what they want. And the reason that he got shot was because people wanted to slow down and stop the peace process with the Palestinians. A group of people wanted to do that. So he was a Jewish prime minister who was shot by a Jew, so, non-Arab, which wasn't what people expected. So, it's complicated, because maybe there are – there are Black Republicans right, in the United States. Like there are people who are against what Obama represents.

BARRY: You can't make assumptions about an entire race of people.

MS. S: Yeah. So was it – did you – Maxx?

BONNIE: Miss, can I go first?

MS. S: Who was next? Who's next? Maxx?

MAXX: I have something funny. You know what Bush tried to do? He tried to make like a – make a rule, not a rule what's it called – like a law, a law that the president that's in a war has to be president till the war ends.

MS. S: Oh really. He tried but that didn't pass, right?

FABIAN: I think another thing is when you think of a Black president all these people I see on the news, on CNN saying he's going to do all these Black things to support Black people but just as she was saying, lots – like the president doesn't make a decision, like he makes a decision, but when he says something he has to talk to all these people, his advisers, those people you never see on the TV, that most of those people are White. Like his adviser to the environment is White, right?

KATHLEEN: That's right.

FABIAN: He has advisers to everything. So he has advisers just to [do] something small like if there was a war resister in America and he comes to Canada, he has someone beside him saying, "Well, I think we should do this. This would help and this would make your public image better." So it's not just him making all the shots. He has so many people behind him. Black, White, Chinese, whatever. They're helping him. (*Ms. S crosses to the blackboard.*) So, I think there's so much more to talk about than the Black thing.

BONNIE: The thing, I just think, I just think that the Americans don't want another war mongrel. 'Cause like Bush puts SO MUCH MONEY into the war. Like it's more than billions of dollars. It has so many zeros. I was reading in the newspaper and they can't even pay for health care.

BELL: Does anyone know if he's staying or not?

FABIAN: What?

BELL: Staying in Iraq or whatever?

FABIAN: He's staying until January 20th.

BARRY: It's Obama's intention to pull out of Iraq and then put more troops into Afghanistan.

ERICA: Yeah, slowly or something.

FABIAN: Bush is still president until January 20th.

BELL: I don't really … Is Guantanamo Bay still going on?

FABIAN: Yes.

BELL: Is he doing anything about that?

DEREK: I heard that Obama was trying to shut down Guantanamo Bay. Hopefully.

BELL: Isn't that what he was doing with Hillary? Like one of the deals like Hillary wanted to close down Guantanamo Bay? And like he wanted to help with that effort too?

BARRY: I don't know, I haven't heard him speaking specifically about it.

CAT: Then what happens when you close down Guantanamo Bay?

BELL: It's closed.

DEREK: It's more peace. It's a good thing if Guantanamo Bay closes.

BELL: Yeah it's good if it closed. Why do you think people will take advantage?

CAT: Well, Guantanamo Bay, isn't that in like Mexico or something?

FABIAN: Cuba.

DEREK: In-between.

CAT: Isn't that where they send like people from the war?

FABIAN: Terrorists.

CAT: Terrorists.

FABIAN: A Canadian one is in there.

DEREK: Omar Khadr.

BELL: Omar Khadr.

BARRY: Alleged terrorists.

CAT: Well, alleged terrorists, don't you think they'd take advantage of, there's not a system that they can – they're scared of?

FABIAN: No, they still have all that stuff. It's not going to go overnight.

BARRY: The thing about Guantanamo is that it's all very secretive and there are torturous practices and everything going on. So it's not like they wouldn't still be trying to protect the US and engage in the war to try and "combat terrorism" so to speak. But Guantanamo is controversial because some of the things that go on there are very sketchy, it doesn't have to obey international law, which everybody else has to do. So it doesn't, you know, it doesn't make political sense. So there's a lot of controversy about that.

FABIAN: And what they're doing is allowed. 'Cause they passed a law. They just wrote something like – to get information they just had like "water treatment" makes it sound, you know, it's little but what they do, they like dunk someone's head under water until they almost pass out. And all these things – they just minimize it to make it sound like they're not doing anything but all these things they're doing, they're allowed to do too. They just minimize, I mean, not minimize but understate, you know, what it actually is.

CAT: You guys think it's a good thing that they get treated that way for the situation that they've done?

FABIAN: I think if it benefits you.

ERICA: 'Cause they haven't done anything wrong. And – think – they're getting tortured for no reason.

DEREK: Omar Khadr isn't even – like he's not even a war – a – shit what's it called –

KATHLEEN: sympathizer.

DEREK: Anyways. They like accused him – they caught him in like the bombing of a building and like he's fifteen or something or he was –

FABIAN: Eighteen. Fifteen at the time.

DEREK: And he's like now being called a war criminal and like what are you there, you're fighting in the war, like how can you be a war criminal?

BARRY: And there are no eyewitnesses to what he did.

DEREK: Yeah, and now he's been there for like how many years? Eight years?

BARRY: He's the only person from the West, from the US and Canada who's in Guantanamo Bay.

BELL: Isn't it that Canada didn't call him back? Like out of all the other countries –

DEREK: Stephen Harper isn't even doing shit.

BELL: They didn't take him back. Isn't he like one of the few who's still there? And there's like this big problem.

BARRY: That's right; with Stephen Harper it's a diplomatic thing, right? That requires Stephen Harper stepping up to the US. So then, it's a complicated thing.

BELL: But I don't understand. Like do you want our citizen back?

BARRY: Well, some people do. Some people ...

DEREK: There's a lot of people what want Omar Khadr back but like Stephen Harper's just not doing anything.

BELL: People fear that will, like, conflict with the Americans like the whole –

FABIAN: I think Bush has influenced him to keep him.

CAT: Well we get smoked like the Americans.

FABIAN: Who?

CAT: Us, Canada, we get (*he slaps his hands together and the shock of it gets a laugh*) slapped.

DEREK: OMARRRRR!

MS. S: It was interesting because they did some Internet looks at internationally who supported Obama and who supported McCain in the international world. So, I don't know if anyone read about that or saw it on TV, what are the countries that – by and large every single country in the world supported Obama and is excited by Obama but there were a couple of major exceptions. Does anyone know what those were?

DEREK: Which places didn't support him?

MS. S: Yeah, which places in the world wanted McCain like in the international vote, like if they were voting.

DEREK: Well Asia didn't give a – any shit 'cause –

FABIAN: What about North Korea?

DEREK: They're communist.

MS. S: The ones I heard about were Iraq and the other one is China and Spain.

MS. M: I would imagine.

BARRY: The Czech Republic – I don't know why.

MS. S: The Czech – so there were –

KATHLEEN: But some countries were more nuanced, like India was concerned because one of the things Obama said was that he wanted to stop the great outsourcing of work in the US. And most of the outsourcing in the technology world goes to India so that has helped their economy. So while they had sympathies with Obama, they were concerned that their own economy would be crushed if the US stopped outsourcing all of their technology to India. And also India is concerned about whatever incoming president's relationship is to Pakistan and to China because they are at odds all the time. So, it's not just based on what it does or doesn't do for your country; that's how you see the interconnectedness of the global world. Who are your friends? It's no different from a student council election here, right? It's not based on the person, but who does she or he hang out with. And that gets our vote or doesn't get our vote.

DEREK: I'm also interested to see because Obama said that they're going to be pulling out of Iraq more and like not depending on them for oil. So now, like, is he going to come to us in, like, in Alberta for oil?

MS. S: What's going to happen with energy in the world?

KATHLEEN: Well, Canada was even panicked for that very reason because Obama started to speak about the environment and about the tar sands in Alberta, and taking a stand on that and suddenly representatives from the Alberta provincial government were on the line to my friend's son [an American friend whose son works on the Democratic environmental policy] saying "what are you doing with these policies because we can't support you in Canada if this will have ramifications for our economy." So it's like a cafeteria line, right – you pick what you like and leave what you don't like. So nobody full on says, "everything you represent I believe in," because people have self-interests, including Canada.

DEREK: Canada is probably going to stand up for itself if Obama is trying to move in and stuff.

BONNIE: Or not.

MS. S: I don't see that.

DEREK: What's that?

MS. S: I don't see America ever invading Canada. But –

DEREK: Oh yeah?

BARRY: And at what point are we just part of the US without them having to invade?

MS. S: Yeah.

KATHLEEN: That's right.

MS. S: The United States has its fingers pretty much everywhere in the world, right? So I can't think of many countries that aren't affected by their foreign policy, their environmental policy, their economic policy. So, it's interesting to see how much Obama can do in the world, right, internationally.

DEREK: And they're going to screw over Mexico too. Mexico's going to like be nothing. 'Cause they do so many trades with them and also our economy is going to go down as soon as theirs does, whatever. So …

MS. S: Ummhmm.

DEREK: We're all screwed. (*Laughter.*)

MS. S: I just thought of something about – you just jogged my memory about something about Mexico that was really interesting recently.

DEREK: Meheeco (*he says in a light falsetto voice*).

MS. S: Oh, Mexico and Chile blocked the – in the United Nations when they were voting on Iraq – on the invasion of Iraq, it was Mexico and

Chile that said "no" and that created a block for the US to go ahead –
and for England and the United States to go ahead and invade Iraq.
And so, 'cause the United Nations was – they were like fifteen votes
against the war and four votes for the war on the UN Security Council
and they still went ahead and invaded Iraq. So the whole relationship
between the United States and the United Nations is a huge ongoing
issue. Like how much power does the United Nations really have if the
United States doesn't listen to the international community and will go
ahead and do whatever they want. So there – there's a lot of conflicted
relationships in the world because of Iraq.

(quiet listening, settled and engaged – pause, laughter)

CHRYSANTHEMUM: [Everyone is] pretty silent.
MS. S: So this was really an interesting conversation with you guys.
(*Everyone claps and smiles.*) And I want to, I want to thank the researchers
for participating and adding to it and congratulate all of you for really
listening to each other and giving over. Um, you know we didn't really
need this (*she refers to the talking pumpkin*).

In thinking through the students' strong and revealing responses
to Obama's victory and about the concepts of hope, desire, and disappointment – all in full display in the classroom dialogue above – I
turned to the analysis of Roberts and Schostak (2012) who argue that
the symbol is always greater and more idealized than the actual person. They write, "Obama the symbol figures the representation of the
promise to come" (p. 380), and that there is a limit to hegemonic coherence and that limit is disappointment. Rowland and Jones (2007) have
argued that Obama's 2004 convention speech redefined the American
Dream and offered a new vision of the dream by creating a narrative
that balanced personal and societal values, but authors Roberts and
Schostak still contend that Obama as symbol became hope for some
and fear for others. Other commentators (Ripley 2004 cited in Roberts
and Schostak 2012) have argued that Obama became "everyone," all
identities – Black, White, male, female – transcending race, gender, and
other forms of difference, using Laclau's (2005) "logic of equivalence,"
or what he refers to as the "play of differences." Laclau explains how,
in populist politics, the particular comes to stand in for the universal.
It is not that differences settle into a clear hegemony, but that different
subject positions are symbolically located together transforming their

Figure 4: Graffiti in the stairwell at Middleview in Toronto

different meanings by their overlapping identifications. It is not that these differences dissolve into a singular, homogenous mass, as Laclau and Mouffe explained in an earlier work (Laclau and Mouffe 1985, p. 127–9), but that differences are preserved though held together in opposition to another group or camp. In the case of our classroom discussion, different subject positions in the room came together in their opposition to those politically unsympathetic to Obama. This "logic of equivalence," then, seemed to play out quite forcefully in our discussion, with one notable exception.

When Maxx interrupts the group, asking why anyone who understood the Black experience from the inside would try to kill Obama, he asks with incredulity, "Why would he do that? Why would you *do* that?" He is asking why anyone, but most especially someone who has been victimized by racism, would murder someone who is promoting equality among races, symbolically or materially? Inconceivable to him, Maxx asks why anyone would do that? Although the teacher helpfully fleshes out what other students seem to be alluding to, that is, that there are other kinds of divisions among people – in this case political divisions that may also explain seemingly irrational hatred – Maxx is challenging the very idea that a Black person could ever have investments more important than surmounting racism. The teacher, at key moments in the discussion, was attempting to subvert such notions of essentialism, reinserting the story of multiplicity within and across social differences. But the narrative surrounding Obama, like the one swelling in the classroom, became a kind of unifying symbol that seemed to be capable of containing the multiplicities present while symbolically unifying them. Maxx's attempt to reaffirm lines of racial demarcation fell upon silence. The focus during the campaign, as the focus in the classroom, was on what binds us as one and what common enemies we might share. Obama the symbol was too powerful that day following the historic election.

Sara Ahmed's work on cultural politics (2004) asks how hate works to align some people and divide others. This is a pertinent question to ask of drama classrooms, which are microcosms of a broader social world, a space where histories of inequality are always present despite unifying narratives that take hold at particular cultural moments. To be sure, the students, on this momentous day, were daring to dream, but they were also anticipating a time when such unifying dreams might meet reality. They were not entirely convinced that Obama could overcome the obvious challenges ahead, although their hope in something better, but as yet unknowable, was palpable.

5 Life or Theatre?

Drama Pedagogy and the Shifting Terrain of (Dis)Engagement

CHRYSANTHEMUM: Lots of times on Monday mornings my alarm clock goes off at seven thirty and I just set it back to nine o'clock.

BERTHAM: Yeah, I do that too.

FABIAN: Because you're already half asleep and you're not really thinking you're just like, "whatever, I'll just miss first period" roll over and go back to sleep.

CHRYSANTHEMUM: I press snooze like four times every day.

ERICA: (*talking over Chrysanthemum*) Yeah, so do I.

CHRYSANTHEMUM: Because I just can't – and then I get more tired because I'm like sleeping and then –

BERTHAM: (*talking over Chrysanthemum*) I put my alarm clock to six thirty so I can press snooze.

FABIAN: (*talking over Bertham and Chrysanthemum*) I doze for like ten minutes.

BERTHAM: My thing is nine minutes for some reason.

BURCU: So could the school do anything better to make it easier for you to come regularly?

ERICA: Yes, start it at a later time. Like that school, I don't know what school it is, but they start at ten or something.

> (Focus Group Interview, Erica, Chrysanthemum, Bertham, Fabian, Middleview, November 24, 2008)

One of the most important understandings we arrived at as we tried to come to terms with the many guises of engagement and disengagement in classrooms is the instability of engagement, the moment-by-moment negotiations between teachers and students. But the pedagogy of drama classrooms does not happen in isolation. It happens in relationship to a larger school, community, and social and political context. It is intimately related to the conditions of the school and the conditions of students' lives. In our coding of data, we looked at forms of engagement along a continuum, knowing full well that it told us only a part of the story. In our coding, we observed "absent" to merely "present" (a body in the room), to "entertained" to "quietly engaged" but non-participatory (silent), to "deeply engrossed" in the work at hand and fully participating both vocally and kinaesthetically. The drama teachers in our Toronto schools cited student absenteeism as one of the greatest challenges they face, as did students when asked about the challenges of collective work in the drama classroom. The Toronto District School Board's research (2009) suggests that there is a clear relationship between neighbourhood income and absenteeism. Students residing in low-poverty/high-income neighbourhoods have much lower absenteeism rates with the reverse also being true. Students living with two parents have lower absenteeism than those in other "family situations." And among secondary students, those taking the majority of their programs in the Academic stream of study have lower absenteeism than those taking other types of courses. Students who were absent at least 20 per cent of the time (missing a day a week or more) were considered to be "at risk" of dropping out and failing to accumulate enough credits to graduate.

Coding for drama pedagogy in our data had to reflect a fuller picture of school life and lives lived outside the classroom. We found that drama pedagogy was intimately connected to the conditions and climate in the rest of the school, the physical plant of the school, and the relations between teachers and students both inside and outside the drama classroom. Conditions external to the drama classroom significantly affect the quality of engagement inside the drama classroom.

Why so much talk about fatigue we wondered in reviewing interview data? In Alex Means's (2013) important ethnographic work in a school in Ellison Square, a disadvantaged neighbourhood in Chicago, he uses the Bureau of Labor statistics to expose the low-wage service jobs that are the fastest-growing employment niches for young people. Read differently, perhaps using the neoliberal discourse of "disengaged youth," urban schools are often blamed for failures of engagement or achievement rather than the effects of disinvestment in schools and youth poverty . This "bottom-tier" schooling, Means argues, effectively sorts poor and racialized youth into low-wage and no-wage futures. This may be the effects of what Richard

Sennett has called "the new capitalism," and what scholars Chadderton and Colley (2012) describe as "neoliberal policies that have promoted economic competitiveness rather than welfare of citizens as the primary task of governments, shifting the risk and responsibility for lifelong education, employment and well-being to individuals (Bauman 2004)" (p. 329).

Later in our focus group, the students explain further:

BERTHAM: That's the only thing that teachers need to understand. We also have lives beyond school, like, some of us have jobs where we work four or five days a week and they don't understand that – then they get upset that we can't do the homework. I work like four or five days a week and three days during the week four to ten thirty so when do I have time to do my homework in those days? I don't.

CHRYSANTHEMUM: I was (*holds up thumb and index finger to measure*) this close to not coming to school today because I didn't feel prepared for a test because I had to work both Saturday and Sunday and there was no chance that I had to study. Like I had to stay up until one, two o'clock to make my study notes to study but like I came because you know, my Mom was like, "you're changing na na na na na and you have to go to school na na na na na" so I was like, "OK, I'm going to school."

ERICA: For me it's just being tired, like exhausted because, like they said, with work and school and all this stuff going on plus like we do have relationships and some of them can be complex sometimes so you just get tired sometimes. Like my Mom – I'm like, "please just let me sleep in today just please for an hour. I need it." like I don't think that I can work without it, like, you know what I mean it ruins your whole day. Sleep is a big issue for me, personally, because I just have so much going on. Or like you'll come in late and they'll be like, "why are you late?" and you're like, "because I slept in" and they think you're a bad kid for doing that but it's like, "I'm sorry I couldn't get my body out of bed." So I think that's a problem.

(Focus Group Interview, Erica, Chrysanthemum,
Bertham, Fabian, Middleview, November 24, 2008)

Every year of the study, in our focus group discussions in both schools in Toronto, the question of work hours arose:

ANNE: Can I go back to – Richard, something you said about arriving on time makes a difference to the quality of the learning that takes place in the class (Richard: Yeah). What could be done to get you here on time?

Like what – what are the things that keep you from getting here on time because there must be something that –

TAYLOR: Do you go to bed late?

RICHARD: Umm, I would say that going to bed late, yeah. And coming home on time. Because I do work late hours at McDonald's.

ANNE: What time does McDonald's close?

RICHARD: It closes at – it doesn't close actually; it's twenty-four hours. But "closing" as they say, it closes at eleven and opens at seven. And they just like change everything up but it's open – it's open to customers.

(Focus Group Interview, Richard, Taylor, Goku, Middleview January 5, 2010)

Within the school, and cumulative in nature, were the myriad distractions of a school suffering material disinvestment creating what Read (2009) describes as a "meteorology of social atmospheres" (p. 49). There were many disruptions to the class and sometimes the students were forced to move elsewhere in the school. One particular day a class had to find another place to work because of the smell of a dead mouse. This event had repercussions on subsequent days as various school board personnel interrupted the class to assess physical plant issues. These interruptions did affect the flow of the class and worked against the teacher as she tried to sustain the work at hand.

At one point the smell was so bad the Middleview students voted to see if they should have class in the library. The disruption of the dead mouse smell was exacerbated by a stink bomb set off in the hallway. Having to decide where to have class created several pedagogical obstacles: it took time away from the work, delayed the settling in process, and dissipated focus. Conditions like these worked against students and teachers trying to sustain engagement with the drama pedagogy:

ERICA: The auditorium.

MS. S.: No, there's an ESL dance class.

FABIAN: That would be fun to watch.

MS. S.: Will you guys have difficulty concentrating?

ALISHA: This is even worse than the first smell.

MAXX: Honestly Miss, I can't stay here much longer. It smells so bad, I can't even describe. Fuck, it's the mouse and now this.

MS. S.: Sorry guys this has sort of got derailed. OK, we're all going to the Library.

ERICA: No. I hate that lady – she's a b –

MS. S.: OK, take a vote. Do you want to stay or go to the library?

ERICA: I think the library might smell as well.

ASHLEY: The whole school has a stink bomb.

(Transcribed classroom discussion,
Middleview, April 6, 2009)

This was one of several such instances where the physical space seriously detracted from the potential engagement of the students, where the pedagogy got lost in the material conditions despite great effort to keep the students engaged socially and academically.

But what became so obvious to us in the first year of the study was that there was not one drama pedagogy that could ensure broad and wide engagement. At Braeburn, the choice of working on a musical production created divisions in the class for some students but clearly offered the pleasure of singing, dancing, and working together for others. Similarly, at Middleview, the choice to collaborate on creating a play text both alienated and engaged the students. The social pedagogy established by Ms. S. at Middleview fostered social bonds for some, while others grew bored with the discussion – however frank and connected it might have been – and they started to resist, causing tensions to erupt. Engagement in the drama classroom is a capricious thing. Sometimes its opposite, disengagement, is strategic and intentional, rather than a simple sign of extrication – the best defence against exposure when questions probe personal understandings rather than book knowledge. Ms. S. explains:

> Usually when we go see a play, I make them write about it, to collect their thoughts. When we talk about it I ask them pointed questions, like "Ask one question about the play – something you didn't understand, something you liked, and something you didn't like." And they have to share that with everybody. In asking the questions we're building our knowledge, too. We're learning about other things. It feels natural. Like having the computer there and googling.
>
> (Interview, Ms. S., Middleview, February 3, 2009)

But youth have been well schooled and they are not all as comfortable with "not knowing," with admitting that learning can be a discovery, a move from ignorance to understanding. Disengagement can sometimes be safer. By disengaging or expressing disinterest, the student can stay protected without having to reveal what they do not know. For some students, revealing the unknown in a secondary school classroom may be more than they can risk. A pedagogical space that prizes the unknown may be too dangerous a place for those who have been made to feel inadequate, or lacking the necessary cultural capital. In many classrooms, teachers participate in this "banking" culture of education and do not enter into the unknown as a place of discovery and intellectual pleasure. The shift for a student then, into this kind of uncertain pedagogy, may be too challenging. How does a student come to trust that in this context it is acceptable *not* to know? Ms. S. speculates:

> But in that collection your knowledge is on show and so your increased knowledge or your limited knowledge is also on show. So there is a compulsion to know more or to distance yourself from that, and that's the student who says, "I'm not interested in that topic anyway." Which may be the case, but may also be the excuse for not wanting to show what isn't known.
> (Interview, Ms. S., Middleview, February 3, 2009)

Teachers and students bring to the classroom a long list of ideals that mostly go unacknowledged. For us, the most palpable ideals in these classrooms were aesthetic and social in nature. We saw aesthetic ideals in the effort to create the conditions for powerful moments of performance, to learn the elements of craft, and to build a polished theatrical production for others to see. We saw social ideals in the desire for open, constructive critical discussion and in the hope that students would be present, engaged, and committed to the work. In *Theatre, Education and the Making of Meanings*, Anthony Jackson discusses the "tension between theatre as education and theatre as 'art': between theatre's aesthetic dimension and the 'utilitarian' or 'instrumental' role for which it has so often been pressed into service" (2007, p. 1). These are complex tensions to negotiate on a daily basis. How do teachers and students use performance and pedagogy in imaginative collaborative work that engages the economic, historical, political, and geographic forces active in their lives? It is from this complex interaction of learning, teaching, and historical context that pedagogy emerges.

Our two Toronto sites, Middleview and Braeburn, presented two radically different pedagogies. The teacher at Middleview demonstrated her profound care for her students' personal and social well-being. There is no doubt that she values drama work for the extent to which it inquires into, and provides an outlet for, her students' personal stories and struggles. *The Doors* project, which we watched unfold over a few months, was a devised piece of theatre that began from individual writing exploring the idea of doors metaphorically, doors as thresholds in our lives. Ms. S likes to work from themes, and often in her process to develop theatrical work she would pick a theme and start the creation process by giving the students various writing prompts that are related to the theme in some way. For *The Doors*, she used writing as a way to develop their personal narratives into material for a play. The students were each given a journal for the process and she began with the prompt, "An open door is ..."

Ms. S's rules for free writing are that students write in silence for a given time period (starting with two minutes and working up to 20 depending on the group's ability to focus). She tells them to always return to the prompt if they get stuck. When she explains the rules to the students, she also lets them know that they will be sharing a selection of what they write with the class. She encourages every student to share something at the end of each free write so that the group gets into the habit of offering feedback to one another and feeling less self-conscious about sharing their work. She explained to us that it's important for the students to share because it gives purpose, incentive, and immediacy to the writing. When students get an immediate peer response to what they have just written, they feel encouraged to write again, she explained. The second prompt was "A closed door is ..."

After these initial prompts to prime their thoughts on the topic, she asked students to write a monologue to a closed door with an imagined person behind it who would either not come out or would not open the door for them. Instead of sharing in the circle, as she did with the two initial pieces, she asked students to perform their monologue (reading from their written text) by choosing someone from the class to be the person behind the door. She had brought in wooden doors for them to work with. The chosen classmate was to try to respond improvisationally on stage, as if they were hearing the words for the first time.

At this point, the students told the teacher that they wanted to write a monologue "in reverse" with the person on the opposite side of the door speaking back to the initial writer. And so they did. Much of Ms. S's planning for such creative projects happens spontaneously; there is plenty of room for students to direct the creative process. After that experiment, the next step was to have students write based on artefacts they brought in from home that were related to doors. She invited them to bring in three artefacts – one had to be written (like a poem or piece of information), one had to be a physical object, and the third was their choice. All of the objects were laid out on the floor and the students had to select one and free write based on the object. They attempted this twice and then shared their writing.

Ms. S explained to us that there comes a point in creating drama when you know that you must stop writing because you have collected enough material. At that point, she presented to the students her own writing based on the door artefacts, and staged it as an example of how you could move from the page to the stage. She also chose key lines from the students' writing for them to take as departure points in developing scene work. She gave each group a line from someone else's monologue and they created scenes based on the text. Ideally, Ms. S would have asked the students to help her dramaturge the work, to create an order for the scenes once they were worked up, but in this case she was feeling pressed for time with the school assembly looming and so she created an order for the scenes, which became the skeleton on which to rehearse and finally stage their collective piece.

For the teacher at Braeburn, such personal exploration was happening, but was incidental to the goal of producing a polished production of a musical (*Joseph and the Amazing Technicolor Dreamcoat*). The class was run like an actor-training workshop, with vocal and physical warm-ups, step-by-step demonstrations of choreography, and singing rehearsals with piano accompaniment. Students were not exploring their own ideas nor how they connected, or did not connect, to the plot of the musical. They were coached in singing and dancing, aiming for flawlessness and professionalism. In this way, the early fieldwork presented two scenarios to us: the classroom that instrumentalizes drama in an effort to carry out some social function, and the classroom that activates theatre as a craft and vocation in an effort to produce an effective performance. It didn't take us long to realize, however, that this easy aesthetic/social split was a seductive but inaccurate description of a more complex reality.

Our discoveries are consistent with O'Toole's (2009) genealogical account of drama in schools. Though O'Toole points to the divisions between those whose pedagogical intentions are either aesthetic or instrumental, he asserts, nonetheless, that "the better the management of the art, the better the learning" (p. 111). In fact, by his account, Harriet Finlay-Johnson's work in 1907, the earliest classroom drama on record, "identified the importance of drama as a motivating factor to help children engage in curriculum" (p. 98). This is perhaps the earliest explicit record of drama being used to enrich engagement with learning across disciplines.

Both of our teachers understood their own work as including the social and the aesthetic agendas simultaneously. As noted, the teacher at Middleview was overwhelmingly concerned with the students' personal and social struggles. But, in ways both overt and subtle, theatre was evoked in the classroom as more than an instrumental set of skills – it was understood (by tacit agreement) as a vehicle for social change. In one student interview, post-performance, we heard clearly the desire for social support and community that small experiences of collective performance might promise for students:

> CHRYSANTHEMUM: We were about to get on stage and we were behind that curtain waiting for the moment when we were supposed to be going out. And we were all back there jumping around like, it was kind of like trying to ramp each other up, and I think that one of the most important things that we were saying to each other was like, "you know what, we're on there. If you make a mistake, you know, we got you" and it was kind of like, you have to be able to tell that person that you're not going up there alone, you're going up there with those people behind you and those people beside you to like catch you when you make a mistake. And I think that if you're able to convince and like make the actors, or like us the students, feel that we're not alone up there when you go up. Because when you go up, you're not thinking like, "OK, well it's us together." You're thinking, "Oh my god, all those people are looking at me." And I think the idea of getting people to think, "it's us rather than me." I think that would help it if we were all talking about it, help each other and know that we're not alone when we're going up there.
>
> (Individual Interview, Chrysanthemum, Middleview, June 2, 2009)

Or Peanut at Braeburn, whose experience in the drama classroom was deeply personal and profoundly consequential:

> I was just gonna say like when I was younger I was a very theatrical person and I would dance and I would sing and I would be a little nerd and when I got lost in my head and into drugs and everything, I lost that side of me. Coming back here, when I saw it on the list, Musical Theatre, I was like, "oh my god, I have to take this chance to be who I was. I'm taking it." And I feel like I was when I was seven. It's amazing. This class has helped me a lot.
>
> (Focus Group Interview, Peanut, Cherry, Kemba, Max, Braeburn, December 1, 2008)

Reflecting on the performances we watched in both schools, the teachers commented on the poor conditions in which they had to work. At Middleview, they lost almost a whole week of rehearsals because their classroom had flooded and they were bounced around from a science lab to an English classroom that was so hot several loud fans had to be running at all times. In the auditorium, the acoustics were poor and the stage was equipped with ineffective microphones. The acoustics were challenging in the Braeburn cafetorium, too, as the "performance space" was filled by hundreds of students eating their lunch. The blocking was compromised because the students were forced to cluster around two microphones on each side of the stage in order to be heard by the audience.

After the performance of *Joseph* at Braeburn, the music teacher expressed his disappointment that 20 of the 40 students who were in the course were not on-stage (although an 11th-hour effort was made to incorporate a few who did show up unexpectedly just prior to the performance to help them salvage their credit). Performance success at Middleview, as at Braeburn, was partially measured in terms of the number of students who showed up. At Middleview, four out of 15 students did not participate in their final performance of *The Doors*. Nonetheless, the teacher felt the performance was a success:

> MS. S: I thought that overall the project was very successful both artistically and pedagogically. Ideally, all the students would have been engaged and perhaps I could have done more to make that happen, but the good thing is that it created an opportunity for the majority of the students to be very engaged, and that is positive. The failure was that Stephanie, Bonnie, K'Thanie and Fabian did not participate in the performance.
> (Email reflecting on performance, January 15, 2009)

She goes on to say that while she initially thought of the lack of attendance and "buy-in" as a failure, she later thought of it as a need for more learning on the part of individual students, "But is that a failure or something for their own learning? I'm not sure. It's been hard getting them to do very much at all this year. Bonnie and Stephanie hardly come to school." (Ms. S, email post-performance, January 15, 2009) This significant question leads us to wonder, what is the place of such "personal work" in learning and how might pedagogies better acknowledge this? Or, indeed, how do teachers separate out their own teaching successes and failures from those successes or failures for which they cannot be responsible?

In our interviews with students, they repeated many times a sense of gratitude for the social and the aesthetic components of their learning. But it seemed to be the case that the sense of social cohesion they sometimes felt in a drama classroom, despite moments of great vulnerability, had a lasting significance and somehow stood apart from other classroom experiences:

> ERICA: You have to know everybody because you have to work with everybody and you're very vulnerable because you're going up and performing in front of these people every day. So you have to feel comfortable with them to, you know, just let yourself go. So that's why everyone gets really close with each other. Like last year, we had conversations about people's lives coming to the point where people are crying because they felt so comfortable with everybody that they could just do that. And I really love that about the Drama class because it's just a place where you could be yourself and you're not worried about "I have to pass this test, I have to stop and pay attention, what did you say? I can't talk to you." It's a lot more of interaction and it's just great.
>
> (Focus Group Interview, Erica, Bertham, Fabian, Chrysanthemum, Middleview, November 24, 2008)

Aesthetics and the Dialogic Turn

The way students thought about their drama class environment is consistent with those theorists who relate aesthetics to the particular practices and social environments in which those practices occur. In the classrooms we observed "the talk" was sometimes the height of aesthetic encounter. Bourriaud's (1998/2002) *Relational Aesthetics* would suggest the same: the social exchange is the art. He states, "as part of a 'relationist' theory of art, inter-subjectivity does not only represent the social setting for the receptions of art, which is its 'environment,' its field (Bourdieu), but also becomes the quintessence of artistic practice" (p. 22).

Ms. S.'s class made us understand this "aesthetic of talk" that we would later see play out in the Prerna classrooms in India. This hard to label and often fleeting sense of connection and resonance that we witnessed in Toronto and Lucknow became a point of particular interest for us in our pursuit to better understand engagement. At several points, I pushed the teacher to extend our thinking about this, as below:

KATHLEEN: So I want to pick up on something really important you just said because right from the beginning of this project we'd been wrestling with the aesthetic and the social and that tightrope that you walk every day in many places, but especially in highly charged places like in your context. When you say those are the most powerful aesthetic moments, I want you to talk more about that because here's the outside critique that's not caring so much about pedagogy but rather "where's the art"? And, "that's not drama necessarily, that's a good group class, that's group therapy that's ... but where's the art in that?" And, you didn't tell us those are the best moments of community or connection; you said those [moments of talk] are the best *aesthetic* moments so I want to push you to say more about that.

MS. S: I don't know if I really thought about it so much in my head but I find those moments to be aesthetic because its really, it's – there's an art in having conversation, in having, um ... Drama is having, at its most basic level, right, it's sharing stories around the fire, so ... that's how drama started, that's, you know, us talking and sharing experiences and listening and building on each other and it's not because I am teaching them to – they're doing it! You know? Because they understand [the importance of sharing through talking].

(Interview, Ms. S., Middleview, February 3, 2009)

Implicit in most understandings of dialogue is the sense that it might build bridges across differences, and because this revered notion of dialogue has surfaced in social practices across a range of fields and geospatial boundaries, it would not be unreasonable to consider it a "dialogic turn" in the social sciences and humanities. Rather than dialogue being unidirectional, a turn-taking but essentially one-way flow of knowledge from one speaker to another, more recent conceptions of dialogue imagine new modes of communication where knowledge is co-created through the meeting, in dialogue, of the different ideas that participants bring into play (see Phillips 2011 for a rich account of the "dialogic turn" in communications studies). Phillips (2011) suggests that, in this regard, difference is understood as a dynamic and positive force in social processes used in developing meaning, rather than an obstacle to coexistence.

Many share Ms. S.'s reverence for the spoken word. When writer Christopher Hitchens (2012) was dying of oesophageal cancer and quite literally losing his voice, he reflected on this power of speech, of engagement earned through conversation:

> In the medical literature, the vocal "cord" is a mere "fold," a piece of gristle that strives to reach out and touch its twin, thus producing the possibility of sound effects. But I feel that there must be a deep relationship with the word "chord": the resonant vibration that can stir memory, produce music, evoke love, bring tears, move crowds to pity and mobs to passion. We may not be, as we used to boast, the only animals capable of speech. But we are the only ones who can deploy vocal communication for sheer pleasure and recreation, combining it with our two other boasts of reason and humour to produce higher syntheses. To lose this ability is to be deprived of an entire range of faculty: it is assuredly to die more than a little. (pp. 53–4)

This self-other consciousness, this sense of the importance of the collective and of dialogue in classrooms, expressed by Ms. S, became a point of discussion with students in interviews as well, as we tried to understand better this interplay of social and artistic dynamics at work in the best kinds of drama pedagogy:

BONES MCCOY: OK, when you're a kid right? Do you remember the, like, giant circle tables and everybody is like this whole community and like we're all friends, but then as you get older you get your own personal space and then your life is your desk. If you do not have things that you need in your desk, then you are disorganized for the world, and then you're separated from other people and yet you're close enough that if you wanted to, you could interact but it's also frowned upon by the overseer, i.e., the teacher who will tell you that some days you should work together, but most of the time you should always be separated, so basically life is (*squaring hands*) desks.

ANNE: Well, OK, well what about drama? How does drama fit in because you don't even have desks in drama.

BONES MCCOY: Well that's just it, like, there are a few cases where, like in my Black history class, for example, we put our desks in a circle about once a month and we talk to each other and stuff. And in drama, it's a very kind of almost raw environment. I find that I always get along with people in my drama class and I'm not afraid to hide anything from them, and in a regular classroom, outside of the teacher, I don't really speak to anyone.

(Focus Group Interview, Bones McCoy,
HLA, Middleview, December 9, 2010)

Later in the focus group, we get two students' coherent articulation of what they think they are learning at school. In this instance, the students discuss the "hidden" and the social curriculum. The passage also demonstrates how the formal interview is built collectively – one student builds on the ideas offered by his peer. It both addresses and illustrates the social curriculum of schooling, and demonstrates how adolescents often have a kind of meta-consciousness about their own evolving understandings. With time, the students perceive the teacher as more complex and dimensional than simply "the boss." Power is ever present in these social lessons:

ANNE: Well, let's go back to that thing that you were saying in schools, the hidden and the not hidden, what do you mean by that?

HLA: Well, umm, there's like the hidden curriculum, the social curriculum, and the academic curriculum (*counting on fingers*) and some people can argue that school isn't actually about the academics, but about the hidden, like how you learn to behave in school, is like how you behave in like the rest of your life. The social curriculum which is like how you learn to interact with people appropriately, not necessarily just close friends and stuff, but also peers and just strangers, and how you end up meeting people and all that stuff … and like teachers could be like your boss 'cause you have to listen to them. That kind of stuff.

BONES MCCOY: So in a way, conformity.

HLA: Sort of.

ANNE: So what do you think you're learning at Middleview in terms of that part?

HLA: The hidden and social curriculum?

ANNE: Yeah.

HLA: Umm, probably at lot. I don't notice it, but probably a lot 'cause I have a group of friends, I talk to people in classes, I don't know.

BONES MCCOY: Oh, how am I learning like socially and stuff from the school?

HLA: Behaviours and stuff.

BONES MCCOY: Behaviour? Easily that I've learned like a great deal of respect for people, particularly in schools. When I was younger, teachers were teachers and, like you said, it was like your boss, but I've actually developed further (*body shifting*). I've developed – I realize that there's two people: there's the teacher, and then there's the person. I've met teachers I disliked, but I've liked the people they are. Like it's very true.

(Focus Group, Bones McCoy, HLA,
Middleview, December 9, 2010)

In India, we found the same prizing of talk and what we learn through the "social curriculum," as HLA calls it. The students engaged in "critical dialogues" around issues of importance, and while we were there they were engaged with other high school students in New York and California (through a program called Kidnet) creating digital stories and communicating via a blog. When we talked to Dr. Sahni about this cross-cultural communication, she again emphasized the centrality of a pedagogy of dialogue despite the other rather high-tech pedagogies the students in the United States were engaging in:

DR. SAHNI: And with Kidnet, it's not so much the online work, it's critical dialoguing that happens around Kidnet.

KATHLEEN: OK, I want to ask about that because I was interested in that. Why are there critical dialogues that happen around Kidnet?

DR. SAHNI: When Kidnet happened, it didn't have a curriculum or anything. All they wanted them to do was just blog and write on the Net, and then children – and I said to them, I'm not about to let them waste their time – you're kind of blogging and things with some distant people who don't really care, but here is the opportunity to use this. And we started with making digital stories, and they weren't able to make those stories unless we had a lot of conversation. Then I said we are going to use these sessions for critical dialogues too. And that's what drove the curriculum for all the other sites. Nobody was doing it like that. And we did it like that so everybody started to do it like that.

(Discussion, Dr. Sahni,
Prerna, January 21, 2012)

In our focus group interview in India, we also sought the girls' perspectives on the importance of the spoken word. The following excerpt from that interview offers some of the girls' thoughts about the "talk pedagogy" of drama and particularly about the place of conversation in their relationships to one another, and their sense of rights and autonomy in the broader social world:

> KATHLEEN: I want to understand what you appreciate about the critical dialogues.
> PREETI: Because it is always related to our lives. So we can share and give our views on that (*nods*).
> KATHLEEN: OK. OK.
> KUSHBOO: We learn more things about (*switches to Hindi, Dr. Sahni translating*) Dr. Sahni: She says we learn a lot from other people's experiences and she says we learn more about our rights, as we discuss.
> LAXMI: (*Dr. Sahni translating*): She says when we all tell our stories then we are kind of bound together and our confidence grows, and more people join us because they feel that if they join us their strength will grow.
> PREETI: And I think we get different ideas than that. And we solve one problem in a different aspect.
> DR. SAHNI: So they get different perspectives.
> POONAM, KUSHBOO: And we make skits.
> KATHLEEN: OK, that was my question. Are the critical dialogues related to the drama?
> DR. SAHNI: Always.
> KATHLEEN: Always. Tell me about that.
> PREETI: If we can't understand – if somebody is not understanding the same situation, they can from the drama. (*Switches to Hindi.*)
> PREETI: (*Dr. Sahni translating*): She says it's a medium for us to express what we are thinking. Our story. If it's more emotional, it helps us understand it much better; let's us talk about it.
>
> (Focus Group Interview, Preeti, Poonam, Sunita, Moni, Kushboo, Prerna, January 21, 2012)

Helen Cahill (2010) nicely captures this active and reciprocal relationship between the performed drama and the construction of identities:

> A reworking of identity requires a dismantling of the categorising that has occurred. But for dismantling to occur we must first see how we are mantled. It is here that drama has a particular potency, for we trade in mantles. However, for the drama to contribute in this way, it must facilitate recognition of the constructed nature of identity, and of the constructing nature of dominant storylines. It must make visible the storying, rather than simply the story. (p. 172)

In writing about art as encounter, Bourriaud (1998/2002) echoes what we witnessed unfolding in both the Toronto and Lucknow sites and supports how our Indian collaborators uncompromisingly used drama as an encounter and an activator of talk. Bourriaud speaks specifically to the potential of art to create dialogue and "inter-human negotiation" (p. 41). He suggests that art is valuable if it is able to stimulate conversation and collective thinking "so there is a question we are entitled to ask in front of any aesthetic production: 'does this work permit me to enter into dialogue?'" (p. 109).

Our interview with the teacher at Prerna, Ms. K, further helped us understand the extent to which dialogue was used in the classroom and her view on the far-reaching implications of this kind of relational pedagogy:

> KATHLEEN: So, critical dialogues, how are they related to taking a position on their own lives?
>
> MS. K: It gives them an identity. They can speak what they feel. And once they can speak what they feel then they can tell others that this is what I want. Otherwise they are doing what others want. They have no place for their own needs, for their own desires. So when we have these types of dialogues, it really helps them to understand this is my need, this is what I like, this is what I do not like. I think it took some time for them also to let their parents know, hey, I do not like this. Or, I like this, I will do this. And I'm so happy, even like I take the critical dialogues quite late, we have the classes at six thirty, seven in summers and they are very confident that they will reach home safely because they are moving in a group, and they have learned the legalities also. They have learned a little bit of law. They have learned what are their rights, through these dialogues, and they understand what are the problems of the society.
>
> (Interview, Ms. K., Prerna, January 20, 2012)

Talk is a double-edged sword in drama classrooms. It often opens up the room to a "social curriculum" that students seem to yearn for, but it also exposes our lack of knowledge, our cultural gaps, our difficult personal feelings. In drama, the talk fuels the performance work and the performance work fuels the talk. It is an unending reciprocity that can invite deep engagement and also induce strategic disengagement. It is a way to discover and reveal that is both desirable and intimidating. The next section on Verbatim theatre exposes a particular kind of pedagogy and genre of theatre that walks a thin line between life and theatre, a thrilling and dangerous line.

Verbatim Theatre and the Desire to Communicate

Our experiences of theatre, both the plays we saw and the devised work we witnessed in classrooms, invited us into the intimate details of strangers' lives. Deleuze (1988) poses the question most germane to the gaze of the researcher and the spectator: "How can a being take another being into its world, but while preserving or respecting the other's own relations and world?" (p. 126).

During the second year of our study, the Verbatim play, *The Middle Place,* produced by Project: Humanity (http://www.projecthumanity.ca) toured schools in the Toronto area, including our Middleview research site. Verbatim theatre is a form of documentary theatre using the actual words of people, often in direct first-person address or testimonial style, to raise issues relevant to a particular community and to activate broader social engagement. Unsurprisingly, Verbatim is a genre that has ignited controversy; its critics are many. If it is purporting to be "real," how might we verify its factual content? Or, if it is real then doesn't it lose the power of metaphor, a dearly held ideal of art itself? In fact, these arguments in my view conflate truth with facts and empty the idea of truths of their potent symbolic value. Trinh T. Minh-ha (1989) has been most elegant on these points, imagining a multiplicity of truths and the perils of a certain imperialism of truth. Trinh suggests that each society has its own politics of truth and that being truthful is being "in the in-between of all regimes of truth" (p. 121). She contends that "thinking true" often means thinking in conformity with a "scientistic" discourse produced by certain institutions. But in shedding this kind of colonizing truth, only then can a story fulfil its pedagogical promise. Trinh writes:

> Why this battle for truth and on behalf of truth? I do not remember having asked grandmother once whether the story she was telling me was true or not. Neither do I recall her asking me whether the story I was reading her was true or not. We knew we could make each other cry, laugh, or fear, but we never thought of saying to each other, "This is just a story." A story is a story. There was no need for clarification – a need many adults considered "natural" or imperative among children – for there was no such thing as "a blind acceptance of a story as literally true." Perhaps the story has become *just* a story when I have become adept at consuming truth as fact. Imagination has become equated with falsification, and I am made to believe that if, accordingly, I am not told or do not establish in so many

words what is true and what is false, I or the listener may no longer be able to differentiate fancy from fact. (p. 121)

In the second year of our study, artistic creators of *The Middle Place* Antonio Cayonne and Andrew Kushnir came in to work with the students at Middleview. They offered a powerful workshop on Verbatim theatre that helped the students undertstand how a "real" life could inspire the interpretation of a character. Pedagogically sophisticated, the leaders invited the students to experiment with how language is lived in our bodies. They led the students in what they call "a punctuation walk," a rehearsal technique designed by the play's director, Alan Dilworth, wherein actors were to physicalize, in a stylized rather than literal way, all the punctuation present in the spoken text. This piece of pedagogy helped the students understand how the actors had worked to get the "real" people – whose words they were speaking – inside their own bodies. This was not at all a process of imitation or mimicry; in fact, the actors had never seen the real people they were depicting. It was an interpretive process that placed great value on how one communicates, not simply what one says.

During the third year of the study, and after a very successful tour of schools in Toronto, *The Middle Place*, a story about the "real," the "true lives" of youth living in a homeless shelter, was picked up by two professional theatres in Toronto, Theatre Passe Muraille and Canadian Stage, where it played to sold-out houses in two separate runs. Many of our youth research participants saw the play a second time at one of these theatres. At that fortuitous moment, our ethnography moved from classrooms into theatre spaces for the next few months, where we conducted 75 post-performance interviews with general and youth audience members to try to understand what the general public was learning about youth, and homeless youth in particular, how this corroborated or interrupted their already well-formed views, and how theatre, as an art form different from others, acted as a forum for social commentary and critique. Project: Humanity's Verbatim play, the extended programming they did through curating the lobby spaces with youth artwork and out-takes of interviews that didn't make it into the final version of the script, their developing of resources for the homeless community and ensuring that community had free tickets to the production, and their continuing commitment to youth in the shelter system constitute acts of political action that both depicted and engaged many of Toronto's marginalized youth. Their unhampered aesthetic and clear

Figure 5: Talk Back session after *The Middle Place* production at Theatre Passe Muraille

public pedagogy provoked a profound reaction in the young people of our study to think through some uncomfortable realities of our shared social context. From our ethnographic perspective, the play effectively initiated a social discourse about responsibility and representation, and incited an experience of theatre making among youth that deepened their experience of spectating. Playwright, Andrew Kushnir, in an early interview with our research team, wished imagined audiences might "sit in the play a little past the curtain call." They did that, and more.

For our research participants, seeing *The Middle Place* and working with its creators was a watershed experience. Inspired by both the content of the play exploring the lives of shelter youth in Toronto, and the form of Verbatim, students back in the classroom at our research sites began to experiment with the genre, and their teacher, Ms. S, worked hard to become proficient in a style of theatre about which she knew very little, a genre that had never been an official part of the drama curriculum in Ontario. Commissioned by the Ontario Ministry of Education, Ms. S then developed a curriculum unit on Verbatim theatre so other teachers could learn about it and teach it to their students. After experimenting pedagogically with the genre, we also communicated the work to our Indian collaborators. After first seeing Verbatim theatre in their school auditorium,

Figure 6: *Globe and Mail* coverage of *The Middle Place* on display in the lobby of Theatre Passe Muraille

the students in Toronto decided to explore the concept of "school cliques" by interviewing their school peers about their experience of social divisions in the school. Upon hearing about the project, the Prerna students also became very interested in this form of theatre making; they took up the challenge of creating a street play about domestic violence based on interviews they conducted with married women in their communities.

The Middle Place took Toronto by storm. Young and old theatregoers gravitated to the theatre and began to learn and speak about the social issue of youth homelessness. And our porous ethnographic methodology took an important turn too; the opportunity allowed us to watch how young people manipulated the genre and became researchers in their own right and of their own cultures. As ethnographers, we helped with developing research skills like interviewing, and the youth learned how difficult interviewing can be and how many ethical considerations come in to play when you are charged with crafting the ideas and words of others, verbatim.

To document and support their process of Verbatim theatre making, we designed a classroom blog so that students could upload their raw data (taped interviews), upload their transcribed interviews, and finally post their monologues devised from their interviews. Then, we invited them to engage with each other's work and provide feedback via the blog. This digital record was enormously useful to us as ethnographers, but it was also a very interesting experiment for the theatre makers. It offered a different kind of feedback to that experienced through shared performances and allowed unmediated responses between peers. The final performance of the monologues was also videotaped and uploaded, completing the whole process. But most importantly, the experiment allowed us to get some insight into the meaning structures used by our research participants when developing their ideas. What questions did they choose for their interview protocols with peers as they aimed to understand how their peers made sense of social divisions that occur in school space? Then, how did they analyse these data? What did they privilege? What seemed less relevant? What were they learning from other young people about a context they knew intimately? It was a terrific experiment methodologically. But it also shifted, once again, the familiar power relations of the research encounter and made space for youth theorizing (see Gallagher and Lortie 2007a).

I had engaged in this kind of methodological work before in previous research projects. Cook-Sather (2012) in a recent article, analysed that earlier methodological work and framed it in a context of "translation." She writes:

As an interpretive framework, "translation" reveals and magnifies the language and culture-based nature of the unfixed and ongoing processes of student experience that must be studied through similarly unfixed and ongoing processes of perception, interpretation, and representation. (p. 2)

Our orientation in research has always been to, as Spivak (1988) has famously urged, listen to the plural voices of those normally "Othered" and hear them as constructors, agents, and disseminators of knowledge. In referencing this methodological orientation, Cook-Sather writes further:

The methodological translations in which Gallagher and Lortie and Fine et al. engaged render some of the basic practices of qualitative research different versions of themselves. Both the methods and those using and participating in them become different versions of themselves – generated within different relationships and productive of different identities. (p. 10)

This is indeed what happened in the research. Students spoke in a vernacular with each other that we likely would not have tapped into. Below, a group of three interviewers from the class interviewing two students they stopped in the hallway:

INTERVIEWER 1: What's your name?

INTERVIEWER 2: No no no no, no names.

INTERVIEWER 1: Oh ... OK. Hi. Um ... what are the cliques at [Middleview]? ... Where do they hang out and what defines them ... music, clothes, or hair.

INTERVIEWEE 1: Um ...

INTERVIEWEE 2: Uh ... I totally didn't understand the question (*Laughing sigh.*)

INTERVIEWER 2: Hi. like, if there were cliques at our school, where would they hang out? Like, uh ... like where they hang out and kind of –

INTERVIEWEE 1: Yeah –

INTERVIEWEE 2: Mmm. We have all the smokers and like all the artsy people that hang out around the arts building and like in the alleyway right there –

INTERVIEWEE 1: Stoners. Yeah, there's like potheads that hang out in crackhead alley, or whatever you want to call it.

INTERVIEWEE 2: Yeah.

INTERVIEWER 3: Where exactly is crackhead alley?

INTERVIEWEE 2: Like the alleyway behind Tim Horton's or something like that.

INTERVIEWEE 1: Yeah, like that little walkway thing by the parking lot.

INTERVIEWEE 2: Yeah, right there. And there's like Malibu Barbie and shit who chills at like Second Cup.

INTERVIEWEE 1: (laughs)

INTERVIEWER 3: Who's Malibu Barbie?

INTERVIEWEE 1: Like all those –

INTERVIEWEE 2: Like, all the fake plastic bit – girls …

INTERVIEWEE 1: (laughs)

INTERVIEWER 3: We have those at our school?

INTERVIEWEE 2: Yeah, we have them at our school.

INTERVIEWEE 1: Yeah, yeah we really do.

INTERVIEWER 3: I definitely need to check that out.

INTERVIEWEE 1: And they all walk around like they run shit and they really don't.

INTERVIEWEE 2: And they all wear Uggs and tights and shit on the same day.

INTERVIEWER 3: Do you know if that's rehearsed?

INTERVIEWEE 1: I really don't know, I think –

INTERVIEWEE 2: I really think they are all naturally insecure about themselves.

INTERVIEWEE 1: Yeah.

INTERVIEWER 3: That's really gross (*pause, then an abrupt change of pace*). Anyhow –

INTERVIEWER 1: (*laugh*) Yeah … OK, so Hi. Do any cliques think they are better than others?

INTERVIEWEE 2: Are you serious? Of course they do.

INTERVIEWEE 1: Yeah.

INTERVIEWEE 2: Like Malibu Barbie.

INTERVIEWEE 1: They're stuck up, think they run, think they run everything … it's really dumb.

INTERVIEWEE 2: When in reality they can't even write their own name.

INTERVIEWER 1: Hmm. Do you belong – is it belong? Yeah it's belong. Do you belong to a clique? Why or why not?

INTERVIEWEE 2: No –

INTERVIEWEE 1: Naw, I wouldn't say we do.

INTERVIEWEE 2: 'Cause, umm, I don't have a label I just wear whatever the hell I wanna wear.

INTERVIEWEE 1: I'm not really into the whole (*puts on high mocking voice*) "oh is that in style, oh that's not in style, you can't be with us. Da da da da da," type thing, you know? So we just do our own thing …

After the interviews, they translated these data into performance monologues to illustrate, through performance, what they had learned both about making Verbatim theatre and about how their peers understand the ways in which school space gets divided up by social categories, fashion, music, interests, and desires. As (drama) researchers, we could not have asked for a more edifying lesson about what young people think, how they access the understandings of their peers, and what performative and poetic sense they make of such ideas for a wider public.

With respect to our methodological use of technology, in subsequent interviews, we asked the students to share their thoughts about the blogging aspect of the Verbatim project. We were interested in how the presentation of self, through digital writing, and their own sense of identity might have been affected by this:

ANNE: Can we ask you just one more question about the blogging? How do you think it changes your writing when you know that other classmates are going to be reading your writing?

MARBLES: Oh, I definitely try and make myself look like a badass. I'm kidding, I'm kidding.

(*Everyone laughs.*)

(Focus Group Interview, Marbles, Joe, Twila, Middleview, January 5, 2010)

However, Marbles does go on to explain that she is not attempting to change herself through writing, though it might happen subconsciously. Many of the students held on to a belief that they are who they are, whatever the medium; that audience and forum do not change who they are or how they present themselves. This is a familiar belief in the stability of an authentic self. Yet, young people seem to be almost chameleon-like in their capacity to adapt to circumstances and changing contexts. Regarding social media spaces, there is no longer any novelty:

GOKU: It doesn't change anything for me ... No, like I'm – like we're on Facebook all the time anyways we don't really – it doesn't, like, change what I would say. Maybe like I'll swear less and I'll be – well, it's not like I'll be nicer. I'll be the same as I normally am.

(Middleview, Focus Group Interview, names here December 11, 2009)

Experts, however, continue to sing the praises of digital forms of literacy learning. Penrod (2007) calculates that adolescents spend about six hours a day online and that they are developing 21st-century literacy skills in the process. Other researchers, too, forcefully argue that digital technologies like blogging have a powerful role to play in primary and secondary education. In one study, Tanti (2012) demonstrated that in addition to the development of traditional literacy skills, skills concerned mainly with the ability to construct well-structured and well-presented texts, the collaborative use of the classroom blog provided students with the means to develop critical literacy skills in relation to interacting with an audience and each other. Even more forcefully, Jabari Mahiri's (2008) work not only explains the significance of digital literacies in the life of urban youth, it also understands the importance of seeking out multimodal research processes to capture the rich digital literacy practices of youth:

> Traditional conceptions of print-based literacy do not account for the richness and complexity of actual literacy practices in young peoples' lives enabled by new technologies that magnify and simplify access to and creation of multimodal texts. Similarly, traditional research processes (that intimately link to traditional conceptions of print-based literacy) are not well suited to capture these widely variable, highly changeable, temporal, and local acts of meaning making and identity construction. (p. 305)

While this may all be true, the blog for us became an especially important way to further engage with the students about their academic, social, and artistic identities as they played with performances online and in their monologues. Wales (2012) found in her research with "at risk" youth in Australia that they also played with "a range of performative identities through the construction of digital and virtual personas." (p. 535)

In our work, we found a particular preoccupation with "the real" in students' lives, eschewing a postmodern sensibility of the performative in exchange for a desire for "the real." What came through most strongly in the interviews with students after they had seen *The Middle Place* was their belief in the communicative power of "the real" and the privileged place "reality" holds in their sense of the value or importance of ideas. Twila was especially forthcoming on this point:

> TWILA: Personally, when the play *The Middle Place* came in, I actually cried, like, OK. Like I don't live in a big house, like I live in Regent Park [public housing]. People think, "oh you don't have the perfect life" but they think "you don't have it bad." I've always been grateful. Like, I have my home, I have my family, I have my friends, I have my school. But I've never really like took in and realized that I have it really good compared to other people and I have to take everything seriously. I have to be grateful for everything because I don't live in a shelter, I'm not pregnant at like a really young age, I don't have an abusive boyfriend, I don't have any of that.
> (Individual Interview, Twila, Middleview, January 14, 2010)

For a message-driven culture, and particularly for young people in schools who are fed a steady diet of moral lessons, Twila pointed out that it was the message as well as the genre – reality-based, documentary style – that heightened the impact of both seeing *The Middle Place* and creating their own Verbatim pieces. They had to work with "reality" and also with creative questions of representation. She reflects an attraction to the form and its impact that is shared by others in the professional theatre world. For instance, renowned Canadian playwright Judith Thompson has, later in her career, been unequivocally turned on to the power of "the real" in her own writing. In a forthcoming chapter on her turn towards working with real and often marginalized communities in her own writing, she explains simply:

> I sculpted a real play with real women; real people, real lives, the idea of REAL had asserted itself. It was hard for me to imagine writing an old fashioned drama with made up characters in a made up situation. Who cares? Any of us could make up a story. It's the real stories that count. And real is ALWAYS more interesting than made-up. (Thompson, in Gallagher and Freeman, forthcoming)

Mary Luckhurst (2008) describes succinctly Verbatim creation in the following way:

> Verbatim Theatre, like other documentary forms, is always stretched on the rack between a pursuit of "facts" – a loaded word in its own right – and an engagement with artistic representation. (p. 203)

I suspect something more was going on in the theatre classrooms with the students, however. Again, Trinh (1989) elaborates on the cultural appeal of story as a vehicle of truth: "Its fascination may be explained by its power to give a vividly felt insight into the life of other people and to revive or keep alive the forgotten, dead-end-ed turned-into-stone parts of ourselves (p. 123). But, in discussing how experiencing Verbatim theatre might have changed her understandings of drama, Twila replies:

> With Verbatim theatre, it all comes – it's all realistic. So like, you can take, I don't know, it just gives you more ideas. Like, you could take something, like a topic, and make it real. Like you can take real inter-views of people and stuff and just make it into something bigger and you can send a real message out to people. I don't know, just, it changes the way you think of writing or it changes your ideas. I don't know. I like Verbatim theatre. I never even knew what Verbatim theatre was and I think it's really interesting, like I never even knew there was Verbatim theatre. I think it's a really good, clear impact of society and stuff.
>
> (Individual Interview, Twila,
> January 14, 2010, Middleview)

Twila is hitting on something quite important here. She, like many adults and young people in our post-performance interviews at the theatres, wish theatre of this kind – theatre that takes from people's "real" stories – would *do* something; could make a social good out of the act of taking stories to justify that act. When one induces theatre into community action, the time frames and desired outcomes also shift. Jan Cohen-Cruz (2010) argues that the "follow-up" becomes equal to, or even more important than, the performance, because the perfor-mance has positioned audiences as witnesses rather than spectators (p. 81). This may explain why Verbatim theatre commonly takes the stories of marginalized groups to produce social or political action. Twila wanted the story to be summoned into action to ultimately change her, and others.

Much has been written about theatre spectatorship and the idea of audience as witness. Implicit in this activist turn is the idea that a witness to an act will be compelled to action more than a dispas-sionate observer. Using "real" lives and taking the audience into the confidence of those represented on stage seems to demand a reciprocity that other art forms may not. Some theatre patrons of *The Middle Place* read this as an affective engagement that also compelled action. In our post-performance interviews in the theatre, we often asked young interviewees how they thought a documentary-style play was different from a documentary film. Many referred to the affective and relational elements that seem especially present in the theatre:

> 1: (*cough*) First of all, a documentary film wouldn't have such a set of monologues in this manner, so in the way the presentation in itself is different.
>
> ANNE: Yeah.
>
> 1: But the main difference I see between a play and a documentary is that when you watch a documentary, it doesn't really feel personal to you; it's more like absorbing information. Like you have the knowledge, it appeals to your mind, but it doesn't really appeal to your heart, like OK, they're homeless youths so they suffer in this way. OK! They're trying to have hope and then go out like that, great for them, it's like you can actually acknowledge those facts and you could cheer them on a little bit, but it doesn't just touch you as much as when actually you come into a play, watch it, it actually comes close to your heart much more than it would in a documentary.
>
> (Post-Performance Youth Interview,
Canadian Stage, March 9, 2011)

Anderson and Wilkinson (2007) in their article citing a resurgence of Verbatim theatre suggest that the form is well suited to intellectual and emotional complexity. At the same time, they maintain that the works are accessible because the drama is built from conversations. My sense, as well, is that Verbatim theatre often elicits ambivalence from its audience, a kind of ambivalence that continues to provoke questions as a productive mode of engagement.

At Theatre Passe Muraille, there were many interviewees who pointed to the sense of immediacy and presence that the theatre offers:

> 2: I think, too, in a play, you are in the moment; you're almost in the play. When you're watching a TV show you can be like using your phone, you're like off doing something – you can leave and even come back – but a play, it's like you're sitting in this one spot and looking and it's like, your attention is always there and you're always going to be in

this play so you're always going to pay attention to it. So I think that helps a lot.

(Post-Performance Youth Interview, Theatre
Passe Muraille, November 3, 2010)

And space mattered too. Many students who'd seen the play at their school and then came the following year to see it at the theatre felt qualitative differences in those experiences:

> C SQUARE: I have actually seen the play twice. It came to my school already. But I liked it better here because at school it was more distracting 'cause it's bigger and more people and more noises and 'cause you are used to the school. And like here, I have never been here before and it's smaller and new people and so you're more focused because you don't know anybody else. And like the white stage, that really caught my attention a lot 'cause you don't see that a lot, like a circle white stage that lights up a lot. I liked it better here than at school or on TV.

(Post-Performance Interview with Middleview
students: Puppy Love, C Square, and Kandy,
Theatre Passe Muraille, November 9, 2010)

But that sense of immediacy and "reality" had disturbing effects too. Because the company ensured that a certain number of seats in each performance were reserved for shelter youth, we also heard stories in interviews where the play was too close and couldn't just be turned off like a television documentary:

> 1: I'm gonna say one thing that killed me in that play. When the actress said, "My dad used to hit me." I was like, "Fuck, I can't deal with this." I turned my head and closed my ears. Last time I saw my dad before I went to CAS [Children's Aid Society] he tried to strangle me, because I cleaned up my bathroom in New Year's. He was like, "Get the fuck out of here." He was screaming at me, choking me. I literally kicked him and ran into the bathroom and locked the door. And then Covenant House [a shelter for homeless youth], until I saw him in June. I was like, "fuck, I can't deal with this." My mom literally told me last week that "I'm going to take you out to the court." I don't need to be there. I'm like, "Why?" She's like, "Because I'm bringing you to the shit of CAS." I'm like, "Don't do this to me." Because I hate to bring stuff like

that up. I had CAS my whole life. My dad always beat the shit out of me. We always had that problem. I had to go to the hospital a bunch of times for that. I cannot sit here and listen. When it happens, I tried to cover my ears. I started crying, and the girl beside me started to cry. It made me cry even more. I really have bad problems with situations like this. It's not something that's easy for me to do it. I have really bad flashback problems. Hearing something like that triggers me so hard. I don't know what to do. I literally almost left the play, but then she stopped talking. So I calmed down.

(Post-Performance Interview with shelter youth,
Theatre Passe Muraille, October 29, 2010)

Many of the students we knew from our research at Middleview also revealed to us, in the post-performance interviews, that they currently live in a shelter or had at some point lived in a shelter for youth. This is not something we knew before we had interviewed them about the play. It certainly gave pause. Going to school has such a normalizing effect that even teachers who may know personal details about their students may not be aware of their fundamental living conditions. Most who shared their shelter stories with us also revealed that no one at school knew they lived in a shelter. Shashaqe, from Middleview, whom we knew very well from our time in her classroom, opened up to us about the impact of the play:

ANNE: So your poem is sort of related then to the play *The Middle Place*?
SHASHAQE: Yes. That's what pushed me to do it.
ANNE: OK, OK. That's really interesting that you've made that connection to the play.
SASHA: From that day, I started to write more poems about what you go through as a teenager, especially in Toronto, especially when you are not used to a certain kind of lifestyle at the centre of downtown. So it's kind of hard.
ANNE: Yes, and how much do you write. Do you write a poem every day, once a week?
SHASHAQE: I mostly write lyrics. I do it in a poem form, and then I make it into a song ... I do that regularly. It expresses what I feel. The part of my poem that really touch me is the part I say "I stand behind," because at that time I was unsure about so much stuff going on. I used to go into my room and cry. When I went there [the shelter], I couldn't do that.
ANNE: You had no privacy.

SHASHAQE: I couldn't have no privacy. I couldn't sleep, I couldn't smile. The things … I have so many different experiences. I had all kinds of stuff around me, so it's like really unbearable. So that was [the play] all summarizing everything living in the shelter. So I was like "Wow!" when I went to see the thing. "Wow, they are actually talking about what I'm going through." So I really enjoyed it.

ANNE: Do you share your songs and your poems with other people at the shelter, or no?

SHASHAQE: No. At the shelter … I'm in a transitional program – still the shelter – but you are more independent. I don't stay in my room. I also see it differently.

ANNE: Do you have your own room now?

SHASHAQE: Yes.

ANNE: OK. So you've got some privacy now. So you could even have quiet to write your poetry and sing your songs.

SHASHAQE: That's what I mostly do. And because I've done that, people have seen a lot about me. That's what I like to have people see about me. But I don't care.

ANNE: Yes.

SHASHAQE: All of this is just summarize from everything from front to the back.

ANNE: Yes, because that was one of the questions we were going to ask you: how does this monologue relate to your own life? What in your own life is living in this monologue?

SHASHAQE: Everything. Especially, like, the first part when I said "I watch myself each day as I stand in front of a mirror. It cures my eyes." I usually literally used to do that, because the person I saw in the mirror was the one the worker saw, or the kids that lived in the shelter didn't see. They saw a different person. I was like "Wow." They are like, "Oh, you are either too fat. You need long hair. You wear too much weave. You need to do this, you need to do that." I used to be afraid to go down the stairs. That's why I buy these big baggy T-shirts in the summer time, put on a jacket, because I was afraid of guys looking at me. It was just …

ANNE: So was a guy saying those comments?

SHASHAQE: Both. Guys and girls.

ANNE: OK. And they felt they have the right to judge you?

SHASHAQE: Yes. It was a whole judgmental thing. So it led to a lot of depression. I don't want to go to school. I tried to run away, I guess. You

know, find some other remedy. I guess praying and hoping. That's what
I thought about.

(Individual Interview, Shashaqe,
Middleview, January 21, 2011)

Again, Trinh's (1989) insights hold sway. She argues that each story is at
once a fragment and a whole – a whole within a whole – and that truth
exceeds meaning and exceeds measure. "It exceeds all regimes of truth"
(p. 123). And what resulted for many youth who came to see the play
was the experience of a shared affective language that came to matter
much more than mere facts.

Another student at Middleview, Asad, a refugee from Kenya, who
had used his actual refugee claim as his monologue to share with others in the class, felt inspired to do so because of seeing *The Middle Place*.
He explained:

> Um, my monologue, I never wrote the monologue 'cause I wrote it also
> to present about my case [as a refugee claimant], so it's like reflecting
> on my image back … explain about where I came from, it's like a dis-
> aster place where I came from … and it's like inside my body – so it's
> like I have decided to give it out. At first I didn't want to give it out
> to school, but … everyone [in this class] … shares … I decided let me
> share my, in my heart, to the school to share what people go through …
> so … sure, my monologue it's about my entire life, through ups and
> down to Canada.

(Individual Interview, Asad,
Middleview, January 11, 2011)

For his Verbatim performance, Asad chose, instead of interviewing others, to mine his own story. I learned in the interview with Asad that he
was the eldest of seven children and had come, alone, to Toronto via
Mombasa, Kenya:

> I am the only male, firstborn child in my family and, as such, I became the tar-
> get when corrupt police raided our home. They demanded bribes – up to five
> hundred dollars – and threatened to lock me up and deport me to Somalia.
>
> My father is basically a street hawker in Somalia and my mother
> makes traditional hats to make ends meet. They managed to save some
> money by selling my mother's jewellery, and with the help of two of

my father's brothers that work abroad, my parents secured enough dollars to pay an agent to bring me to Canada where I hope to be given refuge.

I cannot go back to Somalia as I fear for my life and I cannot return to Kenya where they will harass, imprison, or deport me back to Somalia on trumped up charges.

(Excerpt form Asad's monologue,
performed for his entire class)

Owing to the fact that we consistently asked in our interviews whether the play seemed "real," we learned that people responded to this question on multiple levels: "real" as in "lived" and resonant with one's own life, for those currently or having at one time lived in a shelter; a realistic acting style in which you forget the people onstage are actors; "real" because the script was developed from "real" interviews (the speech is more colloquial, authentic, and less crafted than a fictional account, with minimal theatrical artifice). One young woman shared that she had worked with an organization in Jamaica called J-FLAG (Jamaican Forum for Lesbian, All-Sexuals and Gays) where she was dealing with people who had found themselves homeless because of issues relating to their sexuality. When asked whether the show seemed a true reflection of reality, she replied:

1: This was right on point. It was right on point. Uh, at one point, I ... uh ... I actually couldn't take it. I couldn't take it in a sense where, um, I felt it, like everything they were saying, everything that was being acted out, down to the very teeth, was ... exactly how it is. It was becoming a little bit too much for my heart to handle. I was like, um, "OK, I can't do this. I can't do this." But I thought through it, and I watched, and um ... really, in a sense, it wakes you up. It wakes you to a reality that isn't pushed to the forefront. Like, even in the play, they told us, um, kids in the shelter are not considered a part of society. They are just not talked about, they are just not – that there is nothing much out there, right? So like when I came here, I was watching this, and I was hearing them talking about the drama. And me being in the shelter right now, seeing the drama every day, every day, every day, it hit a note, like (*snapping fingers three times*). Yeah.

(Shelter Youth Interview, Theatre
Passe Muraille, October 29, 2010)

Both inside and beyond the field of theatre, researchers have been paying close attention to the form of Verbatim. As our interviews revealed, and our own experience of *The Middle Place* taught us, Verbatim is a genre with tremendous pedagogical capacity. Derbyshire and Hodson (2008), in their article "Performing injustice: human rights and verbatim theatre" published in the journal *Law and Humanities,* argue that Verbatim theatre allows for the dissemination of information, arousal of compassion, and raising of consciousness in a way that is particular to the form and not possible in a formal, legalistic, and scholarly framework. The latter, they argue, cannot convey the full meaning of human rights, which the writers contend is a cultural process.

The genre of Verbatim was also taken up by our India collaborators. After sharing our experiences in Verbatim at Middleview, Dr. Sahni decided to experiment with the genre at Prerna. Soon after we arrived in Lucknow, the girls wanted to share with us a short documentary film they had created (http://www.youtube.com/watch?v=zQ7rcbgNdP4), which told the story of their exploration of Verbatim and its place in their pursuit of social justice and human rights for girls and women in India. Their performance, *Veerangna* (http://www.youtube.com/watch?v=jyhtljpUutM), began with interviews with women in their communities, their mothers, and grandmothers. They took these Verbatim interviews and began to create a play. They brought their play to the streets in Guari Village where they collected signatures from residents on their petition to stop domestic violence. They invited the local police to the performance, presented them with the petition, and used their presence to inform communities that domestic violence would not be tolerated by the police. They also used this experience to develop a helpline for women and girls, which they continue to support today. Researching the ubiquitous issue of domestic violence, using the Verbatim stories and interviews of their community in the production of their play, engaged the young women of Prerna in a powerful cultural process, helping them to disseminate important legal information, arouse compassion, and raise consciousness exactly as Derbyshire and Hodson (2008) describe above.

Verbatim theatre, as we experienced it in Toronto and in India, is indeed a powerful medium for exploring cultural processes. And, as it turned out for us, a genre that also helped us take a step back from our research, watch the youth of our study conduct research on their own (sub)cultural contexts, and in Toronto also afforded us the chance to have conversations with young and adult theatregoers on the heels of a powerful theatrical experience to see what further sense they make of the cultural representations of, and responsibilities we have for, young, marginalized people.

The Poetics and Politics of Literacy and Language

Brian Street (2001) writes: "literacy can no longer be addressed as a neutral technology as in the reductionist autonomous model, but is already a social and ideological practice involving fundamental aspects of epistemology, power and politics (p. 435)." Street makes very clear the political terrain we are traversing. The ideological model does not attempt to deny technical skills or the cognitive aspects of reading and writing but rather, he would argue, understands them "as they are encapsulated within cultural wholes and within structures of power" (p. 435).

It is the case that in the formal field of literacy, in-school and out-of-school literacy practices have been separated out, assuming the former to be more about reading and writing, while the latter uses digital and aesthetic practices to a greater extent. Although these divisions are often artificial in practice, the scholarly literature still seems to hold implicit hierarchies of literacy practices. I think the drama classroom, as a space, has the potential to be more pluralistic in its conceptions and practices of literacy, to break from the rationalist foundations of literacy. It is a world often also inspired by (digital) image, sound, and other sensory experiences rather than the more traditional literature prompts one might associate with formal literacy teaching. But what is also important in any discussion of literacy is to acknowledge the profoundly political nature of what it means to become literate.

Ms. C at Braeburn was particularly sensitive to the vast world of possible stimuli, a piece of music or a body movement, that might result in literacy engagement. Reflecting her dance background, Ms. C points to the body as the locus of learning and, like Merleau-Ponty (1945/1962 English edition), rejects the body-mind separation. In this sense, the aesthetics of drama draw from a wide range – physical, emotional, cognitive – of what some have termed learning styles, or multiple intelligences (Gardner 1993/2006). Ms. C would begin every class we observed with a physical and a vocal warm-up. She often invited students to lead such warm-ups with physical and vocal ideas of their own.

Literacies seem to multiply in drama. We saw this in the drawing from students in drama classrooms in Taiwan and in writing that became performance in classrooms at Middleview and Prerna. In the area of what I might term aesthetic literacy, Ms. C gave us good insight into her pedagogical choices:

> In general, a lot of them are definitely the kinaesthetic and the visual learner. What I love to do in designing lessons is bringing in at least two learning styles, for example, into one lesson. I would play music, and then I would have them with a crayon on a piece of paper feel the music and make a line of that colour, for example … Or you can do storytelling with music. You can play music and say "What story came to your mind when I played that? OK, now let's tell a story through the physical space, using that music." So like a dance/drama type of context.
>
> (Interview, Ms. C, Braeburn, February 6, 2009)

Literacy researcher Rowsell (2008) suggests the following:

> Art is a symbolic representation of one's internal world made external. Artefacts sediment moments as an expression of how an artist feels or thinks at a moment in time. Art and artistic creation thereby trace social practices used to express how one feels within a social context or social space. (p. 233)

Aesthetic literacy is about giving and receiving, about understanding and producing. This was most acutely observed when we watched the students work with metaphor. In rich drama work, abstract language or symbols are imbued with meaning-in-context. Ms. S at Middleview feels that students "get metaphor differently than they do in English class because the metaphors are applied to them." She's suggesting that students not only can see these abstract concepts being physicalized in space but they also simultaneously interpret what they are seeing. They have the space to discuss these multiple interpretations and come to new understandings. Literacy, then, is both about receiving (understanding) and producing (making new meanings) in the drama classroom.

There were also tremendous social literacies at play in the drama classrooms we observed. One of the interesting things about drama as a literacy practice is that students can receive immediate audience feedback and through this feedback begin to understand how effectively or ineffectively they have communicated their ideas. Ms. S puts it eloquently: "Writing in drama connects to our need as human beings to connect to each other." She reflects constantly on the drama space as a social practice and attempts to create a space of mutual listening, of immediacy, a space without hasty judgements:

> [Students are] more motivated to create this version of themselves through writing because they're sharing it with their peers, and they want to either connect or impress or reveal or flirt ... all those things that we talk about when we're doing scene work in drama, where you're always trying to do something with it. If you're just writing for your teacher, unless you have a real transference with your teacher, and you really want to impress them, it's not as engaging as an audience, as purposeful as an audience.
>
> (Interview, Ms. S, Middleview, February 3, 2009)

The students themselves also realize there is an intimate connection between the making and doing of drama and their social learning, the embodied and physical performance of drama and the collaborative nature of the discipline:

> MARBLES: Well, I think it's because you're interacting with people right? So in the end it's like, "hey, we have to do this skit together, that means we're gonna have to practice together, we're gonna have to talk to each other, we're gonna have to look at each other, we're probably gonna have to even touch each other, like why not be my friend? It just makes sense." And in the end you find that the people are good people and I think this year we just got lucky in that we got a whole pile of good people in one room and it was just like "yay!" and yeah. I think it's the interaction that helps us.
>
> (Focus Group Interview, Marbles, Twila,
Joe, Middleview, December 11, 2009)

For a long time, many drama researchers have been thinking about the role of writing in drama and the role of drama in writing. Cremin et al. (2006) argued that drama created a real context for writing, different from the current context of schooling that has disengaged young writers who "find little purpose in writing and write for their teachers and the curriculum, but not for themselves" (p. 273). Neelands, Booth, and

Ziegler (1993) were writing long ago about the ways in which drama creates the possibility for writers to embed their work in a context that has personal significance. With this, the motivation for writing changes drastically.

Critical literacies, a branch of social literacies, also figure prominently in many drama classrooms. Deborah Appleman's (2009) work talks about the importance of deconstruction in adolescents' learning. Drama engages the impulse to deconstruct because of the multiple layers of meaning often attached to abstract symbols. Appleman and others, such as Moje, Overby, Tysvaer, and Morris (2008), wrestle with what they understand as the complex world of adolescent learning. In my own view, it is both a learning and an unlearning at once. So much of young people's burgeoning social literacies require them to question or challenge their childhood understandings. This can be both an exciting and a disturbing experience. See below Sasha and Anne in an involved conversation about Sasha's experience of shadeism and body image in her home city of Dubai. She wrote about this in her monologue and then performed it for the school, with her class of peers acting as a collective in her scene. In the following excerpt, she is sharing with Anne her thoughts about the issues in her life and also about drama as a space to come to critical consciousness about such life experiences:

ANNE: So, how does your monologue then relate to your life?
SASHA: Well, when I, well it's a true story because it did happen when I was in Grade 5, actually, a girl did say that to me. Um, I studied in Dubai so it was an international school, so um, so mostly the fair people over there – like people from Russia or people from Europe, or people from, like, Egypt and Lebanon – people who are like really beautiful, and like really fair. So, um, it was always, they were always considered "pretty" like compared to people who were darker, like they had better features. Like, I always thought everyone was pretty, but, um, when you're little you're stupid or you act like that. So, that girl did come up and say that to me [that Sasha was ugly because she was dark-skinned], and, um, I felt really bad at that time because it was like a very exciting part of my life because I was, like, chosen to be up on stage, um, from the whole Grade 5, in front of the principal, in front of like seniors, in front of everybody. Uh, and she just comes up to me and says that because – well she just wanted to like – she was fooling around but it does hurt your ... and

then she goes and says oh I was just kidding." But I know you weren't kidding … like for the longest time I thought I wasn't pretty and like, it was just, it was weird. I don't even wanna talk about it, but it's fine, it's fine. But then, when you grow up you realize that these things don't matter and, uh, I decided to lose weight and I did, I kinda changed. Uh, ya.

ANNE: So do you think that there are issues of shadeism happening here in the school?

SASHA: In this school? I don't think so.

ANNE: Or do you think people are –

SASHA: I haven't met anyone like that but I think this happens usually in elementary school, when you're like young and you like to compare. Um, once you're in high school you learn about different cultures and you learn about different countries and you learn – you make friends with people from like – in Toronto there's diversity of people here. Like you can be friends with everybody else, so you know about their culture and where they come from and you start respecting them for that. So, I haven't seen anything like that here. Over there, yes in the East it's a problem, even in my own country it would be a problem, uh, because um, when – I don't know they just have very backwards thinkings and people like to compare their skin colours. 'Cause, I know, 'cause my mom had eight siblings and four of them are dark and four of them are White with green eyes and everything, and people usually like, when my grandfather, when he was younger he would like to take my mom and her sisters out and not take the rest of them out because he didn't want to be seen with them because he wanted to be seen with like his prettier and fairer kids because a lot of people made judgements outside. Some people think that if you're not fair you're not wealthy – it's weird, but that's how they think … Ya, and it's still there in the East, like in the southeastern countries it's still there. Ya, even though people are, like, no there's no race – it's still not racism, its like shadeism … you're like the same race. Like, why talk about colour right?

ANNE: Right, ya. But in your monologue you were also talking about, not only issues of skin colour and race, but you were also talking about body size, right?

SASHA: Yes because well, nobody wants – nobody thinks that like fat people or overweight people are – I wasn't overweight but I was fat, I was chubby and, um, ya, people don't consider you pretty, like, even in the media you see all of these skinny models and everyone wants to be like them and if anyone who looks like them and has a body like them is considered pretty. Because when you see them, you see skinny girls on TV, you see pretty girls on TV – you don't see fat, overweight dark girls on TV. So, people are like "oh, OK, so I see that person on TV, that is beautiful, that's how I want to be," and if anyone who does not look like that they're not pretty, or they're not considered beautiful.

ANNE: So, but your monologue you were really speaking forcefully against that, you know, you were addressing the audience right out there and saying you know, can you believe that this was happening.

SASHA: Because I know how it feels so I can see from the perspective of all of those people who have gone through that, and I know how that feels. I'm – I don't care about stuff like that anymore, it doesn't bother me, but what bothers me is why – don't do that to that person, right? Put yourself in that person's place. It just bothers me because, um, I wouldn't do that to someone and I wouldn't want other people to do that – that's it. I just, I don't like the whole concept of beauty – I don't like talking about it. Everyone is different; everyone is pretty in their own ways – judge them for how they are, like their personalities, like Rayne said that today in the class too. Judge them for their personality not for their body type, body structure, or face, or whatever.

ANNE: Ya, in my experience I find that easier said than done. That it's, you know, of course I totally believe what you say and then you know, in my own life I find it hard to hold on to that sometimes because we are too inundated with those images of what someone else is telling us is beautiful, and then how can you – so you need to …

SASHA: I maintain that at home, too, like if anyone, like my brother is really young so he goes around and says, "oh my god that's ugly, she's ugly! And she's fat!" And I'm like don't say that, so like, because I have experience, like I tell him not to do that and he sometimes listens to me and he like questions me why, and I tell him not to do that. Well, I can't make a difference in the world, I can try to, but I can't like all of a sudden I can't tell people to start looking at people in a different way, but, if someone tells that in front of me I can tell them that what you're saying is wrong and you shouldn't say that because it might hurt other people. How do I know that? I've experienced that, so.

(Individual Interview, Sasha,
Middleview, January 19, 2011)

Rayne, in Sasha's class, had a similar traumatic experience in her elementary school. She decided to write about it in her monologue and share it with her peers. I have elsewhere written about this power of drama to reframe our lives through art as we come to know the world and our sensuous responses to it. The distance provided by the form often affords other ways into a story that may otherwise be "too close to home" (Gallagher 2007, p. 161–2). This notion of distancing was well developed by drama in education pioneer Dorothy Heathcote, and has since been well explored by other practitioners and scholars (see O'Toole 2009; Eriksson 2011). Rayne explains:

RAYNE: I wanted to choose my personal monologue, just because that way it really shows who I am as a person. Being able to – even, my monologue – honestly, that was just a journal entry in my little book like it wasn't even something I literally thought of for school; it was something that one day I thought of and I had to write it down and I showed our teacher and she said it was perfect. So I'm like, this is great – my writing, my feelings and I can share it to other people. So it was a lot better than having something that was scripted kind of thing, so I think it was better.

ANNE: OK, so let's go to your monologue then. How does what you wrote about in your monologue really relate to your life?

RAYNE: Um, well my monologue is about school, mostly elementary school and the way coming to high school it was a big change just because you're younger and you're with different people and then coming here you meet new people; it's kinda changed my way in how I see other kids. Like, in my monologue I had a terrible experience in elementary school. So, coming to high school was a bit of a nice change because I wasn't surrounded by everybody all of the time. Like I have my main group that I hang out with and then I have classmates that I see every day, and that I just need to focus on people who better me and are friends to me. But, in elementary school you're with everyone and every day for however many years it is, and it was hard, and to be able to talk about that I think a lot of people kinda related just like if they had any similar situations.

ANNE: Yours, like Sasha's, was looking back into your past and choosing, well not one moment that was really hurtful but a series of moments that continued over years that were hurtful. What do you feel you got by performing it? What was it like to communicate that to an audience?

RAYNE: It felt empowering just because, I mean, the people that were mentioned in my monologue weren't there, but it's the fact that I got to say it out loud and be like, you know what, by doing this it's helping me grow as a person and be like, I don't wanna deal with that anymore, like I wanna leave that behind in my past and I'm going to move on with my life. I'm not going to let those people bother me anymore. And most of them I don't even talk to anymore so it's kinda like they're out of my life now and I've grown as a person, so it's a lot, it's – it helped to be able to say it. It was good.

(Individual Interview, Rayne,
Middleview, January 19, 2011)

In addition to the drama space, we also became aware of the ways in which our interview space was a place of critical literacy and collaborative knowledge building. Over the course of our research, we always tried to see the plays students were seeing, whether in the school or out in theatres. We wanted to be able to talk with them about their experiences of live theatre. On one occasion, we saw a play that we knew they were seeing, *Secrets of a Black Boy*. In the following excerpt, one can see how Marbles and I are critiquing the piece. It illustrates how these research interviews often became for us important literacy practices in themselves, where the researcher and the student critically engage from a shared experience. Making this kind of knowledge together, sharing questions and concerns, made for very fruitful interviews in which we could address issues of great relevance to our project through the experience of theatre. It was, as I suggested at the outset, a way in the back door or the side door, and one that was extremely useful by creating a kind of mutuality between us and our perspectives. This particular theatre production served as a catalyst into a much broader discussion about race, youth, and representation; ideas of particular interest to us as researchers of youth and drama:

MARBLES: I really enjoyed when we went to see *Secrets of a Black Boy*. That play just like really opened my eyes I guess and changed the way I thought about stuff and things, so I thought that was cool.
KATHLEEN: How? Tell me.
MARBLES: Just like stereotypes in general and like when we – well I guess this doesn't really have anything to do with drama class but we saw it in drama class so that was interesting.

KATHLEEN: Tell me a specific thing that it changed in your thinking.

MARBLES: Basically how people see me as a Black female.

KATHLEEN: How Black men in that play see Black females.

MARBLES: Yes, but I also realized a lot of it – it's not just Black men. A lot of –

KATHLEEN: A lot of people think that.

MARBLES: A lot of everyone.

KATHLEEN: So, OK, let's have a real conversation about this because I saw the play too. I was horrified by how Black women were depicted in that play. Were you horrified too?

MARBLES: Yes I was. I wasn't fully surprised because like a lot of it I saw, too, and I would agree with, but like, wow. I was just like, really? Really?

KATHLEEN: Me too. I thought – I kept thinking, "Am I thinking this because I"m a White woman? What place is that in my reaction to this." But oh my god, I kept thinking if I were a Black girl right now watching this I would be like, "holy crow, this is depressing!"

MARBLES: It is, it is. It almost made me cry. I was like, no! It was really – yeah, I had to think about that for a bit before I shared my opinions with people because I was just like, "what do I say to this?" Because like, it's true, but this is so bad.

KATHLEEN: So what did it make you think about Black men or Black boys? What do you come away with if that's the stuff that they're carrying around and thinking.

MARBLES: Well those guys? Because like, I do have some Black male friends who we are just friends so they talk to me about their relationships and stuff so they're just no different than any other sleazy boy or teenaged boy.

KATHLEEN: So not like those boys in the play.

MARBLES: So not like those boys but those boys in the play, the one was really sweet who had – he had his girlfriend and he was like, "I just want her to know" like, "I just want to know I'm loved" and blah blah blah. And just like, you know, the sweet sappy stuff. Which is cool because, you know like, you don't get a lot of that ever. So …

KATHLEEN: Like he wanted to be needed. That guy, right?

MARBLES: Yeah, he wanted to be needed and I'm like, "yeah, that makes sense." He wanted a good relationship and whatever and I was like, "yeah, that makes sense."

KATHLEEN: Except that he wanted to go to a White woman to get it.

MARBLES: Yeah, I was like – but then again I understand, because like, he went through a lot of Black women looking for that and he never got it. But then when he said that one thing like, "whenever I see a Black woman, it's like, why can't I love you." It's like, you can't just classify all Black women just because like five of them –

KATHLEEN: Dumped you.

MARBLES: Yeah. And I'm pretty sure if that was a true story, which it probably is, he found all those Black women around the same clan … So, you know, boys are just stupid.

(Individual Interview, Marbles, Middleview, January 13, 2010)

Our conversation traversed the terrain of race, racial stereotyping, gender, dreams and desires. Sharing experiences of spectatorship allowed us to occupy a space of critique that was enormously interesting and revealing of the ways in which critical forms of literacy engagement are an effective part of drama engagement.

While all the more traditional literacy skills – writing, reading, listening, and speaking – are also at play in the drama classroom, there remains a large body of research examining the relationship between drama and oral literacy. Ms. S echoes much of this research when she explains what an English Language Learner (ELL) shared with her:

I had a student from the Ukraine who was in my Grade 10 drama class, which was an incredibly unproductive class in terms of the work that we did. But the reason it was so unproductive was because the students just talked constantly to each other. It was really hard to interrupt that ... The three ELLs, who were very motivated to learn in that class, ended up becoming engaged in these conversations... We did do work, but a lot of it was conversation. At the end of the class, I said "I'm sorry we didn't get more done in the class," and he said, "I feel a lot more confident speaking with other people." I think sometimes they see native speakers struggling with language as well, in drama, and it demystifies that fluency that you feel like you need to have.

(Interview, Ms. S, Middleview, February 3, 2009)

Ms. S offers a fresh insight here. The spontaneous nature of conversation in drama means that language can be halting, imperfect. And the benefit to ELLs to see the hesitation of native speakers or the general challenge of the well-articulated idea is significant. With a forgiving and flexible pedagogy, drama has the potential to make people feel more at peace with their humanity and their failings. There is very little in school that accomplishes this kind of life lesson.

There is a further aspect of the drama classroom that Juson, another English Language Learner, shared with us: this sense of the flexibility of traditional, hierarchical power dynamics or the uncertainty about which way the flow of teaching and learning is taking at any given moment:

> Well, I don't really do much in the other classes, because you don't have the opportunity to do that. Like in other courses you are just learning what the teacher is teaching you. But in drama class it's kind of like the teacher is learning from you.
>
> (Individual Interview, Juson, Middleview, January 14, 2011)

The relationship between traditional understandings of literacy and what I have been calling here "social literacies" is perhaps most acute for English Language Learners. Note Joe's sense of himself in the social context as a learner in the following exchange:

ANNE: Have you had any moments in this Drama class where any particular moment was difficult for you? That sort of challenged you?

JOE: Yeah.

ANNE: Can you talk a little bit about it?

JOE: Every moment that – well, this is a challenge now.

ANNE: The interview?

JOE: My English is not that good.

ANNE: I think you're doing great.

JOE: Everybody says the same but I don't feel like my English is enough good or good enough.

ANNE: Good enough.

JOE: Yeah. And the first moment when I arrived here I was like, "OK. My first moment in a school in Canada." So a lot of people were like – and I remember, it was a warm-up exercise, and I thought, "OK, no one here speak my language, and Drama is about talk," well part of it. OK, Miss S said – I don't remember because at that moment I couldn't understand. I just remember, "you just sit there and join us later." And I sat here, right here where I am now, and I stare at everybody and I was so afraid like, "oh my god what am I doing here?" I don't know, it was really, really crazy. And when the first moment after that, the first day Ms. S wrote a lot of things on the board, like the rules of Drama class. And she said, "You have to participate." I said, "OK, I don't think I can yet." That was what I thought. But I think I thought it speaking. And Ms. S stared at me and said, "Well, you already spoke English" but it's not the same saying "I think I can't," and there are a lot of things that I can't. Yeah, a lot of moments like that.

ANNE: When you first spoke, that must have been a big moment for you.

JOE: Well, I have spoken like –

ANNE: Oh, you did.

JOE: But little things. I haven't improved my English very well since I arrived here but I feel more confident a little bit. Just that. I am used to hear and to speak and a little to think in English and that's very important because I was out of practise.

ANNE: Do you think drama has helped you become more confident with speaking or [is it] just time?

JOE: Yeah, everybody here is awesome because – I have to say like nobody told me like, "Oh my god, you have to shut up. If you don't know, just shut up." It would happen in Mexico.

ANNE: Do they? They're impatient with people who don't speak the language?

JOE: Well, if someone can bully you – if someone can like put you down, they do.

ANNE: To get more status from themselves?

JOE: Yeah. More status.

(Individual Interview, Joe,
Middleview, December 11, 2010)

Joe has no objective measures of his literacy, no real sense of whether he has improved. But he has the feeling that he is more confident. He has the belief that his fear of taking risks, and to risk failing, has less of a hold on his participation. He has a sense that his learning has some flexibility because of the social group.

Juson, who emigrated from China offered the following insights:

BURCU: And why do you take drama?

JUSON: First, like, I just like it. Actually, like, drama class is very fun. You have more opportunity to show your feelings because, yeah, I just like drama.

BURCU: You get to share your own feelings.

JUSON: Yeah. Well also another reason, you speak a lot in drama class because there is no Chinese. You practise more your speaking skills. I feel like my speaking skills improve in drama class because we are doing monologues and presentations.

BURCU: Because you are performing and doing presentations that helps with your speaking skills. You don't get that opportunity a lot in the other classes that you take or in life outside the classroom?

JUSON: Not really because, as you can see, there is a lot of Chinese people everywhere in this school. Including in my other classes. Even if you want to speak English with them it's like "why are you doing this, you are Chinese; speak Mandarin it's more easy to communicate." But I am here to learn English so I choose drama.

(Individual Interview, Juson,
Middleview, January 14, 2011)

Researchers who study drama and language learning also signal oral proficiency in foreign language learning through drama. Researchers Kao, Carkin, and Hsu (2011) offer that drama activities facilitate more interactive questioning and, consistent with our interviews with English Language Learners, drama offers more "natural interactions" than most other language learning contexts.

We came to understand the social literacies we encountered in India in two different ways. There were the social literacies that led to critical understanding for the students and the social literacies that were more revealing of the relational aspects of their learning. Critical dialogues were, as I have suggested, a crucial part of the everyday pedagogy in their classrooms. In their group discussions, terms like "rights," "social responsibility," "democracy," "liberty," "equality," and "fraternity" frequently surfaced. But what Prerna also taught us is that critical literacy work sits alongside affective non-rational work in very important ways. Although the "life stories" we witnessed in the drama work and in the digital stories were often harrowing, there was also a great sense of pleasure and even humour present in much of that work. This is consistent with some critical literacy scholars, like Hillary Janks, who in her 2010 book, *Literacy and Power*, considers how the rationalist foundations of critical literacy tend to exclude the affective ways of working "beyond reason," the pleasure and play, desire and unconscious that we observed so consistently with the Prerna students. Janks insists that literacy work can be both serious and playful and implores us to "teach it with a subversive attitude, self-irony, and a sense of humour" (p. 224).

The Prerna students also engaged in critical activities in the community, outside of the classroom. The in-school literacies and out-of-school literacies were more fluid. They interviewed the women in their community about marriage and prepared a documentary from the interviews that focused on the issues of child marriage, patriarchy, and violence against women. They also organized a signature campaign against domestic violence.

Critical dialogues were so much a part of everyday life in the school that even during the formal interviews that we conducted with the students, there were a number of moments when a respondent would engage in a critical dialogue with the teacher or other students present as ideas and issues arose. One of these moments was when a student was musing aloud that it is really difficult for her to think about marrying whom she chooses, and when she chooses to marry, because her uncle and aunt wanted her to marry someone from the village and to share the wedding date with her cousin in order to save money. Dr. Sahni jumped in and engaged her in a critical dialogue, challenging the rights of relatives who were not even there to support, feed, or clothe her and her siblings when her mother was dying. The following passage shows the animated dialogue that unfolded in Hindi during our focus group interview.

DR. SAHNI: She was saying that, you know, they really have no right to be asking when should we be getting married. "No, no we should do it now, your cousin is getting married, it would be much cheaper to do that," so says her mother's brother's wife. So we could get you married at the same time because it would save costs. And she says, "no, I'm not ready, not just now." But they say, in any case, she can't marry anyone from Lucknow because they will never accept that. So I said you're going to marry someone from the village, is it? So then you're done with your dreams of laptops, etc., just forget it, OK? So she says that the reason it should be the village is that they would share the culture. So I say, the man has to be a bit educated. And I say, yeah, like Grade 5 would be good, right? They say, no no, 12th grade. And then I ask if there are educated men in the village? She's not thinking. So I was trying to point out that hey, they have absolutely no right to ask you, they've done nothing for her – her dad still has some right. He raised her for so long, so I say, "but I don't see that this uncle and aunt have any right to ask you any darn thing. Don't get caught up in that trap at all." She says, all of my relatives are in the Yuka territory so you'd better marry someone there. So I told her, I think you are also a little scared about making your own decision, right? Maybe you'll choose wrong. And she says yeah. And I wonder how they have chosen right for anybody, and second, when they make an asinine suggestion like your cousin is getting married and so should you because it will save costs – I was trying to point out that nobody will care as much for you as you do. Don't even get caught up in that.

(Focus Group Interview, Sunita, Laxmi, Kushboo, Moni, Preeti, Poonam, Prerna, January 21, 2012)

Alan Luke, a central figure in the world of critical literacy, makes explicit the "transformation" such a critical approach is seeking. In 2009, he and his colleagues wrote:

Following Freire, critical literacies entail not only a reading of the word, but also a "reading of the world," processes of naming and renaming the world, seeing its patterns, designs and complexities (Mey 1986), and developing the capacity to rewrite, redesign, and reshape it in communities' interests (New London Group 1996). Language, text, and their discourse structures are more than neutral or factual representations of the world. Texts are a means for construing, shaping and reshaping worlds in particular normative directions with identifiable ideological interests and consequences for individuals and communities. Accordingly, critical literacy models have an explicit aim of developing useful, powerful mastery of texts to transform lived social relations and material conditions. (p. 9)

Like Shashaqe at Middleview, the girls at Prerna also engaged in the writing of poetry. I think poetry affords the possibility of heightened language and that language somehow mirrors the extreme emotions they experience. The reading and writing at Prerna is informed, as is the case at Middleview, by their "real-life" experiences. Students write poems and monologues about their own experiences. When the Prerna girls were sharing some of the poetry they wrote in Urdu and Hindi with us, one student Sonita said, "When I write my feelings, I feel lighter." This was interesting because it was exactly the expression shared with us by Puppy Love at Middleview, who'd taken to writing poetry to work through some of his life challenges. The tremendous impact of the digital short (life) stories they created at Prerna, along with the blogging they did with other students across the United States sounded astonishingly familiar to us, echoing clearly the creative writing experiences of students at Middleview. Urcaihi, a student at Prerna, said, "I feel as though I'd shed a very, very heavy burden," because she was able to share the story with many students in other parts of the world. Of her digital story, she said: "I keep wanting to look at it again and again."

What the students in Toronto and the students in Lucknow yearned for was an intimacy between their life experiences and their artistic forms of expression. First, articulating difficult experiences – through language and form – then communicating these to an audience remained the two fundamental drivers of the rich literacy experiences we were witness to in classrooms. Using a range of stimuli and sensory experiences as catalyst for creative expression, and taking a critical perspective on their own lives and their world, brought together the often compartmentalized critical, social, artistic, and academic forms of literacy over which young people desire mastery. Being an interpreter and a producer of meanings through a variety of expressive forms was a social and ideological practice that opened out into the world so that old wounds transformed into new forms of political engagement. The value of performative writing for young people in Toronto and Lucknow, that is, writing undertaken with the distinct desire for its performance for others, was undeniable.

Teacher Discourses: The Pedagogical Dance

Here then is my concluding thought on the question of teacher education as uneven development. If teacher education is to matter, we are obligated to create conditions for learning to live in this time that is out of joint, in discontinuous time and the disjuncture of self/other relations. This means taking responsibility for the discomforting fact of our dependency on the unknown. If we are responsible for a world we have not made, if we have the strange work of trying to understand the minds of others and still keep our own mind, if we have the work of welcoming what cannot be understood and the responsibility for a hospitality without reserve, if we confront a world that is wearing out, if we must work from all this ignorance, we may then begin our teacher education. It will be a teacher education as an unfinished project, more fragile than we ever imagined, now lost and found at the point where our fact of dependency develops within the promise of responsibility. (Britzman 2007, p. 12)

In our research, we often found ourselves wrapped up in the words spoken by teachers about teaching and about their relationships to students. We also listened carefully to students' talk about their teachers. Discussions about "the social," "the artistic," and "the pedagogical" careened into one another as a kind of dance or set of movements that could not escape one another. When teachers talk about their "professional" work, discourses about learning styles, outcomes, and reflexivity emerge, but when teachers talk about their lives in schools – with students – ideas about working environments, stress, health, and isolation begin to pervade the discussions. Both official discourses (teacher as craftsperson, reflexive practitioner) and popular ones (teacher as helper, guide, inspiration, see Moore 2004) set in motion our effusive deliberations about what it means to teach and learn in socio-economically marginalized schools.

"Helping" and "caring" are feelings and actions that were frequently articulated by all the teachers we worked with. Ms. S, in an early interview, put it very honestly:

> I think at age 24 or 25 I felt a really strong desire to be helpful in the world, and I was feeling increasingly dissatisfied with academia because I was doing a master's in English at the time and I just felt like that world was only referencing itself all the time. And there wasn't any connection to the real world. And I really wanted to have – I had been in school for so long, and then I was going back to school essentially, but I really wanted to broaden my own horizons and perspectives on people, and to learn from the world, and be in a profession where I could be in touch with people who were not like me ... And also to be helpful in any kind of way that I could be. Because I feel good about myself if I'm helping others.
> (Interview, Ms. S, Middleview, December 3, 2008)

How we observed this play out in Ms. S's classrooms was unusual. She often wanted to help but rather than construe help as an intervention in a life without logic, she helped by listening carefully to her students and never assuming she knew better than they did. Our fieldnotes are replete with examples of her listening with care and learning alongside her students. She behaved as though she thought she had something to learn from them and something to learn about herself through the openness she cultivated in her classroom. This is the kind of pedagogy that Helen Nicholson (2005) calls "performative" in that it invites the worlds of the students into the work so that the world is not peripheral but central. It's an engagement with the world through the work rather than a pedagogy that shuns the world in order to meet a set curriculum. Leo Tolstoy, in 1860, in an essay on "Popular Education," wrote:

> Every curriculum ought to be a response to answers posed by life, whereas school does not only not come up with questions, but does not even answer those posed by life. School eternally answers the same questions posed by humankind several centuries ago rather than those questions springing from the intellect of the child – the educator is not interested by these (in Blaisdell and Edgar 2000, p. 175).

A believer in the pedagogical imagination, Tolstoy saw teaching as an art and a pedagogical spirit of experimentation its birthright. From our observation, the worlds lived by the students constituted the curriculum and Ms. S's pedagogy aimed to facilitate discussions about those worlds regularly. Most students, in most schools, most of the time, have no expectation of being heard, and so they speak as though they will not be heard, other than in their role or identity as student (good student, bad student, failing student, passing student). But in Ms. S's class, all bets were off. It was both thrilling and dangerous. When I asked Ms. S about this sense of vulnerability as a teacher she connected it to the vulnerability and risk of writing alongside her students:

> MS. S: There has to be some sort of vulnerability or risk that you take as a teacher. I mean sometimes it is to write with them and to read what you write, and I have done it with them before. I think it is important to be in that position where – if you are asking them to constantly create and show their work and share their work, you have to do that too … It's nice to show students that you struggle with language, too, that you struggle to find the words. If they can see that, it's also very helpful.
> (Interview, Ms. S, Middleview, December 3, 2008)

Ms. S's pedagogy and classroom practices made tangible for us Ellsworth's (2005) eloquent description of this dynamic and reciprocal sociality of classrooms:

> … audacious learning selves in the making will risk relationality with the social body that surrounds them, but only if their emergence is met by a particular look on the teacher's face: the look of a teacher in the midst of the experience of her own learning self in the making. (p. 175)

The other aspect of Ms. S's pedagogy was her unrelenting reflexivity, not simply in the context of our interviews, but with herself and her students. She faces failure and challenges with an uncommon candour. In talking with us about a particular group of students in her class, she offers:

> I'm reflecting on my experience in that class. And I feel a moment when I might have gone wrong is this: At a certain point they were all attacking certain kids in the class – the ones who wanted to learn were attacking the ones who didn't want to learn. They were pretty mean. I felt protective of those kids who didn't want to learn. I asked the ones who did want to learn and were attacking them, to be more patient and more polite. In the end, I think that kind of backfired because rather than using that opportunity to then question, in a polite way, those kids and say "Why are you disrupting on a constant basis?" it really gave a lot of power to those kids who were disruptive and sabotaging. The sabotaging kids are really the most vulnerable in a lot of ways. They're masking their insecurities; they don't want to be real. I really feel like, there, I had a chance to turn things around and I kind of screwed it up a bit, because I automatically went to protect them.
>
> (Interview, Ms. S, Middleview, December 3, 2008)

Protecting, helping, and caring – the acknowledgement of affective responses for "the other" – feature in much of the talk about teaching in schools, about "the profession," and about the hope that teachers and students have for more humane social relations and more "success" in learning and life outcomes for students with socio-economic barriers. Although hope is often associated with future prospects, Sara Ahmed (2010) is careful to differentiate it from wishful thinking and states that it guides action in the present. What was especially striking about how Ms. S "helped" her students in the present moment was that this pedagogical orientation could not be separated from her work as an artist. Different teachers perform the role of artist differently as they also differ in the extent to which they see their work as political. The "helping" that Ms. S talks about cannot really be separated from her work as an artist in the classroom. As much as she is an advocate for her students, she is also a fellow artist, helping the students with their play but also participating in its creation. In struggling with her writing and experiencing the vulnerability of bringing it to the class, she shares in the risky aesthetic work alongside the students. Though she has more experience, education, and cultural capital, her artistic and pedagogical struggles are not unlike those encountered by the students. The risks are different, to be sure, but there is something at risk for both teacher and students. It is through the art making that the boundaries between student and teacher become more permeable with a shared commitment to collaborative knowledge building and creative expression. Artistic "helping" then is different from advocacy, and it can surface in the drama classroom at moments of shared vision, shared risk, and shared aesthetic pleasure and despair. Theatre making is a social process, embedded with power relationships. But it is also, as we often witnessed, a place where social relations might be realigned, however temporarily.

How students come to understand how they are "being helped" is also important. In 1947, Percival M. Symonds wrote about the personality of the teacher referring to testimonies of both students and adults. He quotes from previous studies that call into question the teacher's exclusive focus on knowledge and the ability to teach by also looking at "friendliness, helpfulness and appreciation of the child's difficulties" (p. 653). In the following focus group interview, we hear a student nuance this pervasive and long-standing discourse of help, to understand it slightly differently:

ANNE: So you're saying it's the teacher that really helps you engage but also the subject matter itself.

TAYLOR: I strongly believe … it's the teacher.

GOKU: Yeah. It's all about the teacher. Like –

ANNE: So tell me about that. Tell me what you think is great teaching.

GOKU: People who actually care. Like if you're willing to, not even go the extra mile, just like Mr. P is the kind of guy who like he won't lie, he won't really like help you but he'll do things to make sure you have a better chance. Like OK, if you handed in – we do like projects and tests on civilizations at a time so we finished Egypt last time. And it's been like two months since we finished Mesopotamia but we haven't gotten our tests back or our projects because he wants to give people time to hand them in. And what he does with you is he'll write up a page or two to study, and he'll do it in class with you so then you'll get like one class every three weeks just before a big test. And he'll give us the whole day to study and he'll give us the answers to study just as if we got our tests back, but it still gives people the chance to hand in their projects and stuff. They'll probably get less marks but he still gives them the chance.

ANNE: A lot of chances and flexibility.

(Middleview, Focus Group Discussion,
Taylor, Richard, Goku, January 5, 2010)

Goku identifies how important it is for the teacher to care about the students with an unsentimental description of his history teacher: "Mr. P is the kind of guy who – like he won't lie, he won't really like help you but he'll do things to make sure you have a better chance." The student doesn't feel "helped," rather that someone who "cares" gives him a "better chance," a subtle but important distinction. Brian Massumi (2002), drawing on the works of Deleuze and Guattari, suggests that hope springs from how we connect with, and care for, others. Isabelle Stengers (2002), too, believes that we become more hopeful when we find solidarity and connection to others. Richard, in the same focus group, also underscores one of the most highly valued "characteristics" of a teacher by students:

> ANNE: So what is a good teacher in your mind?
> RICHARD: A good teacher in my mind is somebody that's – would give you good chances.
> ANNE: Yeah.
> RICHARD: And is fair to each student. You know? Like, I believe that each student deserves an equal chance – an equal opportunity to get what they want. And the teacher can only do that to a certain extent so.
> ANNE: So fairness.
> RICHARD: Yeah, fairness is a big quality that a teacher must have.
> (Focus Group Discussion, Taylor, Richard, Goku, Middleview, January 5, 2010)

In the above segment, we hear the values of equality and fairness oft repeated by students in many of our discussions that focused on the qualities of a good teacher. The teacher's enjoyment of teaching and their passion for their subject was also outlined in Symonds's early article of student testimonials, some 60 years ago. For Ms. S, the intersection of young people making art was the necessary alchemy for her engagement:

> I find it's very alive with young people. And really creative. I prefer to work theatrically with teenagers than with adults, because teenagers are so interesting. They're coming into their own power. So giving them these opportunities to speak their power, or to find their voice or whatever, it's really thrilling. And the work that I can create theatrically with youth is so interesting. Yeah. And also because the students are so diverse and they come from such interesting backgrounds, the work is really, really

interesting. I find that the theatre world, in the art world, or the indie art world or whatever, there's a lot of the same. So it's not as interesting, it's not as rich. And I don't know how creatively engaged I would be in that environment

(Interview, Ms. S, Middleview, December 3, 2008)

Across the disciplines of education, sociology, philosophy, drama, and health, "hope" and "care" as concepts are widely studied, both quantitatively and qualitatively. From the health literature, Yarcheski, Mahon, and Yarcheski's (2001) study on social support and well-being in adolescents, conducted in a middle school, developed "the Hopefulness Scale for Adolescents," a 24-item visual analogue scale (p. 168). In their study, it allowed them to demonstrate, quantitatively, how social support leads to hopefulness, which, in turn, leads to well-being.

Complementing this quantitative study is a qualitative dissertation on hope among educators. Rose (2007) is careful not to address hope as a personal or individual trait, but through Systems Theory connects it to larger social forces. Particularly relevant to our study, she concludes that one of the foundational needs for a study of hope is "its potential influence on dissipating despair in education so that it is possible to address the broader social conditions that create and perpetuate despair in the first place" (p. 37). Henry Giroux (2006), also concerned with the broader historical and social conditions of youth, in his series of essays, *Politics after Hope,* holds Barack Obama – who was himself using the idea of hope to galvanize a dispirited nation – accountable for the absence of a meaningful focus on issues concerning youth, education, and how this relates to a failing democracy. He describes a "deadening silence from liberals and progressives about crucial issues such as the relationship between democracy and the fate of youth, the persistence of racism, and the central importance of education in providing formative culture for responsibility, engaged citizenship, and public values" (p. x).

Through its connection to democratic life, we are being urged to think of modes of hope and hoping differently (see Hage, 2002). Philosopher Richard Rorty (1999) coins the term, "social hopes,", that is, "hopes for global, cosmopolitan, democratic, egalitarian, classless, casteless society" (p. xii). As a Deweyan pragmatist, the highest good, he argues, is to "trust, cooperate with other people, and in particular, to work together so as to improve the future" (p. xiii). He explicitly ties hope to democracy and suggests that students following a Deweyan education would "acquire

an image of themselves as heirs to a tradition of increasing liberty and ris-
ing hope" (p.121). Philosopher Alphonso Lingis (2002) offers an insight
particularly relevant to the population of our study, that is, students who
have struggled socially and academically in schools because of disadvantages and barriers they face. Lingis claims that "hope" "... doesn't come
out of what went before but *in spite of* what went before" (p. 24).

Scottish education scholars, Hedge and Mackenzie (2012) both acknowledge and critique Noddings's (1984) famous claim that education's purpose is to create caring people. Rather than explicitly identifying caring
acts, they are interested in how emotional sensibilities are cultivated in
classrooms in order to enable care. American Verbatim theatre artist Anna
Deavere Smith (2003) writes, "The theory of the play is that an actor has the
ability to walk in another person's "words," and therefore in their hearts"
(p. 7). Theatre educator, Baz Kershaw (1998), in his article "Pathologies
of Hope in Drama and Theatre" ponders whether drama can produce a
growing number of "carriers of hope" (p. 67) and argues that drama has
the potential to create "currently unimaginable forms of association and
action," what he calls "the *transcendent* sense of the radical" (p. 69).

Helen Cahill (2011), a drama researcher in Australia, attempted to put
this idea to work by bringing in Grade 9 and 10 students to teach her
teacher candidates how to think about the theory behind their practices,
arguing that "we must also uncobble those mind maps that prescribe
and limit what is possible for ourselves and others" (p. 18). Bringing to
her analysis Butler's notion of the necessity of fantasy in imagining differently, she placed the students as coaches so that the pre-service teachers could consider whether or not they can imagine a "learning partner-
ship" (p. 19). Cahill's discussion of discourse is not abstract but comes
through the drama, or as she says, "[the student teachers] get to encounter the construct at an experiential level" (p. 23). Drawing on Foucault,
she suggests that preconceived notions of the teacher are inherited and
that teachers can become "complicit in their own governance" (p. 18).

Sometimes, "good teachers" simply need to resist the orthodoxies
and conventional wisdom of "good teaching," to reject the official discourses and, more and more, to challenge the neoliberal imperatives of
efficiency and expediency:

MS. S: Yeah, and sometimes you're managing a class so much that you're not
allowing for any single moment to – I mean, I think there's a lot of great drama
teachers out there that just keep students busy constantly, so that there is never
a moment of um ... potential like, you know I think it's in the moments where
there's confusion or uncertainty that some of that stuff starts, their anxieties

and their issues start to come out. So, if you're always managing your class so that there is no room for uncertainty and confusion then it's ... you don't get as much, or as many [student] problems maybe?

KATHLEEN: Opening the doors to uncertainty and confusion, what does that do to the art making or the theatre making?

MS. S: It can, you know, it can be productive because from those moments where you're not certain can come new ideas and you know ... fresh understandings. But, it can also just descend into chaos, and not work out very well at all.

KATHLEEN: It's a risk you take.

MS. S: It is a risk you take! You know, doing collective creations I am experiencing that all the time. And there's – I haven't figured out the perfect formula for structuring it, there's no um ... there's no room for uncertainty and confusion. And the dynamics do emerge then, but that's real life. Like, that's ... life is, you're in relationships with people [in classrooms], you know, you're not – you can't structure relationships with your family so that everything goes perfectly, all the time.

KATHLEEN: And different groups create different cultures.

MS. S: Yes!

(Interview, Ms. S, Middleview, March 2, 2011)

Resonant here is the Royal Shakespeare Company's approach to ensemble work. One actor differentiates between the security needed to work effectively in an ensemble and the implied danger of a working environment that has become too comfortable:

> Our ever-growing trust enables us to experiment, improvise and rework on the floor with an astonishing freedom and confidence. This ensemble is a secure environment without ever being a comfort zone. All of us are continually challenging ourselves and being inspired by those around us to reach new levels in all aspects of our work. (in Neelands 2009, p. 183)

When we talk some more about the epidemic of busyness in schools, Ms. S explains further:

MS. S: I think I am trying to like, just work on being more present and actually tuning in and noticing things about students, and listening to them a little more. Because, it's really hard to listen as a teacher because they're – you've got so many of them in the room and then they're all talking at once ... and ... so how do you ...

KATHLEEN: And you do it so well. I mean, you listen so well.

MS. S: But you have to. And, I don't do this well all the time, but you have to stop and just sort of feel the room sometimes. And feel the vibe in the room, like, every day is different and notice what's going on.

(Interview, Ms. S, Middleview, March 2, 2011)

The discourse of helping was also pervasive in India. The teachers at Prerna are unapologetic about how they help and the extent to which they care. After finishing her PhD in psychology, Ms. K found that there were no jobs at the university level. She had not intended to become a teacher, and her own experiences with her teachers as a young person had not motivated her to become one. She explained to us that her work doing marriage-counselling post-PhD opened her eyes to the extent to which domestic violence was prevalent. She started by teaching gender awareness and then became a full-time teacher at Prerna. Bringing her counselling background to her teaching, she describes the student-teacher relationship as one of care, love, and safety. This is teacher as helper and loving ally, but also as a deep listener, problem solver, and one who names injustices. She seems to advocate for teaching as a kind of friendship that creates a "home" but is also the place of broader skill development to enable more equitable lives. This is a pedagogical and social space of sanctuary, holding an expectation of achievement and social amelioration.

Avoiding the framework of "charity" for her work, she recognizes that class and poverty are realities in the girls' lives and she works, through education, to equip her students to negotiate a life that is not determined by these circumstances of birth:

MS. K: You see, I think charity is for a few strata of the society, who can afford really to do that charitable work because of strong financial status. But if you consider me in the profession of teacher, probably through money, I may not be able to help. But if I'm able to give them a good understanding, a good educational base, a feeling of independence, I'm able to give them that care, the love, with which they can stand out in the society, and make an identity for themselves, and then work for others and so that will be more than charity probably.

(Interview, Ms. K, Prerna, January 20, 2012)

Like Ms. S, Ms. K intentionally makes room for the world outside school, knowing that these circumstances are challenging in the extreme and that unless time and effort are spent on these problems, the girls will not move beyond "their tears." They will never feel strengthened by their anger, gaining a capacity to resist and act in solidarity with other girls and the women in their broader community.

> MS. K: For sure, initially I remember that these girls would cry that "my mother said this, my father said this, I do not have this," but you know gradually, it took some time for them, they stopped crying and they want to show their aggression of why that is happening to me. So that feeling of catharsis was there in them, that they were able to speak to us. And when they spoke to each other or they told me "Auntie, this is the problem," or "this child is facing this problem," so we all together were able to give some sort of solution to that problem.
>
> (Interview, Ms. K, Prerna, January 20, 2012)

But unlike Ms. S who spoke often to us about her sense of isolation in the school, Ms. K felt tremendous community with other teachers. The "universe of care" that is cultivated at the school does not reside only between teachers and students but also among the teachers themselves. Ms. K says that they are given leeway to teach in their own way, but that they share knowledge regarding resources in the community that might best serve the girls. The teachers feel respected as professionals, though it is also understood that knowledge is not to be kept to oneself but shared with the community. Interestingly, the teachers are given freedom in the way that they teach, but Ms. K stresses that they share a common purpose. Through retreats and travel together, she says, they develop a cohesive group and strong sense of shared goals.

> MS. K: I think that feeling of oneness, that cohesive feeling that we are all one in the same profession and that we need to work for these children together. It's a feeling that we have the same target, we have the same goal. So that is very important.
>
> (Interview, Ms. K, Prerna, January 20, 2012)

The teachers we met in India, along with our extensive discussions with Ms. S in Toronto, helped us to better appreciate Derrida's (1994) notion of "hospitality without reserve" explored by Britzman (2007) in the opening thought of this chapter. Both Derrida and Britzman, along with Arendt, argue for a commitment to knowing the world in order to take responsibility for it. It is inspiring to be in the company of teachers who heed this call, despite the institutional exigencies and great social challenges they encounter.

Hope is at the centre of the practices we witnessed, but not a naive hope that unwittingly reinforces the status quo. It's a hope that by working together actions could change material lives. No one, in my view, has better articulated this paradoxical hope-in-action than Paulo Freire (1992), who wrote:

> The idea that hope alone will transform the world, and action undertaken in that kind of naiveté, is an excellent route to hopelessness, pessimism, and fatalism. But the attempt to do without hope, in the struggle to improve the world, as if that struggle could be reduced to calculated acts alone, or a purely scientific approach, is a frivolous illusion. (p. 2)

6 Up Close and Personal: Unfinished Stories

KEMBA: If you believe something, you don't know it. If you know it, you don't have to believe it. Belief is in the mind, that's what I know. That's why I use the word "know." Knowing is like – my knowingness comes from within so whatever I'm going to tell you that I know, it's from within. It sparks its feeling within myself and I know; it's a knowing. Belief is like something that I grew up with, my parents or my friends or TV or society tell me: Believe this, believe this, believe this (*points around the room*) but do I know it? If I believe it then I do not know it. I just keep on believing. It's on my mind constantly. All I'm doing is believing believing believing believing. But I never really know for myself. So I don't really use that word. That's one of my words that I'm throwing away.

(Focus Group Interview, Kemba, Cherry, Max, Peanut, Braeburn, December 1, 2008)

Kemba was a very interesting young woman. She shared openly with us and in her interview seemed to set an incredible standard for herself. She purported that she alone was responsible for her accomplishments and failures, and said she'd learned this from her mother. But, she no longer lived with her mother. Instead, she lived on her own and found it a great struggle to get herself to school each day. She liked school when she was there. Braeburn had come through for her where other schools had not, she explained. She appreciated the teachers, the support they provided, their personal sharing, and the high expectations they held. In her first interview, she told us she wanted to be an artist-cardiologist, a heart surgeon and artist in one.

Kemba also taught us that not having bus fare to get to school made it very difficult to maintain good attendance. She wanted to be there, she insisted, but long part-time job work hours, expensive rent, and little money meant that just getting to school was a challenge. Still, she insisted, she was responsible for herself:

> I just want to say I always tell people that, "you are the cause and effect of everything that happens in your life." So whatever is outside of your life happening, it can alter what's going on in school. But it's how you choose to make it affect you. Are you gonna take the positive or the negative or are you gonna take both? Because sometimes we do need to do a lot of the negatives so we can be motivated through that. Some people are motivated in different ways. So it's what you choose to do with whatever is happening in your life outside of school. What are you gonna do? Are you going to leave it alone? Because you need to deal with it, you know what I mean? But how are you going to deal with it because you're not – no matter how you are sad or how blue, there is always someone worse than you, you know what I mean? You have to just push on through.
>
> (Focus Group Interview, Kemba, Cherry, Max, Peanut, Dec 2, 2008)

We learned so many things from Kemba in our interview with her, and from our observations of her in the classroom, our video-recordings of her in-class work, and the joy with which she approached most things. But – and as I've said, there's always a but – Kemba missed the final performance and therefore failed the class she had put so much effort into. Her teacher was unsuccessful in contacting her. It was a puzzle – we never learned what happened. But everything we'd come to understand from Kemba was that she saw herself as solely responsible for her failures and successes; she took up the role of the perfect neoliberal subject. The glimpse we had into her life made us realize how many young people live out such disjunctures in their lives. She also helped us see how important peer relationships are, however transitory, and how momentary connections matter even if the ultimate outcomes and dreams are not realized. Yet, Kemba's disappearance from school was worrying though not unusual; we were left, as we had been many times before, with a troubling question mark.

Maxx was another puzzle. His "outsider" status, as previously noted in the Obama discussion, was, in our view, very consistent with other signs and symbols of his social performance of disconnection we'd been observing over the several months we'd been in his classroom.

Goffman's (1959) explicit framework for understanding social interaction in dramaturgical terms is particularly relevant here. In an expansive metaphor of the world as stage, Goffman talks about the role of expression, or outward performance, in conveying impressions of self to an "audience." We had carefully taken in Maxx's cues, over several months, paying very close attention to his communicative acts. In his final interview, though, we were caught up short by our carefully crafted perception, and Goffman's insight about social interaction came forcefully to light cautioning that "the observer's need to rely on representations of things itself creates the possibility of misrepresentation (p. 251).

Disengaged as Maxx often appeared, and on the periphery of the circle in the classroom, he did not resist in a typical or active way, though his solitude in the classroom and apparent disengagement was a curiosity. Then, we were punctured by an event that happened in 2009 in his classroom at Middleview. It was early in the winter term, a cold February day. We arrived to film the drama students perform their Ibsen scenes in pairs. Maxx and his partner headed up to the front of the class to perform their scene. We weren't sure what to expect from Maxx because he so often appeared disengaged, if body language can be trusted. About halfway through their scene, Maxx "dried," as they say in the acting business. He completely froze and forgot his lines. He backed up and started again, hoping momentum would take over. It didn't. He froze again. During that terrible pregnant pause, we all held our breath, willing the words to come. Then, without warning, Maxx turned to the wall behind him and punched his fist with great force into the concrete block. There was an audible gasp of horror in the room. Maxx stormed out the door.

Months later, on June 2, 2009, we had the opportunity to interview Maxx. It was my intention to run my "interpretation" of that event by him. I had assumed that Maxx was very angry with himself for forgetting his lines. Until that fateful moment, his characterization, his memorization of lines, his focus, and care had surprised everyone. There had been no previous indication that he had enjoyed the Ibsen unit. His clear effort and careful performance had not been anticipated. I imagined that this experience might have been a difficult one to revisit. Early in the interview, Barry asked Maxx about his positioning in the classroom. This exchange was our first surprise:

> BARRY: In class in the fall, I noticed that you often liked to sit at the edge of the room.
> MAXX: What?

BARRY: I don't know if you do that consciously or not, but you would often be sitting in the windowsill or the corner or outside of the circle. You seemed to be more – this is just the way I saw it – you seemed to be more comfortable, like, outside. Were you doing that consciously?

MAXX: I don't know. Was I? I don't even remember.

KATHLEEN: Yeah.

BARRY: Definitely. Almost always.

MAXX: I think I tend to do that everywhere.

BARRY: My question is why do you think that is? Is there something – I know it's hard to think about something you don't do deliberately but like is there a kind of perspective that you get, that you were getting from being out there? Was it some – you didn't want to be a part of the middle?

MAXX: Yeah, I don't get along with people sometimes.

BARRY: You don't get along with people.

MAXX: So I like stay away from them.

KATHLEEN: Right.

BARRY: In all classes?

MAXX: Yeah, most of my classes I sit in the back next to the windowsill. If it doesn't have a window, I'm sitting in the back.

We were surprised by Maxx's response, both the idea that it was perhaps not a deliberate choice or that it was so habitual as to be unrecognizable even to him. The next segment of the interview presented an even greater surprise:

KATHLEEN: I want to ask a question but you can pass on it if you don't want to comment about this. But I remember another moment that really stood out to me.

MAXX: Uh oh, here it comes.

KATHLEEN: Yeah, you know what I'm going say. Let me tell you what my interpretation is, and you can tell me if I'm right or if I'm wrong or if I'm close or if I'm far, OK? (*Maxx: OK.*) So you were doing the Ibsen performance –

MAXX: Yeah, I botched that.

KATHLEEN: Exactly.

MAXX: I liked that guy [Ibsen]. He's so cool.

KATHLEEN: And you – it was a really, that was an intense scene and it was an interesting complicated scene, and – who was your partner again?

MAXX: Ashley.

KATHLEEN: Ashley, that's right. And I think what I saw is that you forgot a line momentarily.

MAXX: Yes, I went dead or blocked or –

KATHLEEN: You dried?

MAXX: Yeah, that word.

KATHLEEN: And you almost broke your hand on the wall.

MAXX: I didn't break my hand. Almost broke the wall.

KATHLEEN: OK. It looked pretty damn hard from my point of view. Pretty hard. And so I did this little thing in my head when I watched that which was to imagine these really high standards that you had for yourself.

MAXX: I don't have high standards for myself! I had high standards for my partner and I let her down. (*Kathleen: Ah.*) And she was so mad, like man. She could have done the play really – she could have gotten a wonderful grade but then I screwed her over really bad.

KATHLEEN: So it was about letting Ashley down or –

MAXX: Yeah. It was bad.

KATHLEEN: So I was wrong. Or I was partly wrong. Because I thought it was about you holding yourself to high standards.

MAXX: If I did a monologue and screwed up I would be like, "oh, I'll try it again." But if I have a partner and I'm in a play then like, if I screw up I'm screwing them up and it's really bad. And I don't like that.

KATHLEEN: Right. That's a – I know that feeling. That's interesting.

(Long pause.)

KATHLEEN: Sorry, just thinking about that …

(Individual Interview, Maxx, Middleview, June 2, 2009)

Obviously caught off guard by my misunderstanding of the event and the premium Maxx had placed on supporting his partner, I wondered how much we get wrong in our observations, how often a particular event that seems consistent with the person you've imagined is completely off the mark. I remembered this experience in the remaining four years and found myself often checking interpretations with participants. In this case, the story of the boy who often placed himself outside the circle, who gazed out the oversized windows rather than fixing his eyes on his teacher or his peers, was deeply engaged in the class, very appreciative of the work they were doing, and committed to others he barely spoke to. As I proposed at the outset of this book, engagement is not an easily observable event, but a complex interior experience.

Another surprise came in the rehearsals to *The Doors* and during the performance and post-performance interviews. Derek had been an interesting student to watch during this process. He had caught our attention early on primarily because his disengagement in class was so intentional, so performative. His relationship with Ms. S was clearly strained. He was a student who would need to be asked to put his cell phone away and take his ear buds out, every day. He made an effort to not join the circle and often lured Ms. S into a confrontation over nothing. Clearly, he was unhappy in the class. One day, during rehearsals, he pressed too far. Speaking imperceptibly softly, missing his lines, laughing while others were speaking, Ms. S remained patient. Finally, when his efforts didn't work, he turned to Ms. S and said, "I respectfully ask that I not be in this play, that I do backstage stuff." Finally giving in to her exasperation, Ms. S told him he could take a zero, was free to leave, and invited someone else to play his role. The other students in the class seemed relieved to have him finally out of the performance, although they helpfully offered that he would be useful doing backstage work.

Despite this particularly difficult rehearsal, Derek was given another chance to play his role, and he did, in the end, join the final performance of *The Doors* for the school. In one part of the play, when Erica was performing her very personal monologue about coming out as a lesbian and fighting her detractors who told her that heaven's door would be closed to her, Derek, who was playing the angel at heaven's door, exclaimed in a very effeminate and highly exaggerated mock homosexual way "SOOOORY," with a limp wrist in the air, signalling that she couldn't get into heaven. The crowded auditorium erupted in laughter and Erica's solemn moment was lost. In the first assembly of Grade 9 and 10 students, Derek had performed his part without this comic exaggeration. But during the Grade 11/12 assembly, in front of his own peers, he broke from character and, as I saw it, distanced himself from the scene by making a joke of her "coming out" moment, thereby distancing himself from it and perhaps protecting himself from homophobic teasing. If he was seen, publicly, to be supportive, what might that mean for his own identity with peers? Needless to say, it was a highly charged moment:

(Erica enters though the door as Derek opens it by acting as its hinge.)

ERICA: There are those that say that heaven is a door that never closes.

BELL: Welcome to heaven. We accept everybody. (*The other girls sigh in unison.*)

ERICA: I've often wondered about heaven and if there is such a place. 'Cause for the last two years, I've been told that I'm going to hell. Why you ask?

BELL: Because you're gay.

BERTHAM: Sorry.

CARMEN: Sorry.

BELLA: Sorry.

ASHLEY: Sorry.

DEREK: (*sends it up to get a cheap laugh*) SOOOORRRYYYYY.

(*Outburst from the audience. When the laughing finally subsides, Erica continues.*)

ERICA: And because of this I stopped believing in heaven and hell altogether. Why believe in a place that's going to reject me? A place that doesn't accept me all because of who I fall in love with. Love. Love is supposed to be a beautiful thing and bring happiness. So I ask myself, "why is it that I'm supposedly going to be punished all because I can only be in love with women?" To me that doesn't seem fair. And if it is so wrong to be gay, why would God have made me? I haven't done anything wrong; I know this. I haven't killed anyone, stolen anything, or caused harm to anybody, I've simply just loved my girlfriend. Now how can you compare these three things to what I've done? You can't. And you never will be able to. So, if there's a door to heaven, I will be opening it one day. (*She exits through the door.*)

(Transcribed from Video-recorded Performance)

We were all concerned over the impact of that public moment on Erica. But in her subsequent interview she was more pleased with her courage to share her story with the school and much less troubled by Derek's betrayal.

The real surprise came in Derek's final interview. Through much of it, he accused Ms. S of being a teacher who couldn't handle students. He blamed her throughout for his boredom in the class:

... like I don't know, it was a stressful class. I mean, we were a bunch of pricks but like, she, I don't know. If you're a good teacher you can adjust and improvise and deal with it (*trails off*). I've never been a teacher so, like, it could be a bunch of bollocks that I'm talking but I think that she could have handled it.

Then, he made a sharp turn towards the end of the interview, which reminded me of how reflexive young people are, how they often experience contradictory emotions, and how privileged we are to be privy to their unfolding learning:

> I'm trying to live my life and experience every emotion, everything included, so I'm trying everything out. Not drugs and stuff but like every kind of experience on a sober level. There's always been stereotypes on youth that they are disturbances and menaces to society but – and it's always going to go on so – there are going to be youth that are asses and there are just going to be youth that are just doing their homework (*long pause*) ... I was a dick in that class.
>
> (Individual Interview, Derek, Middleview, June 2, 2009)

Like the students at Middleview who worked metaphorically with the idea of doors in our lives, what they represent, how they open and close, the students in India translated this concept and theatre pedagogy to explore their own experiences of doors. Performance can achieve this kind of reverberation of meaning, as it clearly did for the young women in India. The following is an update we received from our collaborator Dr. Sahni after having shared digitally the Middleview performance of *The Doors* with her site:

> We did the Doors project in June. I was supposed to take 5 girls to Plymouth, England from Prerna – Kushboo, Laxmi, Sunita, Kunti, and Soni. Kushboo's dad refused to let her go ... not satisfied with that he also refused to let her go back to school. She had just passed her class 10 exam and topped her class. He insisted that he would not allow her to study any further. Kushboo is 17 and her education at our school is heavily subsidised by us. The small amount that she has to pay, she pays herself. Despite this, the father has the authority to forbid her, because she lives in his house. He threatened to throw her out, beat her up, and also threatened to kill her if she defied him and went back to school. We had to intervene with help from the police and Child helpline.

So I sat with the other four girls and we discussed "Doors" – in our lives. The ones that open and the ones that are shut. We discussed Kushboo's life and spoke of the doors that were being shut on her because of the psychological doors that were shut in her father's mind. They then spoke of doors as they experienced them. I asked them to put down as many words as came to their mind when they thought of the term "doors" – they said "protection," "oppression," "happiness," "privacy," "darkness," "safety," "security," "imprisonment." Then we all decided to write poems about our experiences with doors. So that's what we did. Then we read them out to each other. They took them home and then edited them and came back with a fair draft. I edited them very minorly. [Am attaching those.]

Then they acted them out. Most of the movements were theirs, again with minor editing help from me. They then put all their poems together into one long poem. I edited it in order to make sure it maintained its coherence.

Then we choreographed a dramatic movement to the group recitation of this poem too. Will send video.

We also scripted Kushboo's story and dramatised it. We used verbatim theatre. I used Kushboo's Dad, Mom, and her own words almost exactly from a meeting with them the previous day.

So for our presentation in Plymouth at the ARROW Global Congress, we presented a small video clip taken on an Iflip video camera of Kushboo's interview, then presented our playlet, then the enactment of their individual poems on doors, and then the collective poem. Everything is in Hindi, with an English translation in subtitles from me.

Their presentation brought the house down. They received a standing ovation.

We have presented this at least 8 times since then, once at a youth drama festival. It receives a grand response every time we show it.

I will attach the English translations of the poems in this mail and upload the video to the Edublogs page.

Do tell Ms. S about our version of "DOORS." I don't know how she has devised it, but this is how we did it.

We are currently working on a documentary on Child Marriage. The interviews are all being conducted by the girls and I am trying to find professional help to edit it. Can't afford too much though.

Cheers,

Urvashi

(Correspondence, August 15, 2010)

I opened the attachment of Kushboo's translated "Doors" poem and felt the gap between young people in Canada and young people in India shrink ever so slightly.

DOORS
A door –
Open or shut
An open door reveals a vast, wide world
A closed door shuts out the truth
Offers despair, only despair
Hope beckons through the open door …

The door firmly shut
Blocks my path
How shall I come out?
Society closes around me like a prison
No hope for the future
Do I see in this closed space

Nothing to live for
Behind this closed door
Why am I condemned behind it?
What is my fault?
Just this – that I am a girl?
Don't I have a right to know
What lies beyond?

How shall I imagine
The universe of my dreams
Behind this shut door?
Do I not have the right to dream
Do I not have the right to know and
Be my "self"?

And opening that attachment brought me forcefully back to Marcus's (1995) emblematic question to be asked of multi-sited ethnography: "What among locally probed subjects is iconic with or parallel to the identifiably similar or same phenomenon within the idioms and terms of another related or 'worlds apart' site?" (p. 111). The theatre performance and the poetry had brought us full circle.

Dr. Sahni's recounting of the process for her students at Prerna also brought Maxx's interview back to me. He was playing opposite Chrysanthemum's character in her *Doors* monologue, in a scene about her abusive relationship with her stepfather. Maxx was playing her stepfather. There was a moment of disquieting violence in their scene where the stepfather pulled the chair out from under her and she fell to the ground. There erupted an uncomfortable laughter from the audience. Like Kushboo's friends who explored her story, taking on the characters surrounding her story, and even playing Kushboo herself, Maxx was performing Chrysanthemum's story, and when I asked him how he felt about that he explained the following:

> KATHLEEN: Did you ever think when you were developing that character that – I mean, that whole scene was developed from Chrysanthemum's real-life story – and did you feel conscious of that when you were developing your character?
>
> MAXX: No. I kind of put my own character into it. I took someone else from my life and was like, "well, I'm gonna use that character when I do that." It was kind of a mix of me and Chrysanthemum. But they don't know that.
>
> (Individual Interview, Maxx, Middleview, June 2, 2009)

"Me in the role" and "the role in me." Early scholars in drama education attempted to capture the sociality of drama pedagogy, the nature of its collective energy and social relations, the ways in which young people explore their own realities with and through the stories of others, against the backdrop of a larger world. Those early thinkers tried to explain to the broader educational community why such exploratory work mattered profoundly for young people, and how stories and metaphor might offer a way of working together that could have far-reaching implications. Booth and Thornley-Hall (1991) write:

> Role lets children leave the narrow confines of their own worlds and gives them entry into new forms of existence. At the same time, they must find a sense of their own relationships to this fictional life, the "me in the role" and the "role in me". When children participate in drama, they are in charge of building the dramatic experience through their actions and words. They become the drama, discovering ideas and directions that will surprise and change them. Because meanings are being

made and not given, the children will find responses and language powers that are unexpected, engendered by the collective drive for group meaning. (p. 95)

This book, and the ethnography from which it was built, has in some ways been about the desire to insert life into art, but it has been equally about inserting art into life, perhaps even more so. And this insertion of art into big and complex young lives is the preoccupation of many great thinkers of art and human experience. One of which, Jacques Rancière (2011), offers a most fitting summary of the experiences that were shared by young people in Toronto and in Lucknow, working with their own and their peers' "real" lives:

The spectator also acts, like the pupil or the scholar. She observes, selects, compares, interprets. She links what she sees to a host of other things that she has seen on other stages, in other kinds of place. She composes her own poem with the elements of the poem before her. She participates in the performance by refashioning it in her own way – by drawing back, for example, from the vital energy that it is supposed to transmit in order to make it a pure image and associate this image with a story which she has read or dreamt, experienced or invented. (p. 13)

Endings and Beginnings

PEANUT: Can I say "hi" to my Mom? Hi Mom!
BARRY: I'm zooming in for it (*operating the video camera*).
KATHLEEN: Close up.
BARRY: Close up, close up.
KEMBA: Will we be able to get this documentary?
KATHLEEN: This documentary? Well, we're going use it [the video footage] for our analysis, our research.
MAX: What is this research for?
PEANUT: I don't wanna see myself.
KATHLEEN: The study that we're doing on youth engagement in school and Drama class …
KEMBA: Like, this talking, this means a lot to me. Could I, like, have a copy of it?
KATHLEEN: This actual – what we've done today? The focus group?
KEMBA: Yeah, this circle.
KATHLEEN: Absolutely.

BARRY: We can do that.

KEMBA: I'd love a copy.

BARRY: Sure ...

KATHLEEN: Well I really, really, really want to thank you all for this conversation.

KEMBA: Thank you.

PEANUT: Thank you. We would have never done this [without the research as catalyst].

KATHLEEN: You know what? This was an amazing conversation and you were very generous with us and we're basically strangers. So just know that your words, we will handle very responsibly.

KEMBA: You're not strangers. Don't use that word anymore.

(Cherry hugs Kathleen.)

KATHLEEN: Well, not quite strangers, we're a little closer than strangers. But we really appreciate your openness and we will make a DVD – we will all have this conversation as a memory. So thank you. Now go dance and sing.

KEMBA: Thank you very much.

ANNE: Thanks a lot.

BARRY: Thank you.

The lives, and life prospects, of young people have been destabilized by global economic and political uncertainty. Social and educational policies, as well as popular cultural representations of youth, are often sorely lacking youth perspectives and understandings, their agency often reduced to negative representations of anti-social behaviour rather than the great impulses of invention – the unwieldy, unpredictable, and highly changeable forms of engagement we came to recognize and admire. Theirs is a deeply felt humanity to which we must pay better attention if we desire more for our collective future.

Realizing the limits of our capacities as adults to understand, I underscore again our initial desire to create a "youth knowledge base" regarding their experiences of drama pedagogy, of school, of this sociocultural moment; to learn from and with them about their hopes, and for what and whom they care, while endeavouring to keep in dialectical interplay the relationship between social structures and human agency. This book may not, in the end, amount to a "youth knowledge base," but I have attempted to keep young people's voices and their analyses alive in the course of writing it. I have felt guided by them and by my memories of our rich conversations and times together. I have tried to bring my own analyses and that of my team of researchers to this task, knowing that it will fail in so many ways to reproduce the social relations of intimacy, of fear, of anger, of pleasure, and hope that were bound up in its production.

Appendix 1: Social Identity Categories

All pseudonyms and labels were chosen by students. If they do not appear below, they chose not to be identified by social categories.

In addition, many included responses to two questions:

1) Describe yourself in a sentence and 2) If I were to describe you in a book, what should I say?

The students at Prerna, however, wished for their 'real names' to be used in the publication of the research.

Braeburn Year One

Ms. C: Female, White, straight, middle class, Religion: Jewish, Born: Toronto, First Language: English, Other Languages: some Spanish and French
   1) A spiritual, passionate artist/teacher who believes that everyone was born good at heart.
   2) A professional actor/choreographer who transitioned into teaching as she had a passion to bring integrity to art within education.

Peanut: Female, Latina, straight, high class, Religion: Christian, Born: Toronto, First Language: English, Other Languages: Spanish
   1) Caring, open-hearted, funny, and outgoing.
   2) This student is amazing. She is kind, caring, and funny.

Cherry: Female, Spanish/Jamaican/Chinese, heterosexual, high class, Religion: Christian, Born: Toronto, First Language: English, Other Languages: a little Spanish and Chinese, Other: Outgoing and unique

1) I am very open-minded; I love people who are down to earth. Also I hope to become an actress.
2) My past experiences that I had in life have made me a strong and motivated individual.

Kemba Thompson: Female, Afrocentric, straight, Class: I am not categorized, Religion: not religious, Born: Jamaica, First Language: English, Other Languages: speaks Patois, Other: spiritual
1) I am open-minded 18-year-old. Strong, opinionated, Black woman.
2) Kemba is a teenager who is for community. One who strives for her best, for the world.

Sarah: identifiers left blank
1) I am the happiest person in my family.
2) I am the coolest ever.

Ziggy: Male, Bengali, straight, Religion: Muslim, Born: Bangladesh, First Language: English
1) B's up and I like basketball.
2) Horror and gore.

Forty-two Marks: Male, Caucasian, straight, upper class, Religion: Roman Catholic, Born: Yugoslavia, First Language: Serbian, Other Languages: Croatian, English, Other: big
1) That guy.
2) Say what you want.

Gonzalez Sanchez: Male, Mexican, straight, working class, Religion: Catholic, Born: LA, First Language: Spanish, Other Languages: English
1) Randomness and sexual.
2) I [dac] with the nose ring baby and tattoos.

Skeam: Male, Latino, straight, middle class, Religion: Christian, Born: Guatemala, First Language: Spanish, Other Languages: English
1) I am adventurous and outgoing.
2) Nice, outgoing.

Max Fischer: All identity categories left blank. Born: Canada, First Language: English
1) A man of few words.
2) Sorry everyone, the book's not finished.

Middleview: Year One

Ms. S: Female, White, middle class, Religion: Jewish, Born: Toronto, First Language: English
1) I inspire passion in students by promoting emotional honesty in a safe (ish), nurturing environment.

2) Ms. S loves vintage collectibles, brunching hot spots, and traditional Shabbos dinners.

Chrysthanemum: Female, White, straight, middle class, Religion: Roman Catholic, Born: Canada, First Language: English, no other languages spoken
1) I am fun, smart, and I enjoy having fun.
2) Outgoing, talented, strong person, and intelligent.

Erica: Female, White, gay, middle class, Religion: atheist, Born: Canada, First Language: English, no other languages spoken
1) I'm pretty straightforward, open-minded, easy to get along with, and quite mature at times.
2) I'm told by others a lot that I am mature for my age and I have a lot of opinions. Also you could mention I'm the only openly gay student in the class.

Bertham: Female, White, straight, Religion: Catholic, Born: Canada, First Language: English, Other Languages: some French
1) Honest, I tell it like it is, nosy, fun, and I love to try new things and very confident.
2) A strong female with courage and compassion, has acceptance for everyone and a heart of gold – this is what Fabian would write.

Fabian: Male, White, straight, lower middle class, Religion: Catholic, Born: Toronto, First Language: English, no other languages spoken
1) I am a funny, understanding person.
2) I am outgoing, strong, funny, disruptive individual.

Bell: Female, White, straight, middle class, Religion: agnostic
1) I'm me, nobody else. Unique, Outgoing, Creative, Humorous, Trusting.

Bonnie: Female, Black, middle class, Religion: Christian
1) I'm me; I'm different.
2) I like reading books, enjoy music, have a love for money, hate eggs, waffles, and pancakes, have cravings for chocolate, have a thing for piercing.

Mya: Female, African, straight, average class, Religion: orthodox, Born: Eritrea
1) I am caring and myself. Different from other.
2) I am Eritrean, I am 5'6," I am dreamer, I am into fashion.

Maxx: Male (all other indicators are left blank), First Language: English
1) Hmm?
2) The third guy in the class.

Stephanie: Female, African American (American), straight, Religion: Christian, Born: Toronto
  1) Very outgoing, love to have fun.
     Question 2 left blank.
Ashley: Female, White, straight, middle class?, Religion: Catholic, Born: Canada, First Language: English, Other Langugages: a little Portuguese, French, and Spanish
  1) I'm outgoing and fun and can be very shy."
  2) She's shy, quiet, but she's very understanding.
K'Thanie: Female, Black, straight, middle class, Born: Atlanta, Georgia, First Language: English
  1) I'm the type of person who speaks her mind.
  2) Unique.
Bella: Female, Black, straight, middle class, Religion: Seventh-day A., Born: St. Vincent, First Language: English
  1) Chilling low back. Outgoing at times. Love to have fun with family, friends.
  2) I'm me and no one else.
Derek: Male, White, straight, upper middle class, Born: Toronto, First Language: English
  1) Outgoing, striving for success, which will be fulfilled.
  2) Energetic.
Carmen: Female
(Nothing else filled in on her form.)
Cat: Male, Black

Braeburn Year Two: Students

Carl: Male, Jamaican/Barbados, straight, Class: middle on up, Religion: Christian, Born: Toronto, First Language: English, Other Languages: understand a little French
  1) More or less relaxed kind of guy, yet funny.
  2) Smart kid, see potential, sympathetic, empathetic.
Anastasia: Female, Black, straight, Religion: Christian, Born: Jamaica, First Language: English
  1) Entertaining
  2) Outspoken, focus, sociable.
MoMo: Female, Vietnamese, straight, Class: Average, Religion: Buddhist, Born: Canada, First Language: Vietnamese/English
  1) Ambitious, hardworking, motivated, individual.

Middleview Year Two: Students

Eve: Female, Black, straight, Religion: Christian, Born: Toronto, First Language: English
   1) A teenage girl with a passion for clothes.
   2) Say, Eve, the outgoing girl with a passion for fashion.
Varindorf: Male, White, hetro, Class: poor but classy, Religion: Science, Born: Canada, First Language: English
   1) Original.
   2) Laid back.
Daniella: Female, Black, quarter White, Indian, straaaaight, middle class, Religion: not sure, Born: Montreal, Quebec, First Language: French, Other Languages: English, gibberish
   1) I am outgoing, have a good sense of humour (naturally) and I'm easy going.
   2) And whatever you want ☺.
Odinpac: Male, Black, heterosexual, middle class, Religion: don't have one, Born: London, England, First Language: English, Other Languages: Portuguese, some Spanish
   1) I'll give you one word, RANDOM.
   2) I don't know.
Nana: Female, Korean, Sexuality: no, Class: mid-high, Born: South Korea, First Language: Korean, Other Languages: bit of Japanese, English
   1) Outgoing girl.
Unique: Female, Black, straight, Religion: Christian, Born: Toronto, First Language: English, Other Languages: a little French
   1) I'm quiet, but outgoing and very adventurous, but serious and very funny. But there is no one else like me.
   2) Basically what I said above.
Taylor: Male, Italian/Portuguese, straight, middle class, Religion: Christian, Born: Toronto, First Language: English, Other Languages: Italian
   1) My life is amazing.
   2) Whatever you want.
Twila: Female, Mixed (Italian, Black), straight, middle class, Religion: Christian, Born: Toronto, First Language: English, Other Languages: minor French, Other ☺
   1) I am outgoing, too – obsessed and always smiling! ☺
   2) She is nice, smart, never willing to try something new. If she

loves something, she shows it. Like the *Twilight* Saga, she expresses it EVERYDAY! 'Cause she is cool and so is *Twilight*!

Joe: Male, straight, low class, Religion: none, Born: Tijuana, Mexico, First Language: Spanish, Other Languages: a little English, Other: YEAH!
1) I'm a very nice, lovely guy.
2) Whatever.

Ryan: Male, Brown, straight, Religion: Catholic/Christian, Born: Toronto, First Language: English, Other Languages: a bit of Portuguese
1) I am relaxed and laid back.
2) That I'm a well-caring person who loves money.

Mave: Female, Metis, bisexual?, middle class, Religion: none, Born: Toronto, First Language: English, Other Languages: Minor Native, Other: ☺
1) I am so cool. I love photography.
2) She is a creative child, loves cats. Probably gonna be a crazy cat lady.

Marbles: (Female figure drawing), Race: All, Sexuality: All, Class: All, Religion: none, Born: Earth, First Language: (blank), Other Languages: English, French, and a little Spanish
2) Nothing negative please ☺.

Richard: Male, Filipino/Jamaican, heterosexual, middle class, Religion: atheist, Born: Canada, First Language: English, Other Languages: none
1) I am a very down to earth and open with new individuals. I am also very social.
2) I would say I'm creative, thoughtful, generous, and kind towards peers.

Goku: Male, Irish/Spanish/Italian, straight, Class: poooooor, Religion: haven't decided yet, Born: Toronto, First Language: English, Other Languages: I can swear and what not in Gaelic and Spanish
1) I'm a real nerd but I'm also an athlete and I have a lot of different kinds of friends.
2) Big, funny? Nice (hopefully)…

Middleview: Year Three

Kath Brown: Female, Asian, straight, Class: group home (social assistance), Religion: nothing, Born: Nepal, April 15; 2005 I came here, First Language: Tibetan, Other Languages: a bit of Nepalese and understand Hindi a bit

1) I am frank and caring.
2) I am very funny, loveable, very direct, and honest.

Nina: Female, European/Portuguese, straight, working class, Religion: non-practising Catholic, Born: Toronto, First Language: Portuguese, Other Languages: English, Spanish, Brazilian

    1) I think of myself as a strong-willed, hard-headed, kind-hearted Portuguese girl who take shit from no one.
    2) This young woman is a strong-willed and independent person. She has been through many hardships and still keeps her head held high.

Rayne: Female, Canadian/Portuguese (my identity is Canadian but my family is Portuguese), straight, working class, Religion: non-practising Catholic, Born: Toronto, First Language: English, Other Languages: a very little bit of Portuguese,

    1) Lovely, thoughtful, intelligent, intuitive, open-minded.
    2) I am the type of girl who tried to make everyone happy, but I don't know how to make myself happy.

Poke: European (basically all of Europe), straight, lower middle class, Religion: none, Born: Toronto, First Language: English, Other Languages: French, Spanish, Japanese (all, very, very, very small amounts)

    1) Tall, smart, funny, nice, kind. Aware of above-average intelligence but an underachiever. All of the above. Shy as well.
    2) He's left-handed. Do what he says. "You don't want to argue with Poke, trust me." I contradict myself a lot because I can.

Norgen Willis: Male, White, straight, Class: upper/lower, Religion: agnostic, Born: Toronto First Language: English

    1) I can relate to everything, whether or not I have an understanding. I go with what life puts in front of me.
    2) Godly. Epic-ness. Relative. Understanding. Cautious. Polite. Hilarious. Trustworthy. Down.

Daphney Evans: Female, White, single parent, middle class, Religion: Catholic, Born: Canada, November 7, 1994, First Language: English

    1) I am very bubbly, sweet, and sensitive.
    2) Bubbly. Sweet. Sensitive. Sneaky. Moody. Always wants to keep people happy even when I am not happy myself. Fearless. Persistent.

Sasha: Feminine, Indian, straight, Class: Fluctuates from working class to middle class and vice versa, Religion: Muslim, Born: Hyderabad, India, First Language: Urdu, Other Languages: English, Hindi, a bit of French

1) Someone who cares about other people and I'm sensitive to others' feelings.
2) Understanding. Short-tempered. Moody. Caring. Loyal. Someone who wants to help the needy in the near future. Open-minded. Ambitious. Someone who hides her sorrow to make others happy. Stubborn. Hates to be wrong.

Sophia: Female, biracial Latina/Brazilian, straight, working class, Religion: Christian, Born: Canada, First Language: I learned Portuguese (Brazil) and English at the same time
1) Intrepid, bubbly, mysterious, confident.
2) Sophie is intrepid, bubbly, mysterious, confident. She is very easy-going and can shake off things people usually can't tolerate, BUT her pet peeves drive her insane.

Puppy Love/Mr. Loving: Male, African, masculine, working/medium class, Religion: Christian, First Language: Setswana, Other Languages: English
1) I am hard-working, reliable, funny, and I love acting and meeting new people.
2) Friendly. Born to help poor people. A dreamer who's on his journey to his dream. A person who knows what he wants in life. I don't just smile with my mouth, but with my heart too.

Bones McCoy: Female (get nothing = "sorta androgynous"), German/Japanese/various European things, asexual? Class: my own, Religion: Christian but to my own interpretation, Born: Oshawa, Canada, but I have no real connection to it, First Language: English
1) A person of many contradictions.
2) I [am] a thinker first, a speaker second, and a writer only when needed.

HLA: Metro-sexual, White, straight, middle class but just because I have privileges doesn't mean I get them, Religion: I made it up as I go, Born: California, First Language: English, Other Languages: Hebrew
1) I am spectacularly unique and perfectly adequate.
2) Hot and cold, fire and rain – mix polar opposites and that would be me, a mix of a ton of emotions and individual thoughts making me crazy.

Vitamin N: Female, Sudanese, straight, Class: all thanks are due to God, all my basic needs are met and my family is working, Religion: Islam, Born: Toronto, First Language: Arabic, Other Languages: English

1) I am very interested in politics all of a sudden, but I hate it. I don't speak when I am not spoken to/referred to. If I'm given a chance to speak I'll abuse it at times.

2) Interested in the Black revolutionaries of the 1960s. Loves to learn new things. Religious.

Shashaqe: Female – feminine, Jamaican/Indian, straight, single parent; middle to working class, Religion: Christian, Born: Jamaica, First Language: Patois (Jamaican dialect)

1) Observant. Realistic. Courageous. Determined. Hard-working. Intelligent. Honest. Loyal. Easy to snap. Moody. Emotional. Helpful.

2) Shashaqe is a very quiet person. She is very smart. She likes to talk about how she feels. She liked to be in control and thoughtful. She could be sensitive at times but is overall loving.

Sinead Cativa: Masculine female, Sicilian-Canadian, bisexual/pansexual, Class: working poor, impoverished, Religion: I praise and pray to good energy through the language of Christianity, Born: Toronto, First Language: Sicilian, Other Languages: English

1) One confused sorry son-of-a-bitch.

2) Kind of overbearing, good intentions though. Cynical Generation Y who doesn't really appreciate the oblivious opinions and advertisement of other people. Doesn't like working with people but loved 'em! Well, the competent ones.

Asad: Male, Middle Eastern, straight, middle class, First Language: Swahili, Other Languages: Arabic (basic), English

1) Am just me by being what I want.

2) As someone that had dream all over his mind, and the way you would wish to say on me.

Kathy: Female, Vietnamese, straight, middle class, Born: Vancouver, BC, First Language: English, Other Languages: Vietnamese

2) Anyway you want.

C Square: Male, Jamaican, middle class, First Language: English

1) Nice, a football player, funny, loves food.

2) In the NFL, family, kids, successful.

Sarah: Female, middle class, Born: Canada, First Language: English

1) Don't want to answer.

Juson: Male, Chinese, heterosexual

1) I am an outgoing talkative man who likes being outside all the time.

2) Juson is a talkative young man. He likes sports.

Kandy: Female, straight, Born: Grenada, Religion: Seventh-day Adventist
1) Tall, slim, and outgoing.
2) Kandy is a quiet, friendly girl but when angry she can be a totally different person.

Toronto Researchers

Kathleen: Female, White, Scottish descent
Anne: Female, White, European descent
Burcu: Female, White, Canadian/Turkish
Barry: Male, White, Canadian
Heather: Female, White, Canadian

Appendix 2: Tables

Table 1. Survey items from all of the scales as well as extras included in the survey

Student Engagement Scales

ACADEMIC ENTHUSIASM

Intrinsic Motivation

- I'm very interested in school.
- I do not need others to get me to go to school.
- I do school- and class-related activities without anyone pushing me to do them.

Identified Regulation

- The content covered in classes is greatly related to my own interests.
- Most of the time, I find the information in classes interesting.

Affective Connection

- I never feel bored at school.
- Generally, I feel like teachers care about me.
- I enjoy spending time at my school.

ACADEMIC ACHIEVEMENT

Identified Regulation

- Going to school will allow me to learn many useful things.
- I chose to go to school so that I may learn many things.
- It's important to go to school.

External Regulation

- I go to school because it will lead to rewards later on in life.
- I work hard at school to prove to others how smart I am.

Imagined Achievement

- I work hard at school to prove to others how smart I am.
- I see myself going to college or university.
- I feel like my dreams or goals are achievable.

VOLUNTARY INITIATIVE

Extracurricular

- At my school, there are lots of opportunities to get involved in extra-curricular activities.
- At my school, there are lots of extra-curricular activities that reflect my interests.

Assisting Others

- I look for ways to assist others at my school

Within School Space Scales

ACADEMIC PARTICIPATION

Classroom Involvement

- How often do you participate in classroom activities?

Task Completion

- How often do you complete all tasks presented to you?
- How often do you seek out solutions to difficult problems in class assignments on your own?
- How often do you work on class assignments during lunch or breaks?
- How often do you work on class assignments with other students?

Academic Discussions

- How often do you participate in classroom discussions?
- How often do you discuss subject material with peers?

- How often do you discuss subject material with your teacher?
- How often do you speak with your school principal?

SCHOOL PARTICIPATION *(Estimate of how many hours each week the participant spends …)*

- Assisting with a club or organization
- Participating in school governance
- Mentoring a peer
- Volunteering at school events
- Attending school events
- Studying

Outside School Space Scales

FAMILY AND CARING ACTIVITIES *(Estimate of how many hours each week the participant spends …)*

- Preparing a meal for someone else
- Assisting a family member with school work
- Volunteering
- Shopping for your family
- Caring for someone who is sick
- Caring for a family member (feeding, dressing, washing, etc.)

ACADEMICS AND STUDIES *(Estimate of how many hours each week the participant spends …)*

- Assisting a friend with school work
- Studying
- Completing your own school work
- Using a computer for school
- Completing class assignments

ENTERTAINMENT *(Estimate of how many hours each week the participant spends …)*

- Visiting friends
- Playing video games
- Listening to music
- Spending time alone
- Preparing a meal for yourself

- Playing card games or board games
- Using a computer for pleasure
- Watching television or films
- Reading for pleasure
- Shopping for yourself

EXTRA SURVEY ITEMS *(Not assigned to a scale) (Estimate of how many hours each week the participant spends ...)*

- Earning money
- Visiting family members you do not live with
- Attending a local community centre
- Playing sports
- Practising religious activities within your home
- Practising religious activities outside of your home

Table 2. Correlations of the different scales

Scales	AE	AA	AVI	AP	SP	FC	AS	EN
AE	×	×	×	×	×	×	×	×
AA	.727** .000	×	×	×	×	×	×	×
AVI	.666** .000	.535** .000	×	×	×	×	×	×
AP	.660** .000	.550** .000	.524** .000	×	×	×	×	×
SP	.336** .000	.338** .000	.457** .000	.484** .000	×	×	×	×
FC	.423** .000	.386** .000	.473** .000	.534** .000	.544** .000	×	×	×
AS	.182. 059	.175 .069	.276** .004	.390** .000	.632** .000	.302** .001	×	×
EN	−.282** .003	−.034 .725	−.078 .423	−.089 .356	.602** .000	.814** .000	.838** .000	×

** = Correlation is significant at the 0.01 level (2-tailed)
* = Correlation is significant at the 0.05 level (2-tailed)
For all correlations, n = 109.
AE = Academic Enthusiasm; AA = Academic Achievement; AVI = Voluntary Initiative;
AP = Academic Participation; SP = School Participation;
FC = Family and Caring Activities; AS = Academics and Studies; EN = Entertainment

Table 3. Distribution of student responses within each scale

Scales	1 (Low)	2	3	4	5 (High)
AE	2.8% (3)	19.3% (21)	56.0% (61)	20.0% (22)	1.8% (2)
AA	0.9% (1)	8.0% (9)	34.0% (37)	50.0% (55)	6.4% (7)
AVI	1.8% (2)	1.8% (2)	22.0% (24)	42.0% (46)	20% (22)

Scale	Never	Sometimes	Frequently	Always
AP	10.0% (11)	64% (70)	25% (27)	0.9% (1)

Scale	> 1 hour	1 hour	2 hours	3 hours	4 hours	< 5 hours
SP	54.6% (59)	26.0% (28)	10.0% (11)	7.0% (8)	0.9% (1)	0.9% (1)
FC	48.0% (52)	30.0% (33)	11.0% (12)	7.0% (8)	4.0% (4)	0.0% (0)
AS	27.0% (29)	28.0% (30)	23.0% (25)	14.0% (15)	6.0% (7)	2.8% (3)
EN	8.0% (9)	28.0% (30)	35.0% (38)	24.0% (26)	6.0% (6)	0.0% (0)

AE = Academic Enthusiasm; AA = Academic Achievement; AVI = Voluntary Initiative;
AP = Academic Participation; SP = School Participation;
FC = Family and Caring Activities; AS = Academics and Studies; EN = Entertainment

Table 4. Correlations between scales and extra survey items

Scales	Earning Money	Visiting family members you do not live with	Attending a local community centre	Playing sports	Religious activities within your home	Religious activities outside of your home
AE	.212*	.183	.208*	.082	.324**	.190
	.041	.060	.045	.414	.001	.059
	n = 94	n = 106	n = 93	n = 102	n = 97	n = 99
AA	.280**	.305**	.183	.174	.247*	.161
	.006	.001	.079	.081	.015	.073
	n = 94	n = 106	n = 93	n = 102	n = 97	n = 99
	.194	.147	.204*	.234*	.390**	.213*
	.061	.132	.050	.018	.000	.034
	n = 94	n = 106	n = 93	n = 102	n = 97	n = 99
AP	.217*	.226*	.372**	.090	.360**	.266**
	.035	.020	.000	.367	.000	.008
	n = 94	n = 106	n = 93	n = 102	n = 97	n = 99
SP	.199.056	.196*	.298**	.137	.358**	.357
	n = 93	.045	.004	.170	.00096	.00098
		n = 105	n = 92	n = 102		

(Continued)

Table 4. (*Continued*)

Scales	Earning Money	Visiting family members you do not live with	Attending a local community centre	Playing sports	Religious activities within your home	Religious activities outside of your home
FC	.253*	.345**	.386**	.154	.327**	.217*
	.014	.000	.000	.121	.001	.031
	n = 94	n = 106	n = 93	n = 102	n = 97	n = 99
AS	.026	.083	.216*	.010	.201*	.114
	.802	.395	.038	.924	.049	.262
	n = 84	n = 106	n = 93	n = 102	n = 97	n = 99
EN	.089	.155	.131	.260**	.039	−.037
	.945	.112	.210	.008	.702	.718
	n = 94	n = 106	n = 93	n = 102	n = 97	n = 99

** = Correlation is significant at the 0.01 level (2-tailed)
* = Correlation is significant at the 0.05 level (2-tailed)
AE = Academic Enthusiasm; AA = Academic Achievement; AVI = Voluntary Initiative;
AP = Academic Participation; SP = School Participation;
FC = Family and Caring Activities; AS = Academics and Studies; EN = Entertainment

Table 5. Results of *t*-tests on differences between males and females

Scales	t value	Degrees of Freedom	Sig. (2-tailed)
AE	2.63**	107	.009
AA	1.89	107	.061
AVI	0.90	107	.371
AP	1.34	107	.181
SP	2.68**	107	.009
FC	3.53**	107	.001
AS	2.30*	107	.023
EN	0.49	107	.622

AE = Academic Enthusiasm; AA = Academic Achievement; AVI = Voluntary Initiative;
AP = Academic Participation; SP = School Participation;
FC = Family and Caring Activities; AS = Academics and Studies; EN = Entertainment

Table 5a

Survey Items	t value	Degrees of Freedom	Sig. (2-tailed)
Religious activities within your home	2.21*	95	.029
Playing sports	3.25**	100	.002

** = Correlation is significant at the 0.01 level (2-tailed)
* = Correlation is significant at the 0.05 level (2-tailed)

Table 6. Descriptive statistics of the means and standard deviations for scales, and males and females

Scales		Mean	Std. Deviation
AE		3.43	0.07
AA		4.01	0.07
AVI		3.44	0.09
AP		2.61	0.52
SP		2.09	0.10
FC		2.24	0.11
AS		2.90	0.12
EN		3.36	0.09

Scales		Mean	Std. Deviation
AE	M	3.23	0.74
	F	3.61	0.76
AA	M	3.88	0.75
	F	4.15	0.75
AVI	M	3.36	0.90
	F	3.52	0.97
AP	M	2.54	0.53
	F	2.68	0.54
SP	M	1.82	0.83
	F	2.35	1.19
FC	M	1.86	0.84
	F	2.61	1.33
AS	M	2.63	1.13
	F	3.18	1.37
EN	M	3.41	0.94
	F	3.32	0.94

AE = Academic Enthusiasm; AA = Academic Achievement; AVI = Voluntary Initiative; AP = Academic Participation; SP = School Participation;
FC = Family and Caring Activities; AS = Academics and Studies; EN = Entertainment; M = Male; F = Female

Table 6a

Survey Items		Mean	Std. Deviation
Religious activities	M	1.50	1.16
within your home	F	2.17	1.16
Playing sports	M	3.41	1.85
	F	2.30	1.62

References

Ahmed, S. (2004). *The cultural politics of emotion*. New York: Routledge.

Ahmed, S. (2010). *The promise of happiness*. Durham, London: Duke University Press. http://dx.doi.org/10.1215/9780822392781

Akom, A.A. (2008). Ameritocracy and infra-racial racism: racializing social and cultural reproduction theory in the twenty-first century. *Race, Ethnicity and Education, 11*(3), 205–230. http://dx.doi.org/10.1080/13613320802291116

Alrutz, M. (2013). Sites of possibility: Applied theatre and digital storytelling with youth. *Research in Drama Education: The Journal of Applied Theatre and Performance, 18*(1), 44–57. http://dx.doi.org/10.1080/13569783.2012.756169

Amato, P.R., & Ochiltree, G. (1986). Family resources and the development of child competency. *Journal of Marriage and the Family, 48*(1), 47–56. http://dx.doi.org/10.2307/352227

Anderman, E. M. (2002). School effects on psychological outcomes during adolescence. *Journal of Educational Psychology, 94*: 795–809.

Anderson, M., & Wilkinson, L. (2007). A resurgence of verbatim theatre: Authenticity, empathy and transformation. *Australasian Drama Studies, 50*, 153–169.

Anyon, J. (2005). *Radical possibilities: public policy, urban education, and a new social movement*. New York: Routledge.

Appleman, D. (2009). *Critical encounters in high school English: Teaching literary theory to adolescents* (2nd ed.). New York: Teachers College Press.

Appleton, J.J., Christenson, S.L., & Furlong, M.J. (2008). Student engagement with school: Critical conceptual and methodological issues of the construct. *Psychology in the Schools, 45*(5), 369–386. http://dx.doi.org/10.1002/pits.20303

Arendt, H. (1961/1993). The crisis of education. In *Between Past and Future: Eight Exercises in Political Thought*. New York: Penguin Books.

Arendt, H. (1977). *Between past and future*. New York: Penguin.

Arendt, H. (1979). M. Hill (Ed.), *Hannah Arendt: The recovery of the public world*. New York: St. Martin's Press.

Arendt, H. (1982). R. Beiner (Ed.), *Lectures on Kant's political philosophy*. Chicago: University of Chicago Press.

Bhaduri, A. (2008). Predatory Growth. Retrieved from http://development-dialogues.blogspot.ca/2008/02/amit-bhaduri-predatory-growth.html

Barber, M. (1992). *Education in the capital*. London, UK: Cassell.

Barber, M., & Dann, R. (1996). *Raising educational standards in the inner cities: Practical initiatives in action*. London, UK: Cassell.

Barrett, L., Niedenthal, P., & Winkielman, P. (2005). (Eds.) *Emotion and consciousness*. New York: Guilford Press.

Bartko, W.T., & Eccles, J.S. (2003). Adolescent participation in structured and unstructured activities: A person-oriented analysis. *Journal of Youth and Adolescence, 32*(4), 233–241. http://dx.doi.org/10.1023/A:1023056425648

Bauman, Z. (1998). *Globalization: the human consequences*. New York: Columbia University Press.

Bauman, Z. (2004). *Wasted lives*. Cambridge: Polity Press.

Benhabib, S. (1992). *Situating the self: Gender, community and postmodernism in contemporary ethics*. New York: Routledge.

Bickford, S. (1996). *The dissonance of democracy: Listening, conflict and citizenship*. Ithaca, London: Cornell University Press.

Black, A.E., & Deci, E.L. (2000). The effects of instructors' autonomy support and students' autonomous motivation on learning organic chemistry: A self-determination theory perspective. *Science Education, 84*(6), 740–756. http://dx.doi.org/10.1002/1098-237X(200011)84:6<740::AID-SCE4>3.0.CO;2-3

Blaisdell, B., & Edgar, C. (2000). *Tolstoy as teacher: Leo Tolstoy's writings on education*. New York: Teachers and Writers Collaborative.

Bloom, B.S. (1980). The new direction in educational research: Alterable variables. *Journal of Negro Education, 49*(3), 337–349. http://dx.doi.org/10.2307/2295092

Blum, R., & Mann Rinehart, P. (1997). Connections that make a difference in the lives of youths. *Youth Studies Australia, 16*(4): 37–50.

Booth, D., & Thornley-Hall, C. (Eds.). (1991). *The talk curriculum*. Australian Reading Association.

Bourdieu, P. (1999). *Acts of resistance: Against the tyranny of the market*. New York: New Press.

Bourriaud, N. (1998/English version 2002). *Relational aesthetics*. Paris: Presses du reel.

Bowles, S., & Gintis, H. (2011). *Schooling in capitalist American: Educational reform and the contradictions of economic life* (3rd ed.). Chicago, Illinois: Haymarket Books.

Britzman, D. (2007). Teacher education as uneven development: Toward psychology of uncertainty. *International Journal of Leadership in Education*, *10*(1), 1–12. http://dx.doi.org/10.1080/13603120600934079

Brophy, J. (2004). *Motivating students to learn* (2nd ed.). Mahwah, NJ: Lawrence Erlbaum.

Brown, M. (2007). Counting on queer geography. In K. Browne, J. Lim, & G. Brown (Eds.), *Geographies of Sexualities:Ttheory, practices and politics*. (pp. 207–214). Burlington, VT: Ashgate Publishing.

Butler, J. (1990). *Gender trouble: Feminism and the subversion of identity*. London, New York: Routledge.

Butler, J. (1993). *Bodies that matter: On the discursive limits of sex*. London, New York: Routledge.

Cahill, H. (2010). Re-thinking the fiction reality boundary: Investigating the use of drama in HIV prevention projects in Vietnam. *Research in Drama Education: The Journal of Applied Theatre and Performance*, *15*(2), 155–174. http://dx.doi.org/10.1080/13569781003700052

Cahill, H. (2011). Drama for deconstruction. *Youth Theatre Journal*, *25*(1), 16–31. http://dx.doi.org/10.1080/08929092.2011.569299

Campaign 2000 (2010). *Report card on child and family poverty in Ontario*. Retrieved from http://www.campaign2000.ca/reportCards/provincial/Ontario/2010On tarioReportCardEnglish.pdf

Centers for Disease Control and Prevention. (2009). *School connectedness: Strategies for increasing protective factors among youth*. Atlanta, GA: U.S. Department of Health and Human Services.

Chadderton, C., & Colley, H. (2012). School-to-work transition services: marginalising "disposable" youth in a state of exception? *Discourse. Studies in the Cultural Politics of Education*, *33*(3), 329–343. http://dx.doi.org/10.1080/01596306.2012.681895

Christenson, S.L., Reschly, A.L., Appleton, J.J., Berman, S., Spanjers, D., & Varro, P. (2008). Best practices in fostering student engagement. In A. Thomas & J. Grimes (Eds.), *Best practices in school psychology* (5th ed., pp. 1099–1120). Bethesda, MD: National Association of School Psychologists.

Cibulka, J., & Boyd, W.L. (Eds.). (2003). *A race against time: The crisis in urban schooling*. Santa Barbara, CA: Praeger.

Code, L. (2006). *Ecological thinking: The politics of epistemic location*. New York: Oxford University Press. http://dx.doi.org/10.1093/0195159438.001.0001

Cohen-Cruz, J. (2010). *Engaging performance: Theatre and call and response*. London, New York: Routledge.

Coleman, J. (1966). *Equality of educational opportunity*. The United States Department of Education.

Connell, J.P., Spencer, M.B., & Aber, J.L. (1994). Educational risk and resilience in African-American youth: Context, self, action, and outcomes in school. *Child Development, 65*(2), 493–506. http://dx.doi.org/10.2307/1131398

Connell, J.P., & Wellborn, J.G. (1991). Competence, autonomy and relatedness: A motivational analysis of self-system processes. In M.R. Gunnar & L.A. Sroufe (Eds.), *Self processes and development: The Minnesota symposia on child development* (Vol. 23, pp. 43–77). Hillsdale, NJ: Erlbaum.

Cook-Sather, A. (2012). Translating learners, researchers and qualitative approaches through investigations of students' experiences in schools. *Qualitative Research. (Published online 2012, pp. 1–16).*

Cooper, H., Valentine, J.C., Nye, B., & Lindsay, J.J. (1999). Relationships between five after-school activities and academic achievement. *Journal of Educational Psychology, 91*(2), 369–378. http://dx.doi.org/10.1037/0022 -0663.91.2.369

Costigan, A. (2013). New urban teachers transcending neoliberal educational reforms: Embracing aesthetic education as a curriculum of political action. *Urban Education, 48*(1), 116–148. http://dx.doi.org/10.1177/0042085912457579

Council of Ministers of Education (2011). *PIRLS 2011:Canada in context.* Developed by Mélanie Labrecque, Maria Chuy, Pierre Brochu, and Koffi Houme. See http://cmec.ca/Publications/Lists/Publications/Attachments/294/PIRLS_ 2011_EN.pdf .

Cremin, T., Goouch, K., Blakemore, L., Goff, E., & Macdonald, R. (2006). Connecting drama and writing: Seizing the moment to write. *Research in Drama Education: The Journal of Applied Theatre and Performance, 11*(3), 273–291. http://dx.doi.org/10.1080/13569780600900636

Daly, B., Shin, R., Thakral, C., Selders, M., & Vera, E. (2009). School engagement among urban adolescents of color: Does perception of social support and neighborhood safety really matter? *Journal of Youth and Adolescence, 38*(1), 63–74. http://dx.doi.org/10.1007/s10964-008-9294-7

Darling-Hammond, L. (2010). *The flat world and education: How America's commitment to equity will determine our future.* New York: Teachers College Press.

Das, P. (2010). Process of girls dropout in school education: Analysis of selected cases in India. Paper presented at Engendering Empowerment: Education and Equality e- Conference, April 12–May 14. United Nations Girls' Education Initiative: New York http://www.e4conference.org/e4e

Dean, S. (2001). *Hearts and minds: A public school miracle.* Toronto, ON: Penguin.

Deavere Smith, A. (2003). *Twilight—Los Angeles 1992.* New York: Dramatists Play Service Incorporated.

Deleuze, G. (1988). *Spinoza: practical philosophy* (R. Hurley, Trans.). San Francisco: City Lights.

Derbyshire, H., & Hodson, L. (2008) Performing injustice: human rights and verbatim theatre. *Law and Humanities, 2*(2), 191–211.

Derrida, J. (1994). *Specters of Marx: The state of debt, the work of mourning, and the new international* (P. Kamuf, Trans.). New York: Routledge Press.

Dillabough, J., & Kennelly, J. (2010). *Lost youth in the global city: Class, culture and the urban imaginary.* New York: Routledge.

Disch, L.J. (1994). *Hannah Arendt and the limits of philosophy.* Ithaca, London: Cornell University Press.

Dreze, J., & Kingdon, G. (1999). *School participation in rural India.* Development Economics Discussion Paper 18. London: London School of Economics and Political Science.

Dunn, J. R., Hayes, M.V., Hulchanski, J.D., Hwang, S.W., & Potvin, L. (2006). Housing as a socio-economic determinant of health: Findings of a national needs, gaps, and opportunities assessment. *Canadian Journal of Public Health, 97*(s3), 11–15.

Eckersley, R. (2009). Progress, culture and young people's well-being. In A. Furlong (Ed.), *Handbook of youth and young adulthood.* pp. 353–360. London: Routledge.

Ellsworth, E. (2005). *Places of learning: Media, architecture, pedagogy.* New York: Routledge.

Entwisle, D.R., & Hayduk, L.A. (1988). Lasting effects of elementary school. *Sociology of Education, 61*(3), 147–159. http://dx.doi.org/10.2307/2112624

Eow, Y.L., Ali, W.Z.W., Mahmud, R., & Baki, R. (2009). Form one students' engagement with computer games and its effect on their academic achievement in a Malaysian secondary school. *Computers & Education, 53*(4), 1082–1091. http://dx.doi.org/10.1016/j.compedu.2009.05.013

Erickson, F. (1987). Transformation and school success: The politics and culture of school achievement. *Anthropology and Education Quarterly, 18*(4), 335–356.

Eriksson, S. (2011). Distancing at close range: making strange devices in Dorothy Heathcote's process drama teaching political awareness through drama. *Research in Drama Education: The Journal of Applied Theatre and Performance., 16*(1), 101–123. http://dx.doi.org/10.1080/13569783.2011.541613

Fine, M., & Weis, L. (2003), *Silenced voices and extraordinary conversations: Re-imagining schools.* New York, London: Teachers College Press.

Fisher, M. (2009). *Capitalist realism: Is there no alternative.* Winchester, UK; Washington, US: John Hunt Publishing Ltd.

Foucault, M. (1977). *Discipline and punish: The birth of the prison.* New York: Random House.

Foucault, M. (1978). *The history of sexuality an introduction* (Vol. I). New York: Random House.

Foucault, M. (1984). Of other spaces: Utopias and heterotopias. *Architecture, Mouvement, Continuité, 5,* 46–49.

Fredricks, J.A., Blumenfeld, P.C., & Paris, A.H. (2004, Spring). School engagement: potential of the concept, state of the evidence. *Review of Educational Research, 74*(1), 59–109. http://dx.doi.org/10.3102/00346543074001059

Freire, P. (1970). *Pedagogy of the oppressed.* New York: Herder and Herder.

Freire, P. (1973). *Education for critical consciousness.* New York: Seabury Press.

Freire, P. (1976). *Education, the practice of freedom.* London: Writers and Readers Publishing Cooperative.

Freire, P. (1992). *Pedagogy of hope: Reliving pedagogy of the oppressed* (2004 ed., R.R. Barr, Trans.). New York: Continuum.

Freire, P. (1998). *Teachers as cultural workers: Letters to those who dare teach.* Boulder, CO: Westview Press.

Fullarton, S. (2002). Student engagement with school: Individual and school-level influences. *LSAY Research Reports.* Longitudinal surveys of Australian youth research report, n.27. http://research.acer.edu.au/lsay_research/31

Furlong, A. (2013). *Youth studies: An introduction.* London, New York: Routledge.

Furlong, A., & Cartmel, A. (2007). *Young people and social change, new perspectives* (2nd ed.). Maidenhead, UK: Open University Press.

Furlong, M.J., & Christenson, S.L. (2008). Engaging students at school and with learning: A relevant construct for *all* students. *Psychology in the Schools, 45*(5), 365–368. http://dx.doi.org/10.1002/pits.20302

Gager, C.T., & Hickes Lundquist, J. (2004). To work or not to work? A reevaluation of correlates of adolescent employment. Paper presented at the annual meeting of the Population Association of American, Boston, MA.

Gale, F., & Bolzan, N. (2013). Social resilience: challenging neo-colonial thinking and practices around 'risk'. *Journal of Youth Studies, 16*(2), 257–271. http://dx.doi.org/10.1080/13676261.2012.704985

Gallagher, K. (2007). *The theatre of urban: Youth and schooling in dangerous times.* Toronto, ON: University of Toronto Press.

Gallagher, K. (2011a). In search of a theoretical basis for storytelling in education research. *International Journal of Research & Method in Education, 34*(1), 49–61. http://dx.doi.org/10.1080/1743727X.2011.552308

Gallagher, K. (2011b). Roma refugee youth and applied theatre: Imagining a future vernacular. *NJ (National Journal of Drama Australia). 35*:1–12.

Gallagher, K., & Freeman, B. (forthcoming) (eds.) *Why theatre now?: On the virtue and value of Canadian theatre in the new millennium.* Toronto, London, Buffalo: University of Toronto Press.

Gallagher, K., & Fusco, C. (2006). I.D.ology and the technologies of public (school) space: An ethnographic inquiry into the neoliberal tactics of social (re)production. *Ethnography and Education, 1*(3), 301–318. http://dx.doi.org/10.1080/17457820600836939

Gallagher, K., & Kim, I. (2008). Moving towards postcolonial methods in qualitative research: Contexts, cameras, and relationships. In K. Gallagher (Ed.), *The methodological dilemma: Creative, collaborative and critical approaches to qualitative research* (pp. 103–120). London, New York: Routledge.

Gallagher, K., & Lortie, P. (2005). "How does knowin' my business make you any safer": Critical pedagogy in dangerous times. *Review of Education, Pedagogy & Cultural Studies, 27*(2), 141–158. http://dx.doi.org/10.1080/10714410590963848

Gallagher, K., & Lortie, P. (2007). Building theories of their lives: Youth engaged in drama research. In D. Thiessen and A. Cooke-Sather (Eds.), *International handbook of student experience in elementary and secondary schoo,.* (pp. 405–437). Springer Publishing. http://dx.doi.org/10.1007/1-4020-3367-2_16

Gallagher, K., & Wessels, A. (2011). Emergent pedagogy and affect in collaborative research: A metho-pedagogical paradigm. *Pedagogy, Culture & Society, 19*(2), 239–258. http://dx.doi.org/10.1080/14681366.2011.582260

Gallagher, K., & Wessels, A. (2013). Between the frames: youth spectatorship and theatre as curated, "unruly" pedagogical space. *Research in Drama Education: The Journal of Applied Theatre and Performance, 18*(1), 25–43.

Gardner, H. (1993/2006). *Multiple intelligences: New horizons.* New York: Basic Books.

Giroux, H.A. (1990). Rethinking the Boundaries of Educational Discourse: Modernism, postmodernism, and feminism. *College Literature, 17*(2/3), 1–50.

Giroux, H.A. (2003). *The abandoned generation: Democracy beyond the culture of fear.* London: Palgrave.

Giroux, H.A. (2006). *Politics after hope: Barack Obama and the crisis of youth, race and democracy.* Boulder, London: Paradigm Publishers.

Glasgow, K.L., Dornbusch, S.M., Troyer, L., Steinberg, L., & Ritter, P.L. (1997). Parenting styles, adolescents' attributions, and educational outcomes in nine heterogeneous high schools. *Child Development, 68*(3), 507–529. http://dx.doi.org/10.2307/1131675

Glick, P. (2008). *Policy impacts on schooling gender gaps in developing countries: The evidence and a framework for interpretation.* Ithaca, NY: Cornell University.

Grossman, J.B., & Bulle, M.J. (2006). Review of what youth programs do to increase the connectedness of youth with adults. *Journal of Adolescent Health. 39*(6), 788–799.

Goffman, E. (1959). *The presentation of self in everyday life.* New York: Anchor Books.

Guay, F., Chanal, J., Ratelle, C.F., Marsh, H.W., Larose, S., & Boivin, M. (2010). Intrinsic, identified, and controlled types of motivation for school subjects in young elementary school children. *British Journal of Educational Psychology, 80*(4), 711–735. http://dx.doi.org/10.1348/000709910X499084

Gunter, A. (2010). *Growing up bad: Black youth, road culture and badness in an East London neighbourhood*. London: The Tufnell Press.

Hage, G. (2002). "On the side of life" – Joy and the capacity of being. In M. Zournazi (Ed.), *Hope: New philosophies for change*. New York, NY: Routledge.

Hampton, B., Peng, L., & Ann, J. (2008). Pre-service teachers' perceptions of urban schools. *Urban Review, 40*(3), 268–295. http://dx.doi.org/10.1007/s11256-008-0081-2

Harvey, D. (2005). *A brief history of neoliberalism*. Oxford, New York: Oxford University Press.

Hedge, N., & Mackenzie, A. (2012). Beyond care? *Journal of Philosophy of Education, 46*(2), 192–206. http://dx.doi.org/10.1111/j.1467-9752.2012.00844.x

Hitchens, C. (2012). *Mortality*. Toronto, ON: Signal, McClelland and Stewart.

Hirway, I. (2009). *Losing the sparkle: Impact of the global crisis on the diamond cutting and polishing industry in India*. New Delhi: UNDP.

Hyman, S., Aubry, T., & Klodawsky, F. (2011). Resilient educational outcomes: Participation in school by youth with histories of homelessness. *Youth & Society, 43*(1), 253–273. http://dx.doi.org/10.1177/0044118X10365354

IBM Corp. Released 2012. IBM SPSS statistics for Windows, Version 21.0. Armonk, NY: IBM Corp.

Irigaray, L. (2013). *In the beginning, she was*. London, New Dehli, New York, Sydney: Bloomsbury.

Irvine, J.J. (2010). Foreword. In H.R. Milner's (Ed.), *Culture, curriculum, and identity in education*. New York: Palgrave Macmillan.

Jackson, A. 2007. *Theatre, education and the making of meanings: Art or instrument?* Manchester, UK: Manchester University Press.

James, C.E. (2012). Students "at risk": Stereotypes and the schooling of black boys. *Urban Education, 47*(2), 464–494. http://dx.doi.org/10.1177/0042085911429084

Jameson, F. (1991). *Postmodernism, or, the cultural logic of late capitalism*. Durham, NC: Duke University Press.

Janks, H. (2010). *Literacy and power*. London: Routledge.

Joselowsky, F. (2007). Youth engagement, high school reform, and improved learning outcomes: Building systemic approaches for youth engagement. *NASSP Bulletin, 91*(3), 257–276. http://dx.doi.org/10.1177/0192636507306133

Kalantzis, M. (Ed.) (1995). *A fair go in education*. Belconnen, ACT, Australia: Australian Curriculum Studies Association, Inc. (in association with the Australian Centre of Equity through Education)

Kaminski, J.W., Puddy, R.W., Hall, D.M., Cashman, S.Y., Crosby, A.E., & Ortega, L.A. (2010). The relative influence of different domains of social connectedness on self-directed violence in adolescence. *Journal of Youth and Adolescence*, *39*(5), 460–473. http://dx.doi.org/10.1007/s10964-009-9472-2

Kao, S.M., Carkin, G., & Hsu, L.F. (2011). Questioning techniques for promoting language learning with students of limited L2 oral proficiency in a drama-oriented language classroom. *Research in Drama Education: The Journal of Applied Theatre and Performance, 16*(4), 489–515.

Kelly, D., Purvey, D., Jaipal, K., & Penberg, D. (1995). *Exemplary schools project technical report: Balancing diversity and community: A large urban high school adopts the mini-school approach – Case study of Vancouver Technical School.* Toronto, ON: Canadian Education Association.

Kennelly, J. (2011). *Citizen Youth: Culture, activism and agency in a neoliberal era.* London, New York: Palgrave MacMillan. http://dx.doi.org/10.1057/9780230119611

Kennelly, J. & Poyntz, R. (Eds.). (forthcoming). *A phenomenology of youth cultures: Meaning and retrieval in an era of globalization.* New York: Routledge.

Kershaw, B. (1998). Pathologies of hope in drama and theatre. *Research in Drama Education: The Journal of Applied Theatre and Performance, 3*(1), 67–83. http://dx.doi.org/10.1080/1356978980030107

Klem, A.M., & Connell, J.P. (2004). Relationships matter: Linking teacher support to student engagement and achievement. *Journal of School Health, 74*(7), 262–273. http://dx.doi.org/10.1111/j.1746-1561.2004.tb08283.x

Koestner, R., Ryan, R.M., Bernieri, F., & Holt, K. (1984). Setting limits on children's behavior: The differential effects of controlling versus informational styles on intrinsic motivation and creativity. *Journal of Personality, 52*(3), 233–248. http://dx.doi.org/10.1111/j.1467-6494.1984.tb00879.x

Kohfeldt, D., Chhun, L., Grace, S., & Langhout, R.D. (2011). Youth empowerment in context: Exploring tensions in school-based yPAR. *American Journal of Community Psychology, 47*(1–2), 28–45. http://dx.doi.org/10.1007/s10464-010-9376-z

Kortering, L., & Braziel, P. (2008). Engaging youth in school and learning: The emerging key to school success and completion. *Psychology in the Schools, 45*(5), 461–465. http://dx.doi.org/10.1002/pits.20309

Laclau, E. (2005). *Populist reason.* London: Verso.

Laclau, E., & Mouffe, C. (1985). *Hegemony and socialist strategy: Towards a radical democratic politics* (2nd ed.). London, New York: Verso.

Libbey, H. P. (2004). Measuring student relationships to school: Attachment, bonding, connectedness, and engagement. *Journal of School Health, 74*(7), 274–283.

Lingis, A. (2002). Murmurs of life. In M. Zournazi (Ed.), *Hope: New philosophies for change.* New York, NY: Routledge.

Luckhurst, M. (2008). Verbatim theatre, media relations and ethics. In N. Holdsworth & M. Luckhurst (Eds.), *A concise companion to contemporary British and Irish drama*. Malden, MA; Oxford: Blackwell Publishing. http://dx.doi.org/10.1002/9780470690987.ch10

Luke, A., Woods, A., Fisher, D., Bruett, J., & Fink, L. (2009). Critical literacies in schools: A primer. *Voices from the Middle, 17*(2), 9–18.

Lyotard, J.-F. (1984). *The postmodern condition*. Manchester, UK: Manchester University Press.

Mahiri, J. (2008). Literacies in the lives of urban youth. In B.V. Street and N.H. Hornberger (Eds.), *Encyclopaedia of language and education*, 2nd ed., Vol. 2: Literacy (pp. 299–307). New York: Springer Science + Business Media. http://dx.doi.org/10.1007/978-0-387-30424-3_52

Marcus, G.E. (1995). Ethnography in/of the world system: The emergence of multi-sited ethnography. *Annual Review of Anthropology, 24*(1), 95–117. http://dx.doi.org/10.1146/annurev.an.24.100195.000523

Marsh, H.W., & Kleitman, S. (2003). School athletic participation: Mostly gain with little pain. *Journal of Sport & Exercise Psychology, 25*(2), 205

Massey, D. (1994). *Space, place and gender*. Minneapolis: University of Minnesota Press.

Massey, D. (2005). *For space*. London, Thousand Oaks, New Dehli: Sage Publications.

Massumi, B. (2002). *A shock to thought: Expression after Deleuze and Guattari*. London: Routledge.

McConachie, B. (2008). *Engaging audiences: A cognitive approach to spectating in the theatre*. New York: Palgrave Macmillan. http://dx.doi.org/10.1057/9780230617025

McDougall, L. (2003). As the world turns: The changing role of popular drama in international development education. In K. Gallagher & D. Booth (Eds.), *How theatre educates: Convergences and counterpoints with artists, scholars and advocates* (pp. 173–181). Toronto, London, Buffalo: University of Toronto Press.

McKee, K. (2012). Young people, homeownership and future welfare: a policy review. *Housing Studies, 27*(6), 853–862. http://dx.doi.org/10.1080/02673037.2012.714463

McLelland, S., & Fine, M. (2008). Writing on cellophane: studying teen women's sexual desires, inventing methodological release points. In Author (ed.) pp. 232–260. *The methodological dilemma: Creative, critical, and collaborative approaches to qualitative research*. London: Routledge.

McLoughlin, P. (2013). Couch surfing on the margins: the reliance on temporary living arrangements as a form of homelessness amongst school-aged home

leavers. *Journal of Youth Studies, 16*(4), 521–545. http://dx.doi.org/10.1080/1
3676261.2012.725839

McMahon, S.D., Parnes, A.L., & Keys, C.B. (2008). School belonging among low-
income urban youth with disabilities: Testing a theoretical model. *Psychology
in the Schools, 45*(5), 387–401. http://dx.doi.org/10.1002/pits.20304

Means, A. (2013). *Schooling in the age of austerity: Urban education and the
struggle for democratic life*. New York: Palgrave Macmillan. http://dx.doi
.org/10.1057/9781137032058

Merleau-Ponty, M. (1945/1962 English edition). *Phenomenology of Perception*.
(C. Smith, Trans.). London and New York: Routledge.

Metcalf Foundation. (2012). *The working poor in the Toronto Region: Who they
are, where they live, and how the trends are changing*. Written by John Stapleton,
Brian Murphy, & Yue Xing.

Mey, J. (1986). *Whose Language? A Study in Linguistic Pragmatics*. Amsterdam:
John Benjamins Publishing Company.

Milner, H.R. (2013). Rethinking achievement gap talk in urban education.
Urban Education, 48(1), 3–8. http://dx.doi.org/10.1177/0042085912470417

Mirón, L. (1996). *The social construction of urban schooling: Situating the crisis*.
New Jersey: Hampton Press.

Moje, E.B. (2004). Powerful spaces: Tracing the out-of-school literacy spaces
of Latino/a youth. In L.M. Leander & M. Sheehy (Eds.), *Spatializing literacy
research and practice* (pp. 15–38). New York: Peter Lang.

Moje, E. B., Overby, M., Tysvaer, N., & Morris, K. (2008). The complex world
of adolescent literacy: Myths, motivations, and mysteries. *Harvard Educational
Review, 78*(1), 107–154.

Moore, A. (2004). *The good teacher: Dominant discourses in teaching and teacher education*.
New York, NY: Routledge. http://dx.doi.org/10.4324/9780203420270

Muncie, J. (2009). *Youth and crime* (3rd ed.). London: Sage.

National Family Health Survey (NFHS) (2007). Ministry of Health and Family
Welfare. NRHM Health Management Information System. In *School dropouts
or push outs? Overcoming barriers for the right to education*. A. Reddy & S.
Sinha (Eds.). National University of Educational Planning and Administration,
2010. CREATE Pathways to Access, Research Monograph No. 40.

National Sample Survey Organization of India. (2005). *Employment and
unemployment situation in India, January–June 2004, NSS 60th Round, Report
506*. New Delhi: Ministry of Statistics and Programme Implementation.

Neelands, J. (2004). Miracles are happening: beyond the rhetoric of transformation in the Western traditions of drama. *Research in Drama Education: The
Journal of Applied Theatre and Performance, 9*(1), 47–56. http://dx.doi
.org/10.1080/1356978042000185902

Neelands, J. (2009). Acting Together: ensemble as democratic process in art and life. *Research in Drama Education: The Journal of Applied Theatre and Performance, 14*(2), 173–189. http://dx.doi.org/10.1080/13569780902868713

Neelands, J., Booth, D., & Ziegler, S. (1993). *Writing in imagined contexts: Research into drama-influenced writing.* Toronto: University of Toronto Press.

New London Group. (1996). A pedagogy of multiliteracies: Designing social futures. *Harvard Educational Review, 66*(1), 60–92.

Nicholson, H. (2005). *Applied drama: the gift of theatre.* New York, England: Palgrave Macmillan.

Noddings, N. (1984). *Caring: a feminine approach to ethics and moral education.* Berkeley, Los Angeles, London: University of California Press.

Noddings, N. (2001). Care and coercion in school reform. *Journal of Educational Change, 2*(1), 35–43. http://dx.doi.org/10.1023/A:1011514928048

Organisation for Economic Co-operation and Development (OECD). *Programme for international student assessment (PISA* 2004). Retrieved on June 19/07 from http://www.pisa.oecd.org/pages/0,3417,en_32252351_32235731_1_1_1_1_1,00.html

O'Toole, J. (2009). Drama and curriculum. *Landscapes: The Arts, Aesthetics, and Education, 6.* 97–116.

Park, R.E. (1950). *Race and culture.* Glencoe, IL: Free Press.

Patrick, H., Ryan, A.L., & Kaplan, A. (2007). Early adolescents' perceptions of the classroom social environment, motivational beliefs, and engagement. *Journal of Educational Psychology, 99*(1), 83–98. http://dx.doi.org/10.1037/0022-0663.99.1.83

Peña, E. (2007). Lost in translation: Methodological considerations in cross-cultural research. *Child Development, 78*(4), 1255–1264.

Pennington, J.L., Brock, C.H., & Ndura, E. (2012). Unraveling threads of white teachers' conceptions of caring: Repositioning white privilege. *Urban Education, 47*(4), 743–775. http://dx.doi.org/10.1177/0042085912441186

Penrod, D. (2007). *Using blogs to enhance literacy: The next powerful step in 21st-century learning.* New York: Randal Education.

People for Education http://www.peopleforeducation.ca/pfe-news/new-reading-report-shows-parents-a-major-factor-in-student-success/

Perry, A. (2012). A silent revolution: "Image Theatre" as a system of decolonization. *Research in Drama Education: The Journal of Applied Theatre and Research, 17*(1): 103–119.

Phillips, L. (2011). *The promise of dialogue.* Amsterdam, Philadelphia: John Benjamins Publishing Company.

PISA 2009: *Highlights of Ontario student results.* Retrieved from http://www.eqao.com/pdf_e/10/2009_PISA_Highlights_en.pdf

Plan International. (2012). *Because I am a girl: The state of the world's girls—Girls in the global economy, adding it all up.* Woking, UK: Plan International.

Raina, V. (2001). Talk given at Asha Princeton, September 1. http://www.ashanet.org/ Princeton/talks/raina.txt

Rancière, J. (2011). *The emancipated spectator.* London, New York: Verso.

Read, A. (2009). *Theatre intimacy and engagement: The last human venue.* Houndmills, Basingstoke, Hampshire: Palgrave MacMillan. http://dx.doi.org/10.1057/9780230273863

Reddy, A., & Sinha, S. (2010). *School dropouts or push outs? Overcoming barriers for the right to education.* National University of Educational Planning and Administration. CREATE Pathways to Access, Research Monograph No. 40.

Reeve, J., Deci, E. L. & Ryan, R. M. (2004). Self-determination theory: A dialectical framework for understanding the sociocultural influences on student motivation. In D. M. McInerney & S. Van Etten (Eds.), *Research on Sociocultural influences on motivation and learning: Big theories revisited.* (Vol. 4, pp. 31–59). Greenwich, CT: Information Age Publishing.

Reeve, J., Jang, H., Carrell, D., Jeon, S., & Barch, J. (2004). Enhancing high school students' engagement by increasing their teachers' autonomy support. *Motivation and Emotion, 28*(2), 147–169. http://dx.doi.org/10.1023/B:MOEM.0000032312.95499.6f

Reitz, J., & Banerjee, R. (2007). Racial inequality, social cohesion and policy issues in Canada. Institute for Research on Public Policy. Retrieved May 2007 from www.irpp.org

Reschly, A.L., Huebner, E.S., Appleton, J.J., & Antaramian, S. (2008). Engagement as flourishing: The contribution of positive emotions and coping to adolescents' engagement at school and with learning. *Psychology in the Schools, 45*(5), 419–431. http://dx.doi.org/10.1002/pits.20306

Ripley, A. (2004). Obama's ascent: How do you leap from neighborhood activist to US Sentator to perhaps higher office? Even for Barack Obama, it's more complicated than it looks. *Time.* Retrieved from http://www.time.com/time/magazine/article/0,9171,750742,00.html

Roberts, L., & Schostak, J. (2012). Obama and the "Arab Spring": desire, hope and the manufacture of disappointment. Implications for a transformative pedagogy. *Discourse: Studies in the Cultural Politics of Education, 33*(3), 377–396.

Rorty, R. (1999). *Philosophy and social hope.* Harmondsworth, UK: Penguin Books.

Rose, T.A. (2007). *Hope in education: A dialogue with educators.* Unpublished dissertation, University of Oklahoma.

Ross, E.W. (2008). Chapter 35: Social Studies education. In D. Gabbard (Ed.), *Knowledge and power in the global economy: The effects of school reform in a neoliberal/neoconservative age* (2nd ed). New York, NY: Erlbaum.

Rowland, R., & Jones, J. (2007). Recasting the American dream and American politics: Barack Obama's keynote address to the 2004 Democratic National Convention. *Quarterly Journal of Speech*, *93*(4), 425–448. http://dx.doi.org/10.1080/00335630701593675

Rowsell, J. (2008). Improvising on artistic habitus: Sedimenting identity into art. In J. Albright & A. Luke (Eds.), *Pierre Bourdieu and literacy education* (pp. 233–251). London: Routledge.

Ryan, R.M., & Deci, E.L. (2000). Self-determination theory and the facilitation of intrinsic motivation, social development, and well-being. [(Retrieved online from http://www.education.com/reference/article/autonomy-support)]. *American Psychologist*, *55*(1), 68–78. http://dx.doi.org/10.1037/0003-066X.55.1.68

Sahni, U. (2012). From learning outcomes to life outcomes: What can you do and who can you be? A case study in girls' education in India. Centre for Universal Education at Brookings: Global Scholars Program Working Paper Series, Working Paper #4.

Saltman, K., & Gabbard, D. (2010). (Eds.) *Education as enforcement: The militarization and corporatization of schools* (2nd ed.). New York: Routledge.

Salverson, J. (2001). Change on whose terms? Testimony and erotics of injury. *Theatre*, *31*(3), 119–125. http://dx.doi.org/10.1215/01610775-31-3-119

Scott-Jones, D. 1984. Family influences on cognitive development and school achievement. In E.W. Gordon (Ed.), *Review of Research in Education* (Vol.11, pp. 259–305). Washington, DC: American Educational Research Association. http://dx.doi.org/10.2307/1167237

Sennett, R. (2006). *The culture of the new capitalism*. London: Yale University Press.

Sharkey, J.D., You, S., & Schnoebelen, K. (2008). Relations among school assets, individual resilience, and student engagement for youth grouped by level of family functioning. *Psychology in the Schools*, *45*(5), 402–418. http://dx.doi.org/10.1002/pits.20305

Simon, R. (1992). *Teaching against the grain: Texts for a pedagogy of possibility*. New York: Bergin and Garvey.

Sirin, S.R., & Rogers-Sirin, L. (2004). Exploring school engagement of middle-class African American adolescents. *Youth & Society*, *35*(3), 323–340. http://dx.doi.org/10.1177/0044118X03255006

Smyth, J. (2007). Toward the pedagogically engaged school: Listening to student voice as a positive response to disengagement and "dropping out"? In D. Thiessen & A. Cook-Sather (Eds.), *The international handbook of student experience in elementary and secondary school* (pp. 635–658). Dordrecht: Springer. http://dx.doi.org/10.1007/1-4020-3367-2_25

Spivak, G. (1988). Can the subaltern speak? In C. Nelson & L. Grossberg (Eds.), *Marxism and the interpretation of culture* (pp. 280–316). Urbana, Illinois: University of Illinois Press.

Statistics Canada census dictionary, http://www12.statcan.gc.ca/census-recensement/2006/ref/dict/index-eng.cfm

Steinberg, L., Lamborn, S.D., Dornbusch, S.M., & Darling, N. (1992). Impact of parenting practices on adolescent achievement: Authoritative parenting, school involvement, and encouragement to succeed. *Child Development, 63*(5), 1266–1281. http://dx.doi.org/10.2307/1131532

Stengers, I. (2002). A "cosmo-politics" – risk, hope, change: A conversation with Isabelle Stengers. In M. Zournazi (Ed.), *Hope: New philosophies for change* (pp. 244–272). New York, NY: Routledge.

Street, B. (2001). The new literacy studies. In E. Cushman, E. Kintgen, B. Kroll, & M. Rose (Eds.), *Literacy: A critical sourcebook* (pp. 430–442). Boston: Bedford/St.Martin's. http://dx.doi.org/10.4324/9780203468418

Symonds, P.M. (1947). Personality of the teacher. *Journal of Educational Research, 40*(9), 652–661.

Tanovich, D. (2006). *The colour of justice: policing race in Canada.* Toronto: Irwin Law.

Tanti, M. (2012). Teaching English with technology. *Special Issue on LAMS and Learning Design, 12*(2), 132–146.

Tator, C., & Henry, F. (2006). *Racial profiling in Canada: Challenging the myth of a few bad apples.* Toronto: University of Toronto Press.

Taylor, R.D., & Lopez, E.I. (2005). Family management practice, school achievement, and problem behavior in African American adolescents: Mediating processes. *Applied Developmental Psychology, 26*(1), 39–49. http://dx.doi.org/10.1016/j.appdev.2004.10.003

Thomson, P. (2002). *Schooling the rustbelt kids: Making the difference in changing times.* Melbourne: Allen and Unwin.

Toffler, A. (1981). *The Third Wave.* New York: Bantam Books.

Toronto District School Board (2009). [Organizational Development/Research and Information Services. Prepared by Robert S. Brown.]. *Research Today, 4*(1).

Trinh, T. Minh-ha (1989). *Woman, native, other.* Bloomington, Indianapolis: Indiana University Press.

Tuhiwai Smith, L. (1999). *Decolonizing methodologies: Research and indigenous peoples.* London, New York: Zed Books Ltd.

Tyler, K. M., Boelter, C. M. (2008). Linking black middle school students' perceptions of teachers' expectations to academic engagement and efficacy. *Negro Educational Review, 59* (1/2): 27–44, 125–126.

UNICEF *Child poverty in perspective: An overview of child well-being in rich countries.* Innocenti Report Card 7, 2007. UNICEF Innocenti Research Centre,

Florence. Retrieved on June 19/07 from http://www.UNICEF-irc.org/presscentre/article.php?type=2andid_article=49

UNICEF Child well-being in rich countries: A comparative overview. Innocenti Report Card 11, 2013. UNICEF Innocenti Research Centre, Florence. Retrieved on April 18/13 from: http://www.unicef.ca/sites/default/files/imce_uploads/DISCOVER/OUR WORK/ADVOCACY/DOMESTIC/POLICY ADVOCACY/DOCS/unicef_report_card_11.pdf

Vallerand, R.J., Fortier, M.S., & Guay, F. (1997). Self-determination and persistence in a real-life setting: Toward a motivational model of high school dropout. *Journal of Personality and Social Psychology, 72*(5), 1161–1176. http://dx.doi.org/10.1037/0022-3514.72.5.1161

Van der Gaag, J., & Abetti, P. (2011). Using National Education Accounts to Help Address the Global Learning Crisis (Washington: Brookings Institution, 2011); Forbes, P., *National Education Accounts Information on Worldwide Use*. Burlington: Creative Associates.

Wacquant, L. (2009). *Punishing the poor: The neoliberal government of social insecurity*. Durham, NC: Duke University Press. http://dx.doi.org/10.1215/9780822392255

Waiton, S. (2001). *Scared of the kids: Curfews, crime and regulation of young people*. Leicester: Perpetuity Press.

Wales, P. (2012). Telling tales in and out of school: Youth performativities with digital storytelling. *Research in Drama Education: The Journal of Applied Theatre and Performance, 17*(4), 535–552. http://dx.doi.org/10.1080/13569783.2012.727625

War Child Canada and Environics Research Group. (2006). *The War Child Canada report: Canadian youth speak on global issues and Canada's role in the world*. Retrieved on June 19/07 from www.warchild.ca

Waters, S., Cross, D., & Shaw, T. (2010). Does the nature of schools matter? An exploration of selected school ecology factors on adolescent perceptions of school connectedness. *British Journal of Educational Psychology, 80*(3), 381–402. http://dx.doi.org/10.1348/000709909X484479

Wentzel, K.R. (1998). Social relationships and motivation in middle school: The role of parents, teachers, and peers. *Journal of Educational Psychology, 90*(2), 202–209. http://dx.doi.org/10.1037/0022-0663.90.2.202

Wentzel, K. R. (2008). Social competence, Sociocultural contexts, and school success. In C. Hudley and G. Gottfried (Eds,), *Academic motivation and the culture of school in childhood and adolescence*. (pp. 297–310). Oxford, UK: Oxford University Press.

West, P. (2009). Health in youth: changing times and changing influences. In A. Furlong (Ed.), *Handbook of youth and young adulthood* (pp. 331–343). Abingdon: Routledge.

White, A.M., & Gager, C.T. (2007). Idle hands and empty pockets? Youth involvement in extracurricular activities, social capital, and economic status. *Youth & Society, 39*(1), 75–111. http://dx.doi.org/10.1177/0044118X06296906

William T. Grant Foundation (1988a). The forgotten half: non-college youth in America: an interim report on the school-to-work transition. Commission on Work, Family, and Citizenship.

William T. Grant Foundation (1988b). The forgotten half: pathways to success for America's youth and young families: final report. Commission on Work, Family, and Citizenship.

Willms, J.D. (2003). Student engagement at school: A sense of belonging and participation. Results from PISA 2000. Paris: OECD.

Wortley, S., & Owusu-Bempah, A. (2011). The usual suspects: police stop and search practices in Canada. *Policing and Society, 21*(4), 395–407. http://dx.doi.org/10.1080/10439463.2011.610198

Wortley, S., & Owusu-Bempah, A. (2011a). Crime and justice: the experiences of black Canadians. In B. Perry (Ed.), *Diversity, crime and justice in Canada* (pp. 127–150). New York: Oxford University Press.

Yarcheski, A., Mahon, N.E., & Yarcheski, T. (2001). Social support and well-being in early adolescents: The role of mediating variables. *Clinical Nursing Research, 10*(2), 163–181. http://dx.doi.org/10.1177/10547730122158851

Yon, D.A. (2000). *Elusive culture: Schooling, race, and identity in global times.* Albany: State University of New York Press.

Young-Bruehl, E. (1977). Hannah Arendt's storytelling. *Social Research, 44*, 183–190.

Ziegler, S., Hardwick, N., & McCreath, G. (1989). *Academically successful inner-city children: What they can tell us about effective education.* Toronto, ON: Toronto Board of Education.

Index

Page numbers in *italics* refer to photographs and page numbers with *t* refer to tables.

Cross, D., 89, 92, 95–6, 100, 107, 109
C Square (Middleview), 57, 192, 247

dance. *See* music and dance
Daniella (Middleview), 243
Daphney Evans (Middleview), 63, 245
Deci, E.L., 131
Deleuze, G., 49, 180, 218
democracy: educational ideals, 40,
    219–20; listening to diverse views,
    60; political integrity, 149–51;
    social hopes, 219–20; voting
    and political power, 149; youth
    participation, 9
Derbyshire, H., 197
Derek (Middleview), 52, 124, 135,
    143, 145, 147–8, 152–4, 156–9,
    230–2, 242
Derrida, J., 223
Dewey, John, 121, 219–20
dialogues, critical. *See* critical
    thinking
digital technology, computer use for
    pleasure. *See* Entertainment (in
    Outside School Space Scales)
digital technology, computer use
    for study outside school. *See*
    Academics and Studies (in
    Outside School Space Scales)
digital technology, use in research
    project, 8, 13, 17, 23, 107. *See also*
    research project
digital technology and drama
    classrooms: blogs, 184, 187–8, 213;
    Kidnet, 177; literacy, 187–8, 198–9;
    social media, 187–8; storytelling,
    43, 212–13; student Verbatim
    theatre production, 182, 184–8. *See
    also* literacy
Dillabough, J., 135

Dilworth, Alan, 181
Disch, L.J., 16–17
discussions with peers and teachers.
    See Academic Participation (in
    Within School Space Scales)
disengagement: about, xvi–xvii, 93,
    167–8; classroom distractions,
    124–5; and custody arrangements,
    58; Derek's story, 230–2; dropouts,
    11, 77, 90, 164; holiday issues,
    37; humour as, 123–4; Maxx's
    story, 226–30; misinterpretations
    of, 227–30; Prerna dropouts
    and gender, 77; productive
    disengagement, 123–4, 220–1;
    race and ethnicity in *The Middle
    Place*, 57–8; school deterioration,
    36–7, 166–7; student fatigue, 50,
    125, 163–4; and teachers, 52–4;
    work outside of school, 165–6. *See
    also* absenteeism; work outside of
    school
disruption of classrooms. *See*
    disengagement
divorce. *See* marriage and divorce
documentary theatre, 180. *See also*
    Verbatim theatre
domestic violence in Canada:
    audience responses to *The Middle
    Place*, 192–3; role models for
    youth, 57
domestic violence in India: about,
    79–80, 84–6; criminal justice
    system, 80, 84–5; Doors poetry
    project, 232–4; interventions by
    teachers, 84; sexual abuse, 77, 84–5;
    student one-minute storytelling,
    43; student Verbatim theatre
    project on, 184, 197–8, 211. *See also*
    marriage and divorce in India

class struggle, 134; Obama
discussion, 145–8; overlapping
identifications, 160–1;
performance of "toughness,"
127; poverty, 51, 99; and research
project, 17; social identity
categories, 133; youth as "working
poor," 50–1, 56, 75–6
social class in India: about, 32–3;
education goals for economic
independence, 222–3; and
patriarchy, 79–81
social class mobility: international
rankings, 9, 51; Obama discussion,
147–9; resistance to class as fixed,
134–5; and voting, 149; and work
outside of school, 51
social identity categories: about,
133–4; and individual failure
discourse, 119, 134; overlapping
identifications, 160–1; and "the
real," 119, 133; resistance to, 133–4;
student Verbatim theatre project
on cliques, 182, 184–7. *See also*
identity
Social Identity Categories for
research project: about, 5–6,
239; Braeburn, 239–40, 242;
Middleview, 240–2, 243–8;
minority categories, 102–3, 105;
Prerna and "real" names, 239
social literacy. *See* literacy
social media, 187–8. *See also* digital
technology
social relations in drama classrooms.
See drama classrooms
social relations in schools: academic,
social, and hidden curriculum,
176–7; anger, 47–9; cliques, 182,
184–7; dignity preservation, 38;

hardship and solitude, 37–8;
holiday issues, 37; and ideals, 120–1,
168–9; individual responsibility
discourse, 38–9, 119, 134; negative
judgements of peers, 59, 194–5,
203; peer support, 58–9; resilience
of youth, 3–4, 68, 71–4; school
as "start again" space, 37, 70–1,
129–30; schools as constellation of,
21; security and surveillance, 40–1;
students as "working poor," 50–1,
56, 75–6; teacher expectations,
72–3. *See also* engagement;
gender; health and well-being;
hopefulness; race and ethnicity
solitude. *See* Entertainment (in
Outside School Space Scales)
Soni (Prerna), 232–4
Sophia (Middleview), 64, 65, 246
South Asian-born immigrants, 14
speaking. *See* literacy
spectatorship: audience as witness,
190–1; embodied emotions, 67;
research project, 18–19; shared
experiences, 205
Spivak, G., 185
sports, playing, 113. *See also* Extra
Survey Items
Stephanie (Middleview), 50, 145,
148, 153, 172, 242
stereotypes: confrontation incident
at *The Middle Place,* 60–2;
internalization by students of
negative stereotypes, 47; race
and gender in *Secrets of a Black
Boy,* 205–7
storytelling: about, 15–17; art
and life relationships, 213;
and critical thinking, 16–17;
digital storytelling, 43, 177; and